Archiv für Rechts- und Sozialphilosophie

Archives for Philosophy of Law and Social Philosophy

Archives de Philosophie du Droit et de Philosophie Sociale

Archivo de Filosofía Jurídica y Social

Herausgegeben von der Internationalen Vereinigung für Rechts-
und Sozialphilosophie (IVR)
[illegible]

Heft [illegible]

[illegible]

Archiv für Rechts- und Sozialphilosophie
Archives for Philosophy of Law and Social Philosophy
Archives de Philosophie du Droit et de Philosophie Sociale
Archivo de Filosofía Jurídica y Social

Herausgegeben von der Internationalen Vereinigung für Rechts- und Sozialphilosophie (IVR)
Redaktion: DR. ANNETTE BROCKMÖLLER, LL. M.

Beiheft 174

www.steiner-verlag.de/brand/Archiv-fuer-Rechts-und-Sozialphilosophie

UTOPIE EINER NEUEN NORMATIVEN ORDNUNG

Alternativen *im* Recht / Alternativen *zum* Recht

Tagung des Jungen Forums Rechtsphilosophie (JFR)
im März 2023 in Hamburg

Herausgegeben von
Daria Bayer, Sören Deister, Marcus Döller,
Simon Kneip, Hannah Ofterdinger
und Jan-Robert Schmidt

Franz Steiner Verlag

Umschlagbild: Justitia, Landgericht Ulm
Quelle: shutterstock.com / Georg_89

Bibliografische Information der Deutschen Nationalbibliothek:
Die Deutsche Nationalbibliothek verzeichnet diese Publikation in der Deutschen Nationalbibliografie; detaillierte bibliografische Daten sind im Internet über dnb.d-nb.de abrufbar.

Maybachstraße 8, 70469 Stuttgart
service@steiner-verlag.de
www.steiner-verlag.de
Layout und Herstellung durch den Verlag
Druck: Beltz Grafische Betriebe, Bad Langensalza
Gedruckt auf säurefreiem, alterungsbeständigem Papier.
Printed in Germany.
ISBN 978-3-515-13872-7 (Print)
ISBN 978-3-515-13874-1 (E-Book)
DOI doi.org/10.25162/9783515138741

Inhaltsverzeichnis

Utopie einer neuen normativen Ordnung

Alternativen *im* Recht / Alternativen *zum* Recht

DARIA BAYER / SÖREN DEISTER / MARCUS DÖLLER /
SIMON KNEIP / HANNAH OFTERDINGER /
JAN-ROBERT SCHMIDT

Die Vorstellung einer notwendigen Analyse der Form des Rechts und möglicher Alternativen wird heute unter anderem mit dem *Rechtstheoretiker Jewgenij B. Paschukanis* verbunden. Dieser stellte in seinem 1924 erschienenen Buch *Allgemeine Rechtslehre und Marxismus*, das in diesem Jahr sein 100jähriges Jubiläum mit Konferenzen weltweit feiert, die bis heute kontrovers diskutierte These vom „Tod der Rechtsform" im vollentwickelten Kommunismus auf. Für Paschukanis war die Überwindung des bürgerlichen Rechts für eine Gesellschaft, die den Streit um egoistische Besitzinteressen überwunden hat, unumgänglich. Eine echte Alternative könne, so Paschukanis, nur außerhalb der Rechtsform, in einer anderen Form der Regelung sozialer Beziehungen, gefunden werden.

Die in diesem Band versammelten Beiträge *Utopie einer neuen normativen Ordnung* knüpfen an den Gedanken einer notwendigen Analyse der Rechtsform an, beleuchten dabei aber auf doppelte Weise die Möglichkeiten eines neuen Rechts: rechtsformimmanent und rechtsformtranszedent. Gemeinsamer Ausgangspunkt der Beiträge ist die Einsicht, dass jede echte Alternative zur aktuellen rechtlichen Verfasstheit ihren Ausgangspunkt in einer Auseinandersetzung mit dem bestehenden Recht gewinnen, gleichsam aus dieser Kritik hervorgehen muss, möchte sie an diesem nicht eitel vorbeischreiten und es damit verfehlen. Mit diesem Postulat ist jedoch über die Frage nach der Notwendigkeit von Recht (in seiner jetzigen Form) noch nichts gesagt. Vielmehr kann die Utopie einer anderen normativen Ordnung sowohl rechtsimmanent als Alternative(n) *im* Recht, als auch rechtstranszendent als Alternative(n) *zum* Recht konzipiert werden.

Alternativen *im* Recht bedeutet, andere Weisen des bestehenden Rechts zu erdenken und zu erproben. Während in der Beschreibung der immanenten Formulierung von den Alternativen *im* Recht eine Reform der institutionalisierten Rechtspraxis der aktuellen, bürgerlichen Rechtsform in den Blick genommen wird, geht der Gedanke einer Alternative *zum* Recht hingegen weiter, zielt er doch auf eine Transzendierung der institutionellen Ordnung und der normativen Anspruchsbestimmtheit der bürgerlichen Rechtsform ab. Hier wird nämlich danach gefragt, wie es Formen der Praxis geben kann, die noch gar nicht institutionell etabliert sind und im bürgerlichen Recht mit dem Fokus auf individuelle Eigentums- und Besitzrechte auch nicht etabliert werden *können*. Mit dieser Unterscheidung wird klar, dass die Differenz von Revolution und Reform eine Spannung markiert, die sich in der Differenz von Alternativen *zum* Recht einerseits und Alternativen *im* Recht andererseits wiederholt und verschärft. Die Differenz von *Alternativen zum Recht* einerseits und *Alternativen im Recht* andererseits ist dabei selbst eine Differenz, die politisch ausgehandelt werden muss.

Die Tagung, die vom 9. bis zum 11. März 2023 im Warburg Haus in Hamburg stattgefunden hat, nahm beide Lesarten in ihrer Spannung und Gegenläufigkeit in den Blick. Was ist gegen das bürgerliche Recht vorzubringen? Was lässt sich an dieser Rechtsform reformieren, was nicht und warum nicht? Wie ließen sich dann Alternativen im Recht konzipieren? Das sind Fragen, die sich an das Modell Alternativen *im* Recht anschließen. Wie lässt sich das bürgerliche Recht über sich hinaustreiben? Wie lassen sich andere Formen von Recht vollziehen, die im bürgerlichen Recht nicht institutionalisiert sind oder vollzogen werden können? Das sind Fragen, die sich an das Modell Alternativen *zum* Recht anschließen.

Die in diesem Band versammelten Beiträge sind Ausdruck dieses Widerspruchs zwischen Immanenz und Transzendenz, Theorie und Praxis. Sie bewegen sich von einer ästhetischen und materialistischen Kritik an der Form des Rechts über konkrete Alternativen zum Recht etwa bei der Aufarbeitung sexualisierter Gewalt oder der Ausmalung feministischer Verfassungsutopien hin zum Versuch der Transformation des Rechts durch zivilen Ungehorsam. Dabei bleibt insbesondere die Frage offen, ob der formende Begriff der Utopie sinnvoll ist, um über neue Möglichkeitsräume für das Recht nachzudenken – oder ob es in einem ersten Schritt darum geht, durch das gemeinsame Ausprobieren und Sich-Begegnen diese neuen Formen erst zu finden.

Den Auftakt macht *Greta Olson* mit ihrer Keynote. Dort lädt sie uns ein, uns gemeinsam auf die Suche nach zukünftigen Träumen und Begegnungsräumen zu begeben. Sie stützt diese Träume konzeptionell auf etwas – im Einzelnen noch Auszudefinierendes –, das sie in Anlehnung an *Rudolf v. Jhering* „(Menschen-)Rechtsgefühl" nennt. Dieses soll uns nicht nur dazu bringen, das positive Recht zu verstehen, sondern zugleich die Möglichkeit beinhalten, zukünftig selbst Recht zu werden – *Olson* bezeichnet dies als *legality*. Programmatisch endet *Olson* mit den Worten: „Let us speculate, dream, and desire."

Hierzu bauen wir zunächst das Fundament mit den Grundlagen gegenwärtiger materialistischer Rechtskritik. Die ersten beiden Beiträge von *Jan Kerkmann* und *Dana-Sophia Valentiner* beschäftigen sich beide – unter zunächst anderen Vorzeichen – mit einer Begründung rechtlicher Normativität aus der Perspektive leiblicher Verletzlichkeit. So zeichnet *Kerkmann* in seinem Beitrag die Rechtsbegründung *Arthur Schopenhauers* nach, der das Recht anhand des Begriffs des Unrechts bestimmt. Dieses Unrecht, wie *Kerkmann* zeigt, liegt für Schopenhauer in der übersteigerten Selbstbejahung des Einzelnen, in dem sich der Wille immer nur, gemäß dem *principio individuationis*, als egoistischer Einzelwille geltend machen kann. Aus dieser Perspektive muss der Unrechtsbegriff zur Grundlage von (Mitleids-)Ethik wie Rechtslehre werden. Eine nicht unbedingt erwartbare Nähe zu dieser Unrechts-Konzeption zeigt sich in der Rekonstruktion feministischer Utopien bei *Valentiner*. So ruht die frühe feministische Utopie des *Buchs von der Stadt der Frauen* von *Christine de Pizan* auf dem Wunsch nach (körperlichem) Schutz vor Männern. Diesen Rückgang auf feministische Utopien nutzt *Valentiner*, um sich vor diesem historischen Hintergrund dem *Frankfurter Frauenmanifest* zu widmen, an dem sie Hintergründe, Konflikte und Zielsetzungen feministischer Utopiebildung ausleuchtet.

Die feministische Rechts(form-)kritik führt uns sodann ins Strafrecht. In ihrem Beitrag beschäftigt sich *Simone Kreutz* mit der Frage, ob das Strafrecht mit seinem Prinzip der äquivalenten Gerechtigkeit überhaupt ein adäquates Mittel sein kann, sexualisierte Gewalt aufzuarbeiten. *Kreutz* betrachtet dabei alternative Ansätze wie *restorative* und *transformative justice* und orientiert sich insbesondere an einem multidimensionalen Gerechtigkeitsbegriff (*kaleidoscopic justice*). Hierbei rückt *Kreutz* die Forderung nach kollektiver Verantwortungsübernahme, die sich aus einem veränderten Verständnis von Gerechtigkeit ergibt, in den Mittelpunkt und skizziert einige Herausforderungen ebenso wie das utopische Potenzial alternativer Rechtspraktiken.

Ein weiteres Feld, in dem die Rechtspraxis von innen heraus kritisiert wird, stellt die aktuelle Diskussion um zivilen Ungehorsam dar. *Sebastian Tober* untersucht in seinem Beitrag kritisch die breit vertretene Annahme, eine strafrechtliche Rechtfertigung von zivilem Ungehorsam sei in sich widersprüchlich. Zu diesem Zweck verknüpft *Tober* den Begriff des zivilen Ungehorsams mit dem Begriff des Verstoßes gegen verhaltensregelnde Normen. *Tober* widerlegt die These der Unmöglichkeit einer strafrechtlichen Rechtfertigung von zivilem Ungehorsam und zeigt, inwiefern dieser als rechtliche Praxis konzeptualisiert werden kann.

Die Alternativen von Immanenz und Transzendenz nehmen noch einmal und *Rodrigo Muray van den Broek* und *D. E. H. Jacobs* in den Blick. In seinem methodologischen Beitrag zur kritischen Theorie des Rechts versucht *van den Broek* die – vermeintlich unüberbrückbare – Differenz zwischen immanenter und transzendenter Rechtskritik durch einen Rückgriff auf *Jürgen Habermas'* Begriff der „Transzendenz von innen" zu egalisieren. Er will aufzuzeigen, inwiefern der zivile Ungehorsam genau diese Trennung in sich vereint und damit gleichzeitig aufhebt. *Jacobs* hingegen fragt nach der Möglichkeit, ja Notwendigkeit eines kommunistischen Rechts. Die Notwendigkeit ergibt sich für *Jacobs* gerade aus einer recht verstandenen Negation der Gewalt. Diese sei *Karl Marx'* Kritik der politischen Ökonomie ebenso eigen wie dem Recht. Aus dieser Perspektive ist das Recht weniger zu verabschieden als vielmehr notwendige Bedingung freier Sozietät.

Und wenn dieser notwendigen Bedingung doch etwas Tragisches innewohnt? Diesen Gedanken greifen zum Abschluss *William Ross* und *Kristian Schäferling* auf und versuchen zugleich, den Begriff des Tragischen in je eigener Weise zu überschreiten. Das Problem ist schnell einsichtig: Die tragische Konstellation kennt kein Außen, seinem Schicksal kann das tragische Subjekt nicht entfliehen. Auf das Recht gewendet bedeutet das, dass auch das moderne Rechtssubjekt seiner rechtlichen Realität nicht entkommen kann. Es bleibt gefangen in den äußeren Bedingungen seiner Form, die es notwendigerweise perpetuiert und aus denen es sich nicht innerhalb der rechtlichen Form befreien kann. *Ross* versucht, unter Rückgriff auf *Walter Benjamins* Begriff des Trauerspiels und *Christoph Menkes Theorie der Befreiung* diese tragische Konstellation aufzuheben. *Ross* erkennt das emanzipative Potenzial des Trauerspiels in der Möglichkeit, die befreiende Erfahrung eines Bruchs in der zweiten Natur darzustellen, ohne diesen Bruch unmittelbar wieder schließen zu müssen.

Schäferling entnimmt einer Lektüre von *G. W. F. Hegels Phänomenologie des Geistes* ein Spannungsverhältnis zwischen dem Tragischen und dem Komischen. Das komische Subjekt ist das Subjekt des abstrakten Rechts, das dem Sittlichen und seinen starren tragischen Außenbedingungen scheinbar entkommen ist. *Schäferling* zeigt jedoch anhand *Hegels Phänomenologie des Geistes*, dass auch das komische Subjekt der sittlichen Immanenz (bei *Hegel*: des Christentums) und der Subjektivierung durch den Staat unterworfen bleibt. Mit anderen Worten: Auch das komische Subjekt ist ein tragisches Subjekt. Könnte es dennoch ein komisches Subjekt geben, das nicht an die Wiederholung des Tragischen gebunden ist?

Juli 2024, Hamburg / Frankfurt am Main

Daria Bayer
Sören Deister
Marcus Döller
Simon Kneip
Hannah Ofterdinger
Jan-Robert Schmidt

The Utopian Desire for a Just Legal Order and *Rechtsgefühle*

Keynote from the Conference in Hamburg in March 2023

GRETA OLSON

I take the title of my talk from the conference title, which I translate into English as "The Utopia of a New Normative Order – Alternatives in Law / Alternatives to Law." I am honored to speak with and learn from you.[1]

I frankly feel humbled by the concept as well as the history of utopias in law and elsewhere. However, I am also suspicious of utopia. I feel small before this concept and genre, at least given your subject with respect to normative orders. I understand utopian and dystopian texts to be performances of profound social criticism. From Plato's *Republic*, authored around 375 BCE, through Thomas More's *Utopia* (1516) to José Muñoz's vision of a queer utopian future as a horizon in *Cruising Utopia* (2009), utopias imagine an infinitely better counter world to our currently troubled one. They pathologize our messy present by highlighting forms of inequity through a reversed view of what is now the dominant and the hegemonic, or through hyperbole, as in Jonathan Swift's wonderful world of perfectly rational equine beings, the Houyhnhnms, and hideously dirty human-like creatures, the Yahoos, at the end of *Gulliver's Travels* (1726).

Perhaps my difficulty in imagining utopian alternatives in or to the law lies in my training in the un-discipline of cultural studies. I am deeply in concert with the sentiments of the post-humanist feminist philosopher Donna Haraway about the particularity and partiality of any given individual's views on a given subject. Haraway reminds us that there can be no god trick in our scholarship, no *deus ex machina* in

1 I retain the form of this text as a spoken introduction to the conference in Hamburg in March 2023. My great appreciation goes to Birte Christ, Stefanie Rück, Melanie Kreitler, and Laura Borchert for critical feedback on this text and to the editors Daria Bayer and Simon Kneip for their helpful review.

the production of knowledge. Instead, we can only think through and communicate in partial forms of knowledge. Haraway uses "knowledge" in the plural to emphasize the particularity and non-universality of given viewpoints. Situated knowledges, as she writes, produce "a more adequate, richer, better account of a world, in order to live in it well and in critical, reflexive relation to our own as well as others' practices of domination and the unequal parts of privilege and oppression that make up all positions."[2]

For me as a researcher and a facilitator of learning – a term I prefer to more hierarchical terms – this entails using the first person singular in my writings to denote a per force limited view. This is not to be confused with anecdotalism or confessionalism, as the use of the I-voice in Anglophone texts is often misunderstood to be. It entails stating my background. This is as an expatriate U. S. American who has lived more than half of her life in Germany, who is a granny and a civil servant, and also a queer-trans feminist womxn, who aims to be anti-racist and decolonizing in her work,[3] and who has a background in philosophy, studio art, linguistics, literature, and auto-didactically in law. This information might help you to frame what I am saying here within the context of knowing how I was acculturated and under what circumstances. Insisting on the situatedness of partial knowledges also entails admitting to a complete lack of omniscience. There is no communal 'we' doing the enunciating. It also entails describing the errors I make along the way when I am exploring a new hypothesis or topic.

Imagining Utopian Alternatives to Law

To imagine what you, members of the Junges Forum Rechtsphilosophie (Young Forum for Legal Philosophy), might mean by utopian alternatives to law,[4] I look to the work of one of the individuals who kindly invited me to be a part of this event. This is Daria Bayer and her recently published *Tragödie des Rechts* ("The Tragedy of Law," 2021).

On the one hand, Bayer's PhD project included the creation and performance of *Jewgenij: The Tragedy of Law* (2019), a drama concerning the Marxist legal scholar Evgeny Bronislavovich Pashukanis's execution under Stalin. In the play, the non-future of Pashukanis's vision of law in his *The General Theory of Law and Marxism* (1924) is imagined and dramatized. The drama performs not only Pashukanis's call for a change of perspectives within the legal sciences but also his repeated insistence that law and the state will "have withered away" when the next stage of communism has been ar-

---

2 Haraway, Donna (1988): "Situated Knowledges: The Science Question in Feminism and the Privilege of Partial Perspective." In: Feminist Studies 14 (3), 575–599, 579. DOI: 3178066.

3 To unpack how I use this term, see Olson, Greta / Lechner, Elisabeth (2022): "#Feminist – Naming Controversies and Celebrating Points of Connection and Joy in Current Feminisms." In: EJES 26 (2), 292–321.

4 Something that I can only speculate about in the plural.

rived at.[5] Bayer understands this work to be a demystification of law's formal hermeticism brought about through defamiliarization. We witness the death of Pashukanis in a Brecht-like tragedy.[6] *Jewgenij: The Tragedy of Law* also demonstrates the potential of the creative arts to perform legal critique. Elsewhere, I have called this imaginative critique of the current legal order through art a type of performative legal pluralism. Recourse is made to an alternative normative order than the current one when the legal norms and rules of application of the current one fail to solve the conflict at hand.[7]

Yet Bayer's text also offers an avenue for reading Pashukanis's work. It demonstrates how *The General Theory of Law and Marxism* was intended to invite a critical discussion of legal theory and Marxism by demonstrating inherent contradictions within law itself.[8] The published dissertation contains the script of the play. But it is framed by two additional academic texts – one, about the reasons for performing a critique of law via Pashukanis (*Vorbemerkungen*); the other, a discussion of the "withering away" of law that Pashukanis imagined, as well as theater's place in this (*Reflexionen*). Repeatedly, Bayer returns to a central passage from Marx and Engels's *The German Ideology* (1845–6). There, Marx and Engels envision utopia as the freedom from bureaucratic authority that would be acquired through overcoming capitalism and the alienated manner of working and living to which capitalism compels us to adhere.

Bayer quotes a passage from *The German Ideology* (1845/1846) in the play and in the accompanying academic texts. I cite it here in English, having de-gendered the easily available online translation:

> in communist society, no one has an exclusive sphere of activity. Rather, one can become accomplished in any branch, for society regulates general production and thus renders it possible for me to do one thing today and another thing tomorrow, to hunt in the morning, fish in the afternoon, and tend to livestock in the evening, practice criticism after dinner, just as I please, without ever becoming a hunter, a fisherman, a herdsman or a critic.[9]

Quoting Bayer in translation, as she reads this passage:

> Since we cannot now know what living with one another in a communist utopia would comprise in detail, Marx and Engels wish to leave it up to the emancipated subjects of a future society to decide on how they wish to shape their social relationships.[10]

---

5 Bayer, Daria (2021): Tragödie des Rechts. Berlin: Duncker & Humblot, 22, 47.
6 Ebd., 25.
7 Olson, Greta (2022): From Law and Literature to Legality and Affect. Oxford: Oxford University Press, 128, 156, 169, 175, 178.
8 Bayer (2021), 75. Where not otherwise indicated, all translations are by the author.
9 Marx, Karl (1845): "Part I: Feuerbach. Opposition of the Materialist and Idealist Outlook." In: The German Ideology. Marxist Internet Archive, Online Translation, https://www.marxists.org/archive/marx/works/1845/german-ideology/ch01a.htm; access: 12.07.2023.
10 Bayer (2021), 21.

I read spontaneity and freedom in the original and in Pashukanis's rendering of it in the second act of *Jewgenij: The Tragedy of Law* as well as in Bayer's explication of this passage, as an almost existentialist notion of free will. The citation from Marx and Engels describes a process rather than a fixed state. It conceives of being human in terms of performing different kinds of activities at will and without having the entirety of one's identity reduced to the performance of a single type of work. This highly haptic and process-oriented ideal of the human condition – of choosing different activities at various times and not being reduced to any one of them – comes close to Jacob Grimm's aspirations for law as described in his defense of German common-law practices in "Von der Poesie im Recht" (On the Poetry in Law, 1815/1816) against the imposition of Roman-law based legal methodology as championed by his former teacher Carl von Savigny, a point I will come back to.

Reform or Revolution

I do not have the impression that the group gathered here in the Young Forum for Legal Philosophy is interested in pursuing legal abolitionism. Many of you have already survived your legal studies and state examinations and therefore might not wish to get rid of the legal system we are operating in altogether. An equality in suffering creates a special bond and sense of community between lawyers, a *Leidensgemeinschaft* that lends significance to those experiences of pain. Many of your talks feature an emphasis on possible legal defenses for alleged crimes committed by Last Generation activists, who were accused of being a criminal group in 2023. My sense is that your community is more concerned with enacting reform from within the legal system.

Utopia is not something I often dare to dream of in relation to normative orders. In the spirit of Eugen Ehrlich, I have a more *lived law* take on law as the legal and extra-legal set of binding norms that regulate behavior, however imperfectly.[11] This takes in a pluralistic understanding of law beyond the books to include the rules for ordering behavior that precede and extend beyond statutes and precedents and legal institutions. The expanded view of *lived law* that I conceive of, and, with others, have called "legality" has nothing to do with an adherence to state-centered law, as is the more typical usage of the term "legality." Rather, legality, as I use it, describes the totality of whatever people feel to be law-full.[12] People's subjective understandings of what **law as**

---

11 Ehrlich, Eugen (1967): "Die Erforschung des lebenden Rechts (1911)." In: Rehbinder, Manfred (Ed.): Recht und Leben: Gesammelte Schriften zur Rechtstatsachenforschung und zur Freirechtslehre. Berlin: Duncker & Humblot, 11–27.

12 For sources on legality in the sense I am using it, see Olson (2022); Crawley, Karen / Peters, Timothy D. (2017): "Introduction: 'Representational Legality'." In: Peters, Timothy / Crawley, Karen (Ed.): Envisioning Legality. Law, Culture and Representation. London: Routledge, 1–18; and in narrative-based scholarship on subjective relationships to law, see Sharp, Cassandra (2022): Hashtag Jurisprudence. Terror and

legality is determines how they inhabit their legal environments and respond to actual legal processes and institutions. Hence, what they think of as binding norms is legality for them.

Understanding Law as Legality

Forms of legality that are disseminated in medial contexts are what I call **popular law**. Currently, instances of popular law can be most readily found in social media exchanges, where individuals and groups debate noteworthy events, as they are occurring in real time as well as larger cultural-legal issues like migration or climate change.

An example of **popular legality** can be found in the numerous exchanges concerning the lack of attention that was paid to the sinking of a fishing boat carrying at least 750 migrants travelling from Libya to Italy off the coast of Greece, on June 13, 2023. It was estimated that fifty or more of the individuals who drowned were children.[13] The lack of public concern about the drowned migrants was compared negatively to the enormous media interest in the search for the Titan submersible which occurred only days afterwards. After June 18, contact was lost with the miniature submarine containing five men, each of whom had paid $250,000 dollars to visit the underwater remains of the Titanic.

In response to this conjunction of events, the meme "Five rich men get lost on a luxury adventure – Multi-million dollar international rescue operation" was posted on June 21 on Instagram while the enormous search operation for the Titan was still underway.[14] The meme responds to the simultaneity of the two political-legal events in affective terms. Images of the two vessels are juxtaposed so as to demonstrate their visual similarities. I read this similarity as a metaphor that makes an appeal to human rights discourse by asserting the equal worthiness of all the human beings that were involved in the sea disasters on a visual level.[15]

The captions on the mirror images compare the divergent dominant attitudes towards the groups of people on the vessels that carried them to their deaths. The disap-

---

Legality on Twitter. Cheltenham: Edward Elgar Publishing; and Ewick, Patricia / Shelby, Susan S. (1998): The Common Place of Law. Stories from Everyday Life. Chicago: University of Chicago Press.

13 Beake, Nick / Wright, George. (2023): "Greece boat disaster: Capsized boat had 100 children in hold, BBC told." In: BBC News. https://www.bbc.com/news/world-europe-65914476; access: 12.07.2023.

14 redstreamnet (2023): "Five rich men get lost on a luxury adventure – Multi-million dollar international rescue operation …" In: Instagram; https://www.instagram.com/p/Ctv3dRRMyjK/?igshid=NjFiZTEoZDQoZQ==; access: 21.06.2023.

15 This claim rests on the insistence that every human has individual (subjective), fundamental, and universal rights to life, freedom, and dignity. For a definition of human rights, see Bast, Jürgen et al. (2023): "Menschenrechtsdiskurse in der Migrationsgesellschaft. Eine Forschungsagenda." MeDiMi Working Paper No. 1, 7. DOI: 10.22029/jlupub-17716.

pearance of the Titan resulted in a costly multinational effort to save its five passengers, while the sinking of the unnamed boat carrying hundreds of people received very little attention until the two disasters began to be compared. Multiple X (formerly Twitter) and Instagram postings appeared in which the cruel concurrence of the two sets of drownings was discussed. Responses included expressions of violently anti-immigration attitudes as in comments that appeared to condone the drowning of the migrants by pointing out that they were "illegal" or "criminal" as compared to the passengers in the Titan, and equally heated posts about the inhumanness of how the migrants had drowned and also then had been depicted in dehumanizing ways.[16] Larger social issues such as resentments about increasing income disparity were also articulated, as documented in comments such as "eat the rich," and criticisms about how the Mediterranean has become a mass grave for people on flight.[17]

The emotionality involved in exchanges about **law as legality** and the medial means with which legality is expressed substitute for actual legal practices and institutions. These remain highly specialized, linguistically impenetrable, and processually opaque for the majority of lay persons. Legality comprises whatever people perceive to be the norms that order and regulate their behaviors, whether these are legal ordinances or rules created on the basis of agreed upon group regulations.

Such norms of behavior are experienced affectively and often unconsciously in what I call individuals' and groups' *Rechtsgefühle* (legal affects) – their impassioned feelings about law, justice, and their legal environments. Here, I make use of Rudolf von Jhering's discussion of "*Rechtsgefühl*" in his *Der Kampf ums Recht* (1872). Note that Jhering used the term *Rechtsgefühl* – literally feeling about law/justice – in the singular.

Jhering describes the dawning awareness of one's *Rechtsgefühl* using the analogies of childbirth and bodily injury. Only when an individual experiences pain akin to that of an injured limb or an organ failure, or contractions in childbirth, do they recognize what they were previously unaware of – their sense of law and justice as the intensely valued quality that it is. The unconscious then becomes conscious in what Jhering describes as a state of intense feeling comparable to a dawning sense of love.[18] Injured

16 redstreamnet (2023); Jay_rockx (2023): "Because illegal immigration is a crime." In: Instagram, https://www.instagram.com/p/Ctv3dRRMyjK/?igshid=NjFiZTEoZDQoZQ==; access: 12.07.2023; Dayana. (2023): "y'all really acting like being illegal." In: Instagram, https://www.instagram.com/p/Ctv3dRRMyjK/?igshid=NjFiZTEoZDQoZQ==; access: 12.07.2023; victormerinox (2023): "Nah, some dudes here are legal. Others are illegal." In: Instagram, https://www.instagram.com/p/Ctv3dRRMyjK/?igshid=NjFiZTEoZDQoZQ==; access: 12.07.2023.

17 Pérez-Peña, Richard (2023): "5 Deaths at Sea Gripped the World. Hundreds of Others Got a Shrug." In: The New York Times. https://www.nytimes.com/2023/06/23/world/europe/titan-sub-greek-migrant-boat.html; access: 08.08.2023; checkyourdoor (2023): "I get the whole eat the rich ..." In: Instagram, https://www.instagram.com/p/Ctv3dRRMyjK/?igshid=NjFiZTEoZDQoZQ%3D%3D; access: 21.07.2023.

18 von Jhering, Rudolf (1872): The Struggle for Law, Lalor, John L. (trans.) Chicago: Callaghan: "The power of the law lies in feeling, just as does the power of love; and the intellect cannot supply that feeling when it is wanting. But as love frequently does not know itself, and as a single instant suffices to bring it

Rechtsgefühl demands redress, even as Jhering acknowledged that not all social groups have the same means to demand justice.[19]

I use the term in my own work to denote a sense of felt, legally manifested injustice that leads to legal-political protest. I understand *Rechtsgefühle* by necessity to be a multiple concept, first, because of the divergence of opinions about what *Rechtsgefühle* precisely are, and, second, because subjective feelings about law and justice are never singular. They are overlapping, multiple, and sometimes conflicting, and depend on a person's position of relative privilege within their legal environment.[20]

Affective Experiences of Law as Legality in *Rechtsgefühlen*

I wish to imagine with you what the *Rechtsgefühle* in utopian alternatives to law might be. What do they feel and look like? An example of a utopian desire for an altered normative universe, Grimm's poetic essay "On the Poetry in Law" contrasts the abstraction and narrow application of legal rules in contemporary jurisprudence to a way of doing law that was, as Grimm envisions it, once rooted in poetic and performative language. The essay's poetic language and the indivisibility of law and poetry Grimm outlines there, serve to deconstruct the oppositional, binary division that is conventionally made between the fictional (legal) and the non-fictional (aesthetic).

Grimm imaginatively creates an alternative and utopian legal order to contrast his current one, suggesting that a degree of fictionality is inherent to law when it is practiced well and cheerfully (*mit Heiterkeit*) and is rich in belief (*das Glaubensreiche*).[21] Nostalgically, Grimm recalls a distant Germanic common law past in which judges spoke law in an identical manner to the way poets speak poetry. These judges did not possess the law by virtue of their training, specialized vocabulary, and syllogistic methods of application. Rather, they spoke law for and with a people with whom they were in complete unison:

to a full consciousness of itself, so the feeling of legal right uniformly knows not what it is, and what it can do, so long as it is not wounded; but the violation of legal right compels it to speak, unveils the truth, and manifests its force," 61.

19 von Jhering, Rudolf (1872): Kampf um's Recht. Freiburg: Haufe.

20 Similar to situated knowledges, as discussed by Donna Haraway, legal affects are partial, specific, and contextually bound. My thanks to Laura Borchert for this insight.

21 Grimm, Jacob (1822): Kleinere Schriften (6. Band, Erstdruck 1816). Berlin: Ferd. Dümmlers Verlagsbuchhandlung, § 2: "In neither [poetry nor law] is empty statute creation or vain invention at home. The origin of both rests on two essential things, on [the one hand on] that which is wonderful and [on the other hand on] that which is worthy of trust. I understand 'wonder' here as that distant place [a common origin], where for every people the beginning of its laws and its songs meet." The original reads: "in keinem ist blosze satzung noch eitle erfindung zu haus. ihr beider ursprung beruhet auf zweierlei wesentlichem, auf dem wunderbaren und dem glaubreichen. unter wunder verstehe ich hier die ferne, worin für jedes volk der anfang seiner gesetze und lieder tritt," 154.

> everything was available to them [our ancestors] for the most lively and straightforward of uses. And, therefore, everything was theirs in common. And property belonged to everyone. A song belonged to no one poet. Whoever sang it simply knew it better and could sing it more faithfully. [Similarly,] the status of law had just as little to do with [the status of] any particular judge. Judges were not allowed to create new law. Rather, just as singers watched over the property of songs, those who rendered judgement watched over the office of and the service to the law. Without doubt, poetry and law must be understood as proving and as validating one another in archaic times and as closely related to peoples' customs and feasts.[22]

I want to stress the haptic, the unconstrained, and the processual that I read here and also find in the passage from *The German Ideology*, cited above, about a society that would make it possible "to hunt in the morning, fish in the afternoon, and tend to livestock in the evening, practice criticism after dinner, just as I please, without ever becoming a hunter, a fisherman, a herdsman or a critic." As Bayer interprets this passage, a transformed society of "emancipated subjects" would not only leave possibilities of social relationships open but would also no longer identify people on the basis of the type of work they perform.[23]

I discover an expression of utopian longing for an alternative legal order in aesthetic artefacts and performances that are used to protest current legal orders and to supplement them imaginatively with alternated normativities. As mentioned, the arts of Black Lives Matter present haptic responses to systemic racism in the United States and the continued violence against Black life in policing. The photograph *Taking a Stand in Baton Rouge* (2016) by Jonathan Bachman pictures Iesha Evans being arrested by police dressed in riot gear while she was protesting against the racially-motivated killing of Alton Sterling, who was shot after he had already been pinned down by officers.

Evans wears a simple sleeveless dress as she stands upright and faces off against a line of encroaching police, fully decked out in battle gear. The iconic photograph recalls visually arresting images of protest in the face of overwhelming force such as the

22 Ebd., § 2. The original reads: "unseren vorfahren wenigstens würde eine andere ansicht fremd, ja unverständlich gewesen sein. die heutige Wissenschaft pflegt alles haarklein zu spalten, sie aber trennten nichts, sondern genossen alles aus einem vollkommen zureichenden grund; alles war ihnen nur für die geradeste, lebendigste anwendung vorhanden, eben deshalb auch alles gemeines gut und eigenthum jedermanns. keinem dichter gehörte das lied; wer es sang wuste es blosz fertiger und treuer zu singen; eben so wenig gieng das ansehen des gesetzes aus von dem richter, der kein neues finden durfte; sondern die sänger verwalteten das gut der lieder, die urtheiler verweseten amt und dienst der rechte. unbedenklich also müssen die poesie und das recht der alten zeit als für einander beweisend und gültig angenommen werden und beide als mit sitten und festen des volks eng zusammenhangend."
23 Bayer (2021), 21.

"tank man" from Tiananmen Square.[24] Whether in music, in the visual arts, or in performative protest, as in Iesha Evans's demonstrable act of civil disobedience in 2016, aesthetic forms can be employed to critique current legal conditions and/or to perform alternative normative orders.

I find a utopian desire to reform or revolutionize law in Grimm's wish for the legal to, once again, be based in 'the wonderful' and in Iesha Evans's act of aesthetic resistance against arresting police.

Speculation

When legal theory and law look forward and speculate, they are jurisgenerative and perhaps also idealistic and even utopian. Consider, for instance, Jeremy Bentham's footnote about the immorality of harming animals in his *An Introduction to the Principles of Morals and Legislation* (1789), a work that was intended to provide a basis for jurisprudence and punishment based in Utilitarian philosophy. At the end of his analysis, Bentham enters into a discussion of the limits of law that anticipates the work of moral philosophers such as Amartya Sen and Martha Nussbaum on capabilities. He notes the intolerable lack of recognition of the suffering of living beings susceptible to human rule with animals being "tormented" without justification.[25] He then compares their ill treatment to that of enslaved persons:

> The day has been, I grieve to say in many places it is not yet past, in which the greater part of the species, under the denomination of slaves, have been treated by the law exactly upon the same footing as, in England for example, the inferior races of animals are still. The day *may* come when the rest of the animal creation may acquire those rights which never could have been withholden from them but by the hand of tyranny. The French have already discovered that the blackness of the skin is no reason why a human being should be abandoned without redress to the caprice of a tormentor. It may come one day to be recognised, that the number of the legs, the villosity of the skin, or the termination of the *os sacrum*, are reasons equally insufficient for abandoning a sensitive being to the same fate. What else is it that should trace the insuperable line? Is it the faculty of reason, or perhaps,

24 Further, the photograph also recalls iconic photographs of Civil Rights and Vietnam War protesters that resonate in the U. S. American visual imaginary. Earlier protesters stood off against armed police, bearing only flowers as symbolic weapons. Miller, Michael E. (2016): "'Graceful in the lion's den': Photo of young woman's arrest in Baton Rouge becomes powerful symbol." In: The Washington Post, https://www.washingtonpost.com/news/morning-mix/wp/2016/07/11/graceful-in-the-lions-den-photo-of-young-womans-arrest-in-baton-rouge-goes-viral/; access:11.07.2016. See also Rothman, Lily (2016): "Subject of Iconic 1960s Protest Image Speaks About Viral Baton Rouge Photo." In: Time Magazine, https://time.com/4401559/baton-rouge-protest-photo-history/; access: 20.07.2023.

25 Bentham, Jeremy (1823): An Introduction to the Principles of Morals and Legislation. (Erstdruck 1789). Whitefish: Kessinger Reprint, 236.

> the faculty of discourse? But a full-grown horse or dog is beyond comparison a more rational, as well as a more conversable animal, than an infant of a day, or a week, or even a month. But suppose the case were otherwise, what would it avail? the question is not, Can they *reason*? nor, Can they *talk*? but, Can they *suffer*?[26]

Bentham makes two interrelated arguments. First, just as the French had done previously, the English must now recognize that having a darker phenotype does not legitimate a person's enslavement. Second and analogously, the relatively minor anatomical differences between humans and other kinds of living creatures does not entail that these other animals do not suffer. In fact, their capacity for suffering necessitates an enlargement of existing laws to ensure their protection.

Against a history of locating legal subjectivity and personhood in the capacity for speech and rational thought, Bentham insists that experiencing suffering is the central criterion for legal protection. He advocates for expanding laws, which need to be based in the responsibility for the good of others, to include those with fur or fins.

When legal theorists such as Bentham take in affective experiences as a criterion for determining a right to collective protections or even legal personhood, then non-human and non-narrating entities have to be considered as potential rights holders. When conceived of as collective entities that are subject to harm, the environment and individual parts of the environment, such as rivers, can be considered to have a right to redress through the suffering brought upon them via human intervention. When one understands legal systems to bear responsibility for addressing affective states such as acute suffering, then they take on a responsibility for advocating for the rights of non-human beings.

Legal tools to advocate for the non-human are found in the Rights of Nature (RoN), which has been used to argue for the inherency of ecosystems' rights to thrive and to be protected from harm.[27] Various Articles from the European Convention of Human Rights (ECHR) have also been used in cases appearing before the European Court of Human Rights (ECtHR) to enact environmental measures based on the harms done to humans in that environment and the violation of their human rights.[28]

More speculatively, Malte Gruber envisions a private law that would move away from a bilateral model of liability, individual responsibility, and definable chains of harm to concepts of collective climate responsibility and endangered legal entities. In this, Gruber takes up Gunther Teubner's call for a utopian political law, a law for the

---

26 Ebd., 311.

27 See, for example, Kersten, Jens (2014): "Das Anthropozän-Konzept." In: RW Rechtswissenschaft 5 (3), 378–414. DOI: 10.5771/1868-8098-2014-3-378.

28 European Court of Human Rights (2022): "Factsheet – Environment and the ECHR." In: Press Unit, https://www.echr.coe.int/documents/d/echr/FS_Environment_ENG; access: 12.07.2023.

future.[29] A newly envisioned private law would advocate for the subjective rights of collective entities that are worthy of protection. This jurisgenerative private law would include vulnerable entities that currently cannot advocate for themselves:

> a future law can no longer be content with analysing everything "private" counterfactually into bilateral relationships of human individuals, which are then contrasted with the communal interests of a "public" [...]. future law must develop civil procedures that give a voice to those affected by various climate and environmental damages, especially those who are still unheard. This enables an adequate negotiation of ecological damages.[30]

Gruber recognizes the many difficulties that impaired previous legal claims to environmental protections and collective liability. Yet he claims that law can no longer divorce itself from political change and political conflict. Liability law, in particular, must be developed creatively in order to address the insurmountable environmental problems that influence us all:

> Helping the "politics of the law" (Politik des Gesetzes) gain legal force can therefore provide substantive legal flanking and procedural support for an otherwise insufficiently enforceable yet existentially urgent climate protection – almost in the sense of a "climate politics of the law," which has an independent function for a law of the future.[31]

In work that I am embarking on now in the research group "Human Rights Discourse in Migration Societies" (DFG FOR 5321 "Menschenrechtsdiskurse in der Migrationsgesellschaft" (MeDiMi)), I am inquiring about the applicability of the concept of *Rechtsgefühle* in the context of human rights. Working with images of migration in conventional news sources and in social media, my colleagues and I analyze the affective states that are created when people engage with images of migration. I want to understand if *Menschenrechtsgefühle* (feelings for/about human rights) could provide the basis for a decolonized human rights discourse and praxis. I am wondering if these 'feelings for human rights' might have the jurisgenerative potential to enable people to alter their current legal orders. I wish to see if *Menschenrechtsgefühle* have a utopian potential.

In previous work, I speculated that a large number of images of migration serve to dehumanize those they depict by either likening them to natural disasters (a tsunami of migrants) or comparing them to predators. Another group invokes humanitarian discourse to depict migrants as perpetual victims in need of being saved by their view-

29 Teubner, Gunther (1990): "Die 'Politik des Gesetzes' im Recht der Konzernhaftung. Plädoyer für einen sektoralen Konzerndurchgriff." In: Baur, Jürgen F. et al. (eds.): Festschrift für Ernst Steindorff zum 70. Geburtstag. Berlin: de Gruyter, 261–279.

30 Gruber, Malte (2024): "The Anthropocenic Cupola. On Future Models of Climate Change Liability." In: Zeitschrift für Restssoziologie 44 (1), 67–110, 77. DOI: 10.1515/zfrs-2023-1004.

31 Ebd., 72.

ers. Yet a third type of image gives individuals names and stories and presents them as legal subjects and rights bearers who have moral and legal agency. This last group, I hypothesize, can move people beyond typically distant viewing practices and move them to want to take up political action, thus rendering a more utopian legal order a plausible reality.[32]

Examples of Utopian Desire as Expressed through New Visions of Law

In the last part of this talk, I want to address the reformist work you are doing here and also to highlight the research of some younger colleagues. These colleagues are all working in various legal-cultural environments to inch closer to more utopian legal orders.

I quoted Daria Bayer at the beginning of this talk. I described her performance and explication of the tragic suppression of the possibilities presented by Marxist law as speaking out of a utopian desire for change. This performance finds an echo in the dramatic reading of cultural-legal texts that your group will open this conference with when I am done speaking.[33] Your performance here tonight, like Bayer's *Jewgenij: The Tragedy of Law* demonstrates that law and legal philosophy are an iterative and performative practice that can also be enacted, lived, and fleshed out in new, changing ways. I want to finish this text by gesturing to the work of younger colleagues besides the ones gathered here. Their work, like yours, imagines an altered normative future. (Note that "young" is relative. As my beloved and long departed dad used to say, "old" is always your own age plus fifteen years. You should cultivate older friends.)

In her recent monograph *EU Law as a Creative Process – a hermeneutic approach for the EU internal market and fundamental rights protection* (2021), the Dutch legal scholar and European Court of Justice litigation expert, Pauline Phoa, analyzes European Court of Justice cases that work to balance fundamental and economic rights. Phoa is interested in identifying the vision of humanity that underlines these judgements and the multiple narrative choices that went into their construction. Embracing James Boyd White's and Jeanne Gaakeer's ideas of narrative jurisprudence and Paul Ricœur's model of meaning making in prefiguration, configuration, and transfiguration, she traces the various and at times also conflicting images of humanity that inform the Court's role in deciding on EU law. Her detailed narrative readings of the ECJ's judgements and the ideas of selfhood, humanity, and EU citizenship that indirectly inform them are intend-

32 See Olson/Wessels (2020); Olson (2022); Olson, Greta (2023): "Metaphor" / "Metaphoric Fictionality in Poems about Migration and in Anti-Immigration Discourse." In: Gammelgaard, Lasse Raaby et al. (eds.): Fictionality and Literature. Core Concepts Revisited. Athens: Ohio State University Press, 182–211.

33 Larissa Reissner (1925): "Die Barrikade," Elfriede Jelinek (1975): Die Liebhaberinnen, and Ursula K. Le Guin (1974): Die Enteigneten, moderated by Liza Mattutat, Daria Bayer, and Marcus Döller.

ed to enable law to better enact justice: "I believe that asking such questions will lead to more clear, consistent and just judgements, irrespective of the particular field of law."[34]

Ultimately, Phoa's text imagines a legal life that can be deeply transformative. She invites her sister and fellow legal practitioners to practice legal process in consciously self-reflective and critical creative ways.

> Legal life, therefore is a literary, creative life. We constantly create texts, and tell and retell stories as we shift between the concrete facts of a case and the abstract rules of statutes and, in more complex cases, the higher legal order norms of general principles of law and/or international and super-national institutions, or even the abstract idea of justice.
>
> As legal professionals, we have the responsibility to ask ourselves; how do we do that, by what art?[35]

Closer to home, a colleague at the University of Giessen, Germany, the cultural-legal studies, scholar Laura Borchert recently completed a dissertation titled *Beyond Bostock: Towards a New Queer Rights* (2022), which will be published as the monograph *Suspect Subjects* in early 2025. In this text, Borchert argues that law can potentially play a "role in and for queer emancipation" and proposes a queer hermeneutics of law.[36] Her intention is to move away from the "legal sexual orientationalism" which she accurately detects at the basis of U. S. American law, that renders anything other than heterosexuality and cisgenderism marginal and deviant. To avoid this orientationalism, Borchert proposes to 'queer' the legal criteria currently necessary for LGBTQIA+ persons to receive protections according to Constitutional law.

In order to envision how the Supreme Court might "judg[e] more queerly," she presents a series of "queer legal imaginaries." This includes suggestions for post-categorical anti-discrimination laws that do not essentialize identity, thereby reducing members of the groups these laws are aimed to protect to their gender- or sexuality-based minority status. Borchert outlines how rights could ideally be based on a collective understanding of mutual needs and networks of care. Finally, Borchert argues against abolishing the legal system altogether in favor of "re-thinking, re-conceptualizing and re-creating" law and cultural-legal education to be emancipatory endeavors, for "law can also serve as an agent for uncovering de-equalizing conditions."

Finally, American law professor Almas Kahn's recent work conceptualizes a new category of Black Lives Matter judicial opinions in the United States. Kahn describes these opinions' formalist readings of the Fourth Amendment with its prohibitions against unreasonable searches and seizures as a legal strategy for combating racial bias

---

34 Phoa, Pauline (2021): EU Law as a Creative Process. A Hermeneutic Approach for the EU Internal Market and Fundamental Rights Protection. Zutphen: Europa Law Publishing, 263.
35 Ebd., 2.
36 Borchert, Laura (2022): Beyond Bostock. Towards a New Queer Rights (unpubl. Diss. Giessen).

in U. S. law.[37] She analyzes judicial opinions that "advance fundamentalist critiques of the U. S. legal system through formal subversion" and calls this strategy a "creative formalism [intended] to promote racial justice." By uncovering the creative potential of judicial opinions, particularly dissenting opinions, in cases in which the court had insisted that it was color-blind, and in trials that insist on "color-conscious decision-making" in their procedures, Kahn delineates inventive means to address the systemic racism that continues to operate at the heart of American law:

> Black Lives Matter opinions fundamentally endeavor to close the fissure between law and justice that has been a defining feature of Black life since the colonial period. While acknowledging the judiciary's complicity in creating the racial inequities that continue to roil U. S. law and society today, Black Lives Matter opinion authors retain hope in reparation through genre re-formation.[38]

For reasons of space, I have only gestured to the innovative work of the scholars mentioned here. No abolitionism is called for. Rather these legal thinkers sketch out or document the specific, well-thought-out steps that are necessary for changing and ameliorating the legal conditions of current normative realities. I see them and you as the legal actors and thinkers who can alter legal futures.

Dreaming of and Desiring Utopia

Returning to a utopian vision that has inspired me in my own work and life, I wish to finish this talk by quoting from the late José Esteban Muñoz on queer utopia. He describes a queer desire for the unattained, the not yet here, yet also still possible. This queer desire allows us to dream. As Muñoz writes:

> Queerness in not yet here. Queerness is an ideality. Put another way, we are not yet queer. We may never touch queerness, but we can feel it as the warm illumination of a horizon imbued with potentiality. […]
>
> To see queerness as horizon is to perceive it as a modality of ecstatic time in which the temporal stranglehold that I describe as straight time is interrupted or stepped out of. […] Seeing queerness as horizon rescues and emboldens concepts such as that have withered by the touch of neoliberal thought and assimilationist politics.[39]

---

37 Kahn, Almas (forthcoming): "Black Lives Matter in the Judiciary and the Re-formation of Legal Narratives". In: Olson, Greta / Stern, Simon (eds.): Law, Narrative, Narratology. Interdisciplinary Essays.
38 Ebd.
39 Muñoz, José Esteban (2009): Cruising Utopia. The Then and Now of Queer Futurity. New York: New York University Press, 1, 32.

In the spirit of Ernst Bloch, Muñoz advocates for concrete utopias in contrast to abstract ones, arguing that the former represent "the realm of educated hope" and comprise "the hopes of a collective, an emergent group, or even the solitary oddball who is the one who dreams for many."[40]

It is this concrete form of dreaming for many that I want to dwell on with you and the concrete utopias I see you desiring. I see a vision for an alternative normative order in the very concrete possibility of a feminist constitution that Dana Valentiner explores in her talk, a possibility that was already in place in the Frankfurt Women's Manifesto from 1991. Utopian desire is also found in the various forms of civil disobedience with which your talks engage. Many of you reference the protests by the Last Generation here in Germany. I see you defending these individuals and their *Rechtsgefühle* in the future and your finding the creative legal means needed to do so. With you, I wish to dream alternative future normative orders.

Allow me, if you will, – an older human – to share your vision of the future. Let us speculate, dream, and desire.

About the Author: Greta Olson is Professor of English and American Literary and Cultural Studies at the University of Giessen and Director of the Center for Diversity, Media, and Law. She was Fellow at the Käte Hamburger Center for Advanced Study in the Humanities "Law as Culture" in Bonn (2014, 2016). She is a general editor of the *European Journal of English Studies* (EJES), and the co-founder of the European Network for Law and Literature.

Prof. Dr. Greta Olson
Justus Liebig University of Giessen, Department of English, Otto-Behaghel-Straße 10 B, 35394 Gießen, Germany, greta.olson@anglistik.uni-giessen.de.

---

40 Ebd., 3.

Die Normativität des Leibes in Schopenhauers Rechtstheorie

JAN KERKMANN

The Normativity of the Body in Schopenhauer's Theory of Law

Abstract: In this essay, I would like to show that Schopenhauer derives the genesis of the state from the collective longing for bodily integrity. For Schopenhauer, the hypothetical consent of each individual is necessary for the constitution of the state. It follows from this that the state has to secure the corporeality of the individual, which is always endangered in the state of nature. Therefore, *in* and *with* law, the state violates its own conditions of existence as soon as it seeks to extend its powers to the body of the individual. On the basis of the state- and law-founding dimension of corporeality, it is possible to argue against both the arbitrariness of a legal positivist formalism and the metaphysical tendency of natural law normativity.
Keywords: Corporeality, pure legal theory, contract theory, constitution of the state, political liberalism, Schopenhauer

1 Einleitung

In der Willensmetaphysik Arthur Schopenhauers nimmt der Leib eine zentrale Rolle ein. Während die ontologische und naturphilosophische Bedeutung des Leibes durch facettenreiche Untersuchungen[1] erschlossen werden konnte, wurde die politisch-rechtstheoretische Begründungsdimension der Leiblichkeit in der Schopenhauer-For-

1 Den metaphysischen und systematischen Status des Leibes in der Philosophie Schopenhauers analysieren besonders die vielschichtigen Beiträge in, vgl. Koßler, Matthias / Jeske, Michael (Hg.): Philosophie des Leibes. Die Anfänge bei Schopenhauer und Feuerbach (2012). Würzburg: Könighausen und Neumann. Zum hermeneutischen Element in Schopenhauers Analogiebildung zwischen dem Leib und dem Willen vgl. Dörpinghaus, Andreas (2000): „Der Leib als Schlüssel zur Welt. Zur Bedeutung der Funktion des Leibes in der Philosophie Schopenhauers". In: Schopenhauer-Jahrbuch 81, 15–32.

schung bislang nicht mit derselben Intensität erörtert.[2] In diesem Aufsatz soll gezeigt werden, dass Schopenhauers Gleichsetzung des Leibes mit dem individuellen Willen fruchtbringende Impulse für eine immanente Kritik des Rechts liefern kann. Auf den ersten Blick kann und soll Schopenhauers Theorie – auch im Selbstverständnis des Frankfurter Denkers – keine utopische Alternative zum Recht anbieten. Sie kann aber dazu dienen, innerhalb eines bestehenden Rechtssystems die legitimen Grenzen eines staatlichen Zugriffs auf den Einzelnen ins Bewusstsein zu rufen, ohne auf strittige, normative Annahmen zurückgreifen oder eine entwicklungsgeschichtliche Auffassung des Rechts vertreten zu müssen. Im gemeinsamen Dialog zwischen Philosophie und Rechtswissenschaft, kann Schopenhauers „individualistische Rechtslehre auf moralischer Grundlage"[3] für die Suche nach Alternativen *im* Recht herangezogen werden.

Um diese Lesart zu plausibilisieren, soll besonders der § 62 aus dem vierten Buch der *Welt als Wille und Vorstellung* beleuchtet werden. Die leitende These lautet, dass Schopenhauer den individuellen Leib respektive den Willen in seiner Ethik als genetischen und systematischen Grund des Rechts begreift. Schopenhauer kann den Kategorien von ‚Recht' und ‚Unrecht' eine überpositive und vorstaatliche Gültigkeit zusprechen, indem er sie in dem leiblich erfahrbaren Phänomen eines Einbruches in die „Gränze der fremden Willensbejahung"[4] verankert. Gerade weil Schopenhauer das Recht von der staatlichen Wirksamkeit entkoppelt und seine Existenz bereits im primordialen Naturzustand verortet, spürt er im Begriffsgehalt des Rechts einen Maßstab für die immanente Kritik desselben auf. Eine immanente Kritik kann *zum einen* überzeugen, wenn sie in der beanspruchten Begründungslogik des kritisierten Bezugssystems Widersprüche, Inkonsistenzen oder fehlerhafte Regressargumente freilegt. *Zum anderen* kann sie zu ihrem Gelingen aber auch auf ein vorauszusetzendes Fundament ausgreifen, das bei Schopenhauer – so die hier verfochtene Auffassung – in einer normativ konnotierten Leiblichkeit wurzelt. Von diesem Sinnhorizont oder Grundsatz kann und muss die Kritik alsdann zeigen, dass er jeden einzelnen Schritt der vermeintlich autarken Entfaltung des betrachteten Referenzgefüges im Verborgenen leitet und dessen Schlussfolgerungen bis in die letzten Filiationen trägt. Dass Schopenhauers

---

2 Auch Rudolf Neidert exponiert die Leib-Wille-Identität in seiner insgesamt sehr verdienstvollen Arbeit nicht als Ausgangspunkt und Begründungszentrum der reinen Rechtslehre. Vgl. Neidert, Rudolf (1966): Die Rechtsphilosophie Schopenhauers und ihr Schweigen zum Widerstandsrecht. Tübingen: Mohr. Es ist ein dezidiertes Anliegen des vorliegenden Artikels, einer Lesart entgegenzuwirken, die das vonseiten Neiderts scharfsinnig beobachtete ‚Schweigen zum Widerstandsrecht' als etatistisches Relikt innerhalb der liberalen Staatstheorie Schopenhauers dechiffrieren möchte. Vielmehr muss Schopenhauer gemäß der hier zu verfechtenden und einzulösenden Auffassung das Widerstandsrecht gegenüber staatlichen Willkürmaßnahmen nicht eigens thematisieren, weil es sich aus seiner Konzeption einer legitimen Abwehr des am jeweiligen Leib verübten Unrechts notwendigerweise ergibt.

3 So lautet die treffende Charakterisierung Petersen, Jens (2017): Schopenhauers Gerechtigkeitsvorstellung, Berlin/Boston: De Gruyter, 24.

4 Schopenhauer, Arthur (2017): „Die Welt als Wille und Vorstellung". In: ders.: Sämtliche Werke. 10 Bände. Hg. Hübscher. Zürich: Diogenes. Band I, 2. Teilband, § 62, 417

Version einer immanenten Kritik des Rechts dem zweiten Typus zuzuordnen ist, soll im Folgenden anhand einer textnahen Lektüre des § 62 veranschaulicht werden. Zuvor ist allerdings Schopenhauers Konzeption der Willensmetaphysik in aller gebotenen Kürze vorzustellen, da diese die Rechtstheorie des Philosophen grundiert.

2 Die Willensmetaphysik Schopenhauers im Grundriss

In den §§ 26–28 seines Hauptwerkes *Die Welt als Wille und Vorstellung* entfaltet Schopenhauer seine Willensmetaphysik, wobei er sich zunächst auf die naturphilosophische Grundlegungsebene konzentriert. Das metaphysische, monistische Prinzip des Willes offenbart sich nach Schopenhauer in der Erscheinungswelt und differenziert sich innerhalb von Raum und Zeit verschiedenartig aus:

> Wie eine Zauberlaterne viele und mannigfaltige Bilder zeigt, es aber nur eine und die selbe Flamme ist, welche ihnen allen die Sichtbarkeit ertheilt; so ist in allen mannigfaltigen Erscheinungen, welche neben einander die Welt füllen, oder nach einander als Begebenheiten sich verdrängen, doch nur der *eine Wille* das Erscheinende, dessen Sichtbarkeit, Objektität das Alles ist, und der unbewegt bleibt mitten in jenem Wechsel: er allein ist das Ding an sich: alles Objekt aber ist Erscheinung, Phänomen, in Kants Sprache zu reden.[5]

Der Wille erweist sich nicht nur als die individuelle Lebenskraft in jedem Menschen, sondern expliziert sich zuvor in den großen Objektivationsstufen der anorganischen Kräfte, der Flora und der Tierwelt. Erst am Ende dieses vertikal aufsteigenden Naturprozesses manifestiert sich der Wille auch in der menschlichen Gestalt.[6] Der Wille konstituiert das „Jedem unmittelbar Bekannte“[7], das sich im Raum-Zeit-Kontinuum als Materialität des individuellen Leibes ausdrückt. Nach Schopenhauer ist jeder „wahre Akt“ des Willens „sofort und unausbleiblich auch eine Bewegung“[8] des Leibes. Der jeweilige Leib fungiert demzufolge als notwendige Bedingung sämtlicher Handlungen sowie des äußerlichen Affiziert-Werdens. Der Leib enthüllt sich als Träger jeder faktischen Willensentscheidung, die über einen „veränderliche[n] Vorsatz“[9] oder bloßen Zukunftswunsch hinausreicht.

Insofern die Kapazitäten der Raum und Zeit vereinigenden Materie begrenzt sind und alle Lebewesen darauf drängen, ihr Existenzrecht gegen andere Willenserscheinungen zu sichern, muss die Materie beständig ihre Form wechseln. Dergestalt bezeugt sich für Schopenhauer – und dieses naturphilosophisch hergeleitete Theorem

5 Schopenhauer (2017), Bd. I/2: § 28, 205.
6 Schopenhauer (2017), Bd. I/2: § 26, 179.
7 Schopenhauer (2017), Bd. I/2: § 18, 143.
8 Schopenhauer (2017), Bd. I/2: § 18, 143.
9 Schopenhauer (2017), Bd. I/2: § 18, 143.

zeichnet die pessimistische Textur der Philosophie Schopenhauer aus – „die dem Willen wesentliche Entzweiung mit sich selbst".[10] Weit entfernt, die Natur im romantisch-rousseauschen Sinne als eine harmonische Idylle zu verklären und sie der menschlichen Kultur als unverfälschte Kontrastfolie gegenüberzustellen, ist sie nach Schopenhauer durch „Streit, Kampf und Wechsel des Sieges"[11] geprägt. Entsprechend referiert Schopenhauer in seiner tragischen Schilderung der Natur auf die destruktive Rücksichtslosigkeit, mit der jener Streit ausgefochten wird:

> Die deutlichste Sichtbarkeit erreicht dieser allgemeine Kampf in der Thierwelt, welche die Pflanzenwelt zu ihrer Nahrung hat, und in welcher selbst wieder jedes Thier die Beute und Nahrung eines andern wird, d. h. die Materie, in welcher seine Idee sich darstellte, zur Darstellung eines andern abtreten muß, indem jedes Thier sein Daseyn nur durch die beständige Aufhebung eines fremden erhalten kann; so daß der Wille zum Leben durchgängig an sich selber zehrt und in verschiedensten Gestalten seine eigene Nahrung ist, bis zuletzt das Menschengeschlecht, weil es alle andern überwältigt, die Natur für ein Fabrikat zu seinem Gebrauch ansieht, das selbe Geschlecht jedoch auch [...] in sich selbst jenen Kampf, jene Selbstentzweiung des Willens zur furchtbarsten Deutlichkeit offenbart, und *homo homini lupus* wird.[12]

Diese Textstelle ist vor allem deswegen von Bedeutung, weil Schopenhauer die zivilisationstheoretisch-aufklärerische Trennlinie zwischen der vermeintlich ‚schonungslosen' Natur und der vernunfterfüllten Fortschrittsgeschichte der Menschheit aufhebt. Dadurch untermauert er die Allgegenwart der in der gesamten Vorstellungswelt dominierenden Selbstentzweiung des Willens. Die Ausprägungen des ewigen Streits lassen sich überall in der Natur *und* in der Kultur entdecken. Im zwischenmenschlichen Konfliktzusammenhang des *homo homini lupus* stattet sich der Streit nach Schopenhauer mit den Waffen der List und der Verstellung aus. Es kommt zu einer Fortsetzung desselben Kampfes mit anderen Mitteln. Im Hinblick auf die leitende Fragestellung dieses Aufsatzes ist also festzuhalten, dass die Natur in Schopenhauers Monismus des Willens keineswegs axiologisch als Refugium ursprünglicher Güte aufgerufen wird, das erst durch den Einfluss des vermeintlich jäh in diese Ordnung hineinragenden Menschen korrumpiert wurde. Daher können die menschliche Geschichte und Kulturentwicklung nicht beanspruchen, jemals gänzlich aus dem ruinösen Naturgeschehen herauszutreten. Der dunkle Grund des an sich selbst zehrenden Willens durchzieht die anorganischen Körper ebenso wie die sublimierten, menschlichen Institutionen.[13]

---

10 Schopenhauer (2017), Bd. I/2: § 27, 198.
11 Schopenhauer (2017), Bd. I/2:§ 27, 197.
12 Schopenhauer (2017), Bd. I/2: § 27, 198.
13 Vgl. Schopenhauer, Arthur (2017): „Parerga & Paralipomena I". In: ders.: Sämtliche Werke. 10 Bände. Hg. Hübscher. Zürich: Diogenes. Band IX, 2. Teilband, § 128, 280 f.: „Ueberall und zu allen Zeiten hat es viel Unzufriedenheit mit den Regierungen, Gesetzen und öffentlichen Einrichtungen gegeben; großentheils aber nur, weil man stets bereit ist, diesen das Elend zur Last zu legen, welches dem menschlichen Daseyn

Es ist die zentrale These dieses Aufsatzes, dass es gerade diese überzeitliche und das gesamte Naturgeschehen prägende Erstreckung des Pessimismus ist, die es Schopenhauer gestattet, den Staat nicht mit dem gefährlichen, normativen Anspruch einer Verwirklichung chiliastischer Zustände zu überfrachten. Schopenhauers naturphilosophisch untermauerte und in einem liberalen Sinne weiterzuführende Beschränkung der staatlichen Eingriffsberechtigung ist im Folgenden anhand der Rechtstheorie zu erläutern.

3 Schopenhauers Definition des Unrechts

Es kann gemäß der hier vertretenen Leitthese nicht als Zufall betrachtet werden, dass Schopenhauer bereits zu Beginn des § 62 auf die Leib-Wille-Relation abhebt. Auch an diesem Ort beschreibt er den zweckmäßig organisierten Leib als eine Selbstdarstellung des Willens, die sich in der Abfolge zeitlicher Akte versinnlicht. Entsprechend wird die basale Willensbejahung als „Erhaltung des Leibes, mittels Anwendung der eigenen Kräfte desselben“[14] gefasst. Entscheidend für Schopenhauers Staatstheorie ist die auf dem Gedanken des *principii individuationis* fußende, metaphysisch-anthropologische Grundannahme, dass der „Wille jene *Selbstbejahung* des eigenen Leibes in unzähligen Individuen neben einander darstellt“.[15] Obzwar dieser Wille *an sich* ein und derselbe in allen Lebewesen ist, kann der Einzelne die äußere Natur mitsamt den anderen Individuen nur im Medium der Vorstellung wahrnehmen. Demgegenüber wird er sich der Realität seines eigenen Wollens permanent über die leibhaft gespürten Handlungsvollzüge gewahr. Deswegen begreift sich jedes Individuum nahezu zwangsläufig als Mittelpunkt der Welt. Es ist sogar bereit, „die Welt zu vernichten, um nur sein eigenes Selbst, diesen Tropfen im Meer, länger zu erhalten“.[16] Es liegt in der Konsequenz dieses Egoismus, dass der Wille dazu neigt, über die anhand der eigenen Leibessphäre abgesteckten Bejahungsgrenzen hinauszugehen. Dergestalt bricht er in die „Gränze der fremden Willensbejahung“[17] ein. Diese Überschreitung der angemessenen Erhaltung des eigenen Leibes benennt Schopenhauer terminologisch als ‚Unrecht‘. Zur Verdeutlichung sei die zentrale Textstelle aus dem § 62 ausführlich zitiert:

> Dieser Einbruch in die Gränze fremder Willensbejahung ist von jeher deutlich erkannt und der Begriff desselben durch das Wort *Unrecht* bezeichnet worden. Denn beide Theile erkennen die Sache, zwar nicht wie wir hier in deutlicher Abstraktion, sondern als Ge-

selbst unzertrennlich anhängt, indem es, mythisch zu reden, der Fluch ist, den Adam empfieng, und mit ihm sein ganzes Geschlecht.“

14 Schopenhauer (2017), Bd. I/2: § 61, 410.

15 Schopenhauer (2017), Bd. I/2: § 62, 417.

16 Schopenhauer (2017), Bd. I/2: § 61, 415.

17 Schopenhauer (2017), Bd. I/2: § 62, 417.

> fühl, augenblicklich. Der Unrechtleidende fühlt den Einbruch in die Sphäre der Bejahung seines eigenen Leibes, durch Verneinung derselben von einem fremden Individuo, als einen unmittelbaren und geistigen Schmerz, der ganz getrennt und verschieden ist von dem daneben empfundenen physischen Leiden durch die That, oder Verdruß durch den Verlust. Dem Unrecht-Ausübenden andererseits stellt sich die Erkenntniß, daß er an sich der selbe Wille ist, der auch in jenem Leibe erscheint, [...] nicht *in abstracto*, sondern als ein dunkles Gefühl dar: und dieses nennt man Gewissensbiß, oder näher für diesen Fall, Gefühl des *ausgeübten Unrechts*.[18]

Bemerkenswert ist, dass Schopenhauer den ‚unmittelbaren und geistigen Schmerz' von dem ‚physischen Leiden' unterscheidet. Dennoch sollte diese Differenzierung nicht vorschnell in einem dualistischen Sinne verstanden werden. Vielmehr könnte hierin ein aspektrelativer Monismus gesehen werden. So kann sich der geistige, mit dem äußeren Einbruch in die eigene Bejahungssphäre verknüpfte Schmerz niemals ohne das leiblich verortete Leiden herausbilden. Zudem kann die leibliche Dimension durchaus einen Vorrang beanspruchen, da sich der als ungerecht zu beurteilende Angriff auf den einzelnen Leib in dem aufkeimenden Gefühl gewissermaßen ausfaltet und konturiert. Die somatische Ebene bleibt auch dahingehend bestimmend, dass es nach Schopenhauer ein intuitives Gefühl ist – und keine diskursive Abstraktion oder logische Schlussfolgerung – welche die Verletzung der Willensbejahung indiziert. Überleitend ist zu betonen, dass der Ursprung des Unrechts nach Schopenhauer weder in der Abweichung einer Handlung gegenüber dem kategorischen Imperativ noch in der Missachtung einer allgemeingültigen Norm zu suchen ist. Das originäre Unrecht beruht aber auch nicht in dem Verstoß gegen eine konventionelle, rechtspositivistische Satzung.

4 Die Herleitung des Eigentumsrechts

Nach Schopenhauer sind es fünf hauptsächliche Punkte der *reinen Rechtslehre*, welche die Philosophie sachhaltig auszuarbeiten und der *positiven Gesetzgebung* als Maßstab vorzulegen hat. In Schopenhauers hierarchischer Explikation des Verhältnisses von reiner Rechtslehre beziehungsweise der Moralphilosophie auf der einen Seite und den innerstaatlichen, rechtspositivistischen Regeln des menschlichen Zusammenlebens auf der anderen Seite wird das Potenzial für eine immanente Kritik des Rechts bereits virulent: Schopenhauer legt dergestalt nahe, dass sich das Recht nicht durch sich selbst begründen kann. Deswegen ist es immer wieder im Lichte desjenigen Prinzips zu kritisieren, das die Begründung in Wahrheit legitimiert. Neben der Erklärung des

18 Schopenhauer (2017), Bd. I/2: § 62, 417.

inneren Wesens der Begriffe von Recht und Unrecht (1), der Herleitung der moralischen Gültigkeit der Verträge (2), der Rekonstruktion der Staatsentstehung (3) sowie der Deduktion des Strafrechts (4) bezeugt sich die normative Richtliniensetzung der Philosophie auch in der Ableitung des Eigentumsrechts (5).[19] Schopenhauer schränkt die Funktion der Ethik also nicht auf die deskriptive Erfassung moralischer Tatsachen ein. Es ist besonders der letztgenannte Aspekt des Eigentumsrechts, in dem die eminente Bedeutung der Leiblichkeit in Schopenhauers Theorie des Rechts markant hervortritt.

So könne das Eigentum einem Menschen nur dann ohne Unrecht *nicht* genommen werden, wenn es zuvor durch seine leiblichen Kräfte bearbeitet worden sei. Diese prominent bereits bei John Locke anklingende Eigentumstheorie[20] wird von Schopenhauer gegen Kants Votum für das Präokkupationsrecht aufgerufen. Eine Gründung des alleinigen Nutzungs- und Besitzanspruches auf eine bloße Willenserklärung kann nach Schopenhauer nie erschöpfend sein. Der triftige Rechtsgrund wird erst durch den im eigenen Leib objektivierten, zur Bearbeitung einer Sache aufgewendeten Willen geschaffen. Dessen Kräfte sind alsdann mit der korrespondierenden Sache „gleichsam verwachsen und identificirt".[21] Entsprechend bricht der Delinquent auch hier in die Sphäre der fremden Willensbejahung ein. Durch den Diebstahl oder die vollständige Zerstörung des leblosen Dinges entzieht der Unrecht-Ausübende dem im anderen Leib erscheinenden Willen jenen Grad an Mühe, der zuvor in die aneignende Modifikation der Sache einging.

5 Zwei potenzielle Einwände gegen Schopenhauers leibliche Fundierung des Naturrechts

Nun ließen sich *zwei* mögliche Einwände gegen Schopenhauers Theorie vorbringen: *Erstens* liegt es nahe, Schopenhauers leiblich-physische Verwurzelung des Unrechts angesichts der kognitiv geleiteten Vergehen wie Betrug, Vertragsbruch, Erpressung usw. als unterkomplex zu beurteilen. Mit seinem Fokus auf die leibhaften Grenzen der

19 Vgl. Schopenhauer (2017), Bd. I/2: § 62, 432.

20 An dieser Stelle ist einschränkend anzumerken, dass Locke die Formierung des Eigentums zwar über den vorgängigen Akt einer eigenständigen Bearbeitung des Gegenstandes begründet. Anders als Schopenhauer, bedenkt Locke die darin ausgedrückte Arbeitsleistung jedoch nicht als existenzielle Äußerung einer individuellen Selbstbejahung des Willens. Locke stützt seine Eigentumstheorie primär mit dem Hinweis auf den göttlichen Auftrag, sich die Erde durch die Arbeit untertan zu machen. Vgl. Locke, John (2003): Über die Regierung (The Second Treatise of Government. Stuttgart: Mayer-Tasch. V § 32, 25 f.: „Soviel Land ein Mensch bepflügt, bepflanzt, bebaut, kultiviert und soviel er verwerten kann durch die Nutzung seines Ertrages, soviel ist sein eigen. Durch seine Arbeit grenzt er es gleichsam gegen das Gemeingut ab. […] Als Gott die Welt der ganzen Menschheit zu gemeinsamem Besitz gab, gebot er dem Menschen auch, zu arbeiten – der überdies durch seinen armseligen Zustand dazu gezwungen wurde."

21 Schopenhauer (2017), Bd. I/2: § 62, 419.

Willensbejahung scheint Schopenhauer nur einen reduzierten Bereich moralisch qualifizierter Handlungen thematisieren zu können. Dass Schopenhauer sich dieser Problematik vollends bewusst war, wird daran deutlich, dass er neben der körperlichen *Gewalt* auch die *List* als zweiten Stamm der Unrechtsausübung benennt. Während der Weg der Gewalt dem Satz vom zureichenden Grunde des Werdens und damit der physischen Ursächlichkeit folgt, bedient sich die List des Gesetzes der Motivation im Sinne der durch das Erkennen hindurchgegangenen Kausalität. Dennoch hält Schopenhauer selbst hier an seiner leibeszentrierten Grundthese fest. Im Falle der List werden dem Willen des fremden Individuums Scheinmotive vorgehalten, indem dessen Erkenntnis als Medium der Handlungsgründe verfälscht wird. Die List durchschaut den fremden Intellekt als ein zu täuschendes Mittel, das wiederum bestimmend auf den Willen und damit auf die leibliche Handlungspraxis des Anderen einwirken soll. Der Paradefall für diesen Vorgang bekundet sich nach Schopenhauer in der Gestalt der „Lüge", deren „vollkommenste" Form durch den *„gebrochene[n] Vertrag"*[22] bezeichnet wird.

Zweitens könnte sowohl aus einer rechtspositivistischen Perspektive als auch unter dem Index eines von der Würde des Menschen oder der Gottesebenbildlichkeit her argumentierenden Naturrechts ein gewichtiger Vorwurf erhoben werden. Demzufolge könnte das vonseiten Schopenhauers aufgerufene Gefühl des „geistige[n] Schmerz[es]"[23] aufgrund seiner bewusstseinsimmanenten Unzugänglichkeit niemals hinreichend sein, um die Kategorie des Unrechts allgemeingültig zu begründen. Diese Kritik unter rechtspositivistischen Vorzeichen fortsetzend, könnte darauf beharrt werden, dass die Sachverhalte von Unrecht und Recht nur dann bestehen können, wenn die zu ahndenden Straftatbestände gesetzmäßig niedergelegt sind. Um den Gesetzen ihre Wirksamkeit zu verleihen, müsste sich jedoch ein institutionell-politisches Gewaltmonopol herausgebildet haben. Auch diese Einrede hat Schopenhauer im § 62 der *Welt als Wille und Vorstellung* vorweggenommen. Als Antipoden wählt Schopenhauer dabei jenen weichenstellenden politischen Denker der Neuzeit, mit dem ihn eine vergleichbar desillusionierte Anthropologie verbindet. Der *bellum omnium contra omnes* des Naturzustandes mündet in Hobbes' *Leviathan* bekanntlich in einer autoritären Staatskonzeption. Im Gegensatz dazu, zieht Schopenhauer das gleiche Urszenario zur Profilierung eines minimalstaatlichen Liberalismus heran.[24] In wirkmächtiger Weise hat bereits Thomas Hobbes eine vorstaatliche Gültigkeit der Begriffe von Unrecht und

---

22 Schopenhauer (2017), Bd. I/2: § 62, 421.

23 Schopenhauer (2017), Bd. I/2: § 62, 417.

24 Der Grundgehalt von Schopenhauers staatskritischem Liberalismus wird von Jean-Claude Wolf angemessen und stringent zusammengefasst. Vgl. Wolf, Jean-Claude (2014): „Bejahung und Verneinung des Willens (W I, §§ 60–67)". In: Arthur Schopenhauer: Die Welt als Wille und Vorstellung (= Klassiker auslegen Bd. 42), hrsg. v. Hallich, Oliver / Koßler, Matthias. Berlin: De Gruyter, 155: „Die rechtliche Bejahung des Willens besteht darin, dass jedermanns vitale (und egoistische) Interessen, nicht an Leib, Leben und Eigentum geschädigt zu werden, gleichermaßen affirmiert und mit der ganzen Autorität des Staates garantiert werden. Damit wird nicht ein sozialer Fürsorgestaat anvisiert, sondern eher ein liberaler Minimalstaat.

Recht vehement bestritten.[25] Schopenhauer sieht hier die problematische Maxime eines erkenntnistheoretischen Empirismus walten. So könne Hobbes die These eines „konventionelle[n] und willkürlich angenommene[n]"[26] Anfangsgrundes des Rechts allein deswegen einlösen, weil er sich ausschließlich auf äußere Wirkungen und Handlungserfolge konzentriere.

In der direkten Wendung gegen Hobbes' materialistischen Empirismus begreift Schopenhauer Recht und Unrecht als innere, moralische Kategorien. Die gewissenhafte Selbsterkenntnis leitend, soll durch sie schon im Naturzustand der Punkt angezeigt werden, „wo die Bejahung des eigenen Willens zur Verneinung des fremden wird, d. h. den Grad seiner Heftigkeit, […] durch Unrechtthun angiebt".[27] Insgesamt wäre jedoch zu fragen, ob diese Verinnerlichungstendenz Schopenhauers lebensweltlich-leiblicher Verankerung des Unrechts nicht widerspricht. Wie oben veranschaulicht werden konnte, hatte er das Unrecht ausdrücklich als handfesten Einbruch in die Leiblichkeit einer Alterität herausgestellt. Die Problematik, inwieweit das Unrecht in einer äußeren Missachtung der subjektiven Willenssphäre besteht oder ob es sich in der inneren Selbstreflexion des Täters als Grad des Unrechttuns manifestiert, ist im Folgenden zu erörtern.

6 Das Recht als abgeleiteter Begriff und die Priorität des Unrechts

Im Gesamtzusammenhang des § 62 muss Schopenhauers Verlagerung der moralisch-juridischen Zentralbegriffe in die Innenwelt des Subjekts überraschend anmuten. *Zum einen* hatte er die Begriffe von Recht und Unrecht wenige Seiten zuvor nicht gleichursprünglich behandelt. *Zum anderen* hatte er sie dort keineswegs zu Reflexionsstützen der mit dem Unrechttun verbundenen Gewissensausprägung herabgestuft. Ein wesentliches Element der Rechtstheorie Schopenhauers äußert sich nämlich in der asymmetrischen Anordnung, der gemäß er das Recht im § 62 aus dem *leiblich* vermit-

---

Die liberale Seite wird insbesondere dadurch betont, dass der Staat nicht als moralische Erziehungsanstalt konzipiert wird, welche sich anmaßt, neue (d. h. nicht-egoistische) Menschen zu schaffen."

25 Dass Schopenhauers kritischer Interpretation des englischen Denkers beizupflichten ist, lässt sich anhand des prinzipiellen Diktums Hobbes' unterstreichen, wonach nicht die Wahrheit, sondern einzig die Autorität das Recht setze und über die Grenzfälle seiner Einhaltung entscheide. Zum souveränitätstheoretischen Grundsatz des „auctoritas, non veritas facit legem" und zur Exklusion der Unrechtskategorie aus dem Verhältnis zwischen dem Souverän und den Untertanen vgl. Hobbes, Thomas (1996): Leviathan. Hamburg: Meiner, XXI, 180: „Denn es ist schon dargelegt worden, daß nichts, was der souveräne Repräsentant unter irgendeinem Vorwand einem Untertan antun kann, im eigentlichen Sinne als Ungerechtigkeit oder Unrecht bezeichnet werden kann; denn jeder Untertan ist Urheber jeder Handlung des Souveräns, so daß diesem nie das Recht auf irgend etwas fehlt, abgesehen davon, daß er selbst der Untertan Gottes und zur Einhaltung der Naturgesetze verpflichtet ist."

26 Schopenhauer (2017), Bd. I/2: § 62, 426.

27 Schopenhauer (2017), Bd. I/2: § 62, 426.

telten Unrecht ableitet. Durch diese Herleitung kann Schopenhauer den möglichen Einwand der Naturrechtstheoretiker zurückweisen, wenn diese die Ursprünglichkeit oder transzendente Überzeitlichkeit des Rechts unterstreichen.

Auch in dieser Deduktion greift Schopenhauer auf den konkreten, empirisch-zeitgebundenen Leib als Ursprungsort des innerstaatlich gültigen Rechts zurück. Dies erhellt schon daraus, dass er die erste Entstehung und maßgebliche Anwendung des Rechtsbegriffes in Fällen vorfindet, wo „versuchtes Unrecht durch Gewalt abgewehrt wird".[28] Diese Abwehrhandlung kann nach Schopenhauer nicht ihrerseits als Unrecht bewertet werden. Der Angegriffene reagiert innerhalb der Sphäre der eigenleiblichen Willensbejahung, die ihm *qua* Natur und Dasein zugehört. Der Unrecht-Leidende initiiert damit nur eine Negation der an ihm ausgeübten Negation. Zugleich stellt er die mit dem Dasein des Leibes zusammenfallende Bejahung der eigenen Erhaltungskräfte wieder her.

Das Unrecht wird in diesem Textstadium definitorisch mit der „Verneinung des fremden Willens"[29] gleichgesetzt, wohingegen der derivierte Gegenbegriff des Rechts an die „Verneinung jener Verneinung"[30] angebunden wird. Also kann Schopenhauer auf einem genuin leibphilosophischen Wege das Erkenntnisziel stützen, dass die Moral eine absolute Gültigkeit jenseits historisch-politischer Konventionen zu beanspruchen vermag. Gleichzeitig könnte jedoch die Frage gestellt werden, ob Schopenhauer die Möglichkeit einer immanenten Kritik des Rechts nicht signifikant abschwächt, wenn er es aus der Faktizität des prioritären Unrechts entwickelt und es als bloßen Restitutionsakt der vormaligen, leiblichen Integrität begreift. Um die Relevanz des Rechts im Naturzustand zu sichern, ist nochmals zu prononcieren, dass Schopenhauer über die Anwendung des Rechts-Unrechts-Gegensatzes auf die innere Gewissensprüfung hinausgeht. Die Semantik des Rechts beschränkt sich im § 62 nämlich nicht auf eine moralische Bestimmung, auf deren Basis der Anfangspunkt des eigenen Unrechttuns taxiert werden kann. Vielmehr existiert nach Schopenhauer bereits im Naturzustand ein unaufhebbares *„Zwangsrecht"*.[31] Insofern sich dieses jedoch in der Abwehr der „eindringende[n] äußere[n] Gewalt"[32] manifestiert, wird auch hier deutlich, dass Schopenhauer ein indifferentes Gelten-Lassen verschiedener Individualinteressen innerhalb des Naturzustandes *noch nicht* als Recht klassifizieren möchte.

Es ist ebendiese paradoxale Absenz des Rechts – das *prima vista* als ‚Zwangsrecht' marginalisiert und in seiner Genese zudem über die Vermittlungsfigur einer ‚Negation der Negation' erschlossen wird – die Carl Schmitts frühe Kritik an Schopenhauers Rechtsphilosophie motiviert hat. Schmitt ist zunächst zuzustimmen, wenn er – sei-

28 Schopenhauer (2017), Bd. I/2: § 62, 423.
29 Schopenhauer (2017), Bd. I/2: § 62, 422.
30 Schopenhauer (2017), Bd. I/2: § 62, 423.
31 Schopenhauer (2017), Bd. I/2: § 62, 424.
32 Schopenhauer (2017), Bd. I/2: § 62, 423.

nem eigenen, anti-individualistischem und etatistischem Ansatz verpflichtet – hervorhebt, dass „die Ausdrücke Bejahung und Verneinung des individuellen Willens" offenkundig „selbstständige Individualitäten" voraussetzen, die „*als solche* sich gegen eine Verneinung verteidigen dürfen, und deren Wert somit in ihrer Individualität besteht".[33] Daran anknüpfend, überdehnt Schmitt jedoch die Argumentation. Schmitt moniert, dass Schopenhauer die Begriffe des Rechts und des Unrechts „durch die Worte Bejahung und Verneinung" substituiere, die „gänzlich leer sind, solange sie nicht durch eine Angabe darüber, wann die Bejahung berechtigt ist und wann die Verneinung unberechtigt ist, einen Inhalt bekommen".[34]

In seinem Vorwurf, dass Schopenhauer die Existenz ‚selbstständiger Individualitäten' schlichtweg postuliere, lässt Schmitt die willensmetaphysische Einbettung des Einzelnen unberücksichtigt. Wie oben demonstriert werden konnte, begründet und erklärt Schopenhauer anhand der metaphysischen Doktrin einer All-Einheit des Willens den normativ konnotierten, „unmittelbaren und geistigen Schmerz"[35], mit dem sich der Unrecht-Leidende konfrontiert sieht. Aus diesem Faktum des Schmerzes generiert sich wiederum die von Schmitt eingeforderte „Angabe, wann die Bejahung berechtigt ist".[36] Des Weiteren ist Schmitts Urteil zu widersprechen, dass sich in Schopenhauers Rechtslehre „keinerlei Anhaltspunkte ergeben, wo die Grenze zwischen Bejahung und Verneinung ist".[37] Dass Schopenhauer diese eingeklagten ‚Anhaltspunkte' sehr wohl zu benennen vermag, könnte einerseits mit der nicht interpretationsbedürftigen, evidenten Unmittelbarkeit der geistigen Schmerzerfahrung untermauert werden. Andererseits könnte gegen Schmitt darauf hingewiesen werden, dass jeder Wille beziehungsweise individuelle Leib nach Schopenhauer nur begrenzte physische Kapazitäten zu seiner Selbsterhaltung besitzt. Eine Verlagerung dieser lebensnotwendigen Kräfte in die Dienste eines fremden Willens muss daher apodiktisch als Unrecht bewertet werden, *sobald* sie die individuelle Existenz des Dienenden selbst aufzuheben beginnt.

Gerade vor dem Hintergrund der Kritik Schmitts ist nun die Frage zu diskutieren, ob sich die Bedeutung und der Funktionsmodus des Rechts – das im Naturzustand allein als Negation eines vorherigen Unrechts gefasst wird – in Schopenhauers Theoriebildung ändern, sobald der Übergang in eine staatliche Ordnung vollzogen ist.

Den Übergang vom Naturzustand in die Staatsordnung schildert Schopenhauer ähnlich wie die klassisch-neuzeitlichen Vertragstheorien Hobbes' und Samuel von Pufendorfs. Schopenhauer bezieht sich zunächst auf die wiederholten Erfahrungen

---

33 Schmitt, Carl (1914): „Schopenhauers Rechtsphilosophie außerhalb seines philosophischen Systems". In: Monatsschrift für Kriminalpsychologie und Strafrechtsreform, März/April 1914, 27–31, hier 28.
34 Schmitt (2014), 28 f.
35 Schopenhauer (2017), Bd. I/2: § 62, 417.
36 Schmitt (1914), 29.
37 Schmitt (1914), 30.

der leiblichen Vulnerabilität und des zufällig verteilten, schmerzhaften Unrechtleidens. Im Zuge dieser Widerfahrnisse sieht sich die „allen diesen Individuen gemeinsame Vernunft“[38] schließlich zu der Überlegung veranlasst, ein „gemeinschaftliches Opfer“[39] darzubringen. Auf dieser Basis soll einem überwiegenden und ebenso kollektiv wirksamen, „daraus hervorgehenden Vortheil“[40] Geltung verschafft werden. Der sich im Genuss des Unrechttuns bestätigende „Egoismus des Einzelnen“, wird durch einen „methodisch verfahrenden [...] Egoismus“[41] abgelöst. Die „das Ganze überdenkende Vernunft“[42] legt sich einen *„Staatsvertrag“*[43] auf. In diesem drückt sich das jedem Einzelnen innewohnende Bedürfnis einer Vermeidung des Unrechtleidens aus. Somit wird die ursprüngliche Machtlosigkeit des Rechts, das im Naturzustand der physischen Gewalt hilflos gegenüberstand, mit Hilfe der vereinigten Kraft aller Vertragssubjekte auf die Seite der legitimen Autorität transferiert.

Für die (rechtspositivistische) Gesetzesordnung des Staates ist die Gesinnung der Bürgerinnen und Bürger irrelevant, da er sich allein an der Verhinderung des *Unrechtleidens* orientiert. Die Moral zeichnet hingegen zunächst die Grenzen vor, bis zu welchem Grad die Bejahung des jeweiligen Leibes geduldet werden kann, ohne in ein *Unrechttun* umzuschlagen. Weil es demnach ohne die den Tatbestand des Unrechttuns definierende Moral beziehungsweise die reine Rechtslehre keine Grundlage für den Ansatzpunkt, die Erstreckung und die Tragweite der innerstaatlichen Gesetzesgültigkeit geben könnte, bleibt auch innerhalb des Staates der gravierende Einfluss der leiblichen Einbettung des Rechts spürbar. Angesichts Schopenhauers luzider Unterscheidung der Kompetenzbereiche der Moral und des positiven Rechts offenbart sich noch einmal die Fragwürdigkeit des Schmitt'schen Kritikpunktes, wonach Schopenhauer nicht über die „Grenze zwischen Bejahung und Verneinung“[44] reflektiere. Wie oben verdeutlicht werden konnte, fasst Schopenhauer das Recht im Naturzustand als bloße Wiederherstellung eines zuvor durch das Unrecht suspendierten Zustandes. Trotz seiner begründungstheoretischen *Nachrangigkeit im Hinblick auf die Natur* kann das so verstandene Recht aber einen temporalen wie logischen *Vorrang gegenüber dem Staat* respektive *vor* jeder positiven Rechtsnorm beanspruchen.

---

38 Schopenhauer (2017), Bd. I/2: § 62, 427.
39 Schopenhauer (2017), Bd. I/2: § 62, 427.
40 Schopenhauer (2017), Bd. I/2: § 62, 427.
41 Schopenhauer (2017), Bd. I/2: § 62, 427.
42 Schopenhauer (2017), Bd. I/2: § 62, 427.
43 Schopenhauer (2017), Bd. I/2: § 62, 428.
44 Schmitt (1914), 29.

7 Zusammenfassung und Schluss

Die Ergebnisse dieses Vortrages seien abschließend in einem Hierarchisierungsvorschlag der Begründungsebenen gebündelt. Als Austragungsort der Bejahung des Willens kann der Leib in rechtlich-ethischer Hinsicht die schlechthin primäre Stellung beanspruchen. Allein durch den Leib wird der Schmerz der äußeren, in die jeweilige Willenssphäre eingreifenden Einwirkung wahrnehmbar, sodass die Phänomene von Unrechttun und Unrechtleiden ihren realen Gehalt gewinnen (1). Die zweite Ebene wird von dem moralischen Naturrecht eingenommen, das sich seinerseits auf die aus der leiblichen Leidenswahrnehmung entwickelte Kategorie eines vorstaatlichen Zwangsrechtes stützt (2). In ihrem leiblichen Rückbezug unterscheidet sich Schopenhauers Erklärung des Naturrechts maßgeblich von theologischen oder anerkennungstheoretischen Ansätzen. Als drittes Element nach der primordialen Leiblichkeit und dem Naturrecht kann Schopenhauers Anleihe bei dem klassischen Kontraktualismus beurteilt werden, wodurch der Danziger die Entstehung und den Zweck des Staates zu bestimmen sucht (3). Erst auf der vierten Ebene siedelt Schopenhauer den staatlichen Rechtspositivismus an (4).

Zusammenfassend lässt sich sagen, dass der Leib als konstitutive Ursprungszone des Rechts gedeutet werden kann, indem Schopenhauer die Genese des Staates aus dem kollektiven Wunsch nach *leiblicher* Unversehrtheit derivieren lässt. Schopenhauer berücksichtigt hierbei, dass das bereits im Naturzustand bestehende, negativ über die Verneinung des Unrechts definierte Recht des Individuums erst innerhalb eines intakten Staatsgefüges effektiv operieren kann. Zur Konstitution des Staates ist aber – wie Schopenhauer mit Hobbes postuliert – die hypothetische Einwilligung jedes Einzelnen erforderlich. Diese erfolgt für Schopenhauer aufgrund einer Schutz-Gehorsam-Reziprozität, wobei der Staat garantiert, die im Naturzustand stets gefährdete Leiblichkeit des Individuums im Austausch gegen dessen Unterordnung unter ein staatliches Gewaltmonopol zu sichern. Daher verstößt der Staat *im* und *mit* dem Recht gegen seine eigenen Daseinsbedingungen, sobald er seine Machtbefugnisse auf den Leib des Einzelnen auszuweiten sucht. Somit erweist sich der Leib in Schopenhauers Rechtstheorie als gestaltgewordene Grenze der staatlichen Wirksamkeit. Auf der Basis der staats- und rechtsbegründenden Dimension der Leiblichkeit lässt sich sowohl gegen die Beliebigkeit eines rechtspositivistischen Formalismus wie auch gegen die problematische, metaphysische Tendenz der naturrechtlichen Normativität argumentieren. Stattdessen kann der Ursprung des Rechts im existenziell nachvollziehbaren, leiblichen Selbsterhaltungsinteresse des Einzelnen fundiert werden. Die mit der Bejahung des Willens zusammenfallende Erhaltung des individuellen Leibes hat für Schopenhauer einen unauflöslichen, normativen Wert, weil erst auf dieser konkreten Grundlage moralische Bestimmungen des gerechten Handelns geleistet und weiterführende Erwägungen des Staatszweckes entfaltet werden können.

Zur Person: Jan Kerkmann ist Privatdozent am Philosophischen Seminar der Albert-Ludwigs-Universität Freiburg. Zu seinen systematischen Schwerpunkten zählen Metaphysik, Politische Philosophie und Naturphilosophie.

PD Dr. Jan Kerkmann
Albert-Ludwigs-Universität Freiburg, Philosophisches Seminar, Platz der Universität 3,
79085 Freiburg i. Br.

Sind Frauenrechte utopisch?

Feministische Verfassungsutopien am Beispiel des Frankfurter Frauenmanifestes

DANA-SOPHIA VALENTINER

Utopia of Gender Equality?

Exploring Feminist Constitutional Utopias through the Frankfurt Women's Manifesto

Abstract: This article deals with feminist constitutional utopias. It focuses on the intersection of feminist, utopian and constitutional visions. The study highlights the lack of attention given to feminist constitutional utopias in contemporary utopian research. This oversight may be attributed to the inadequacy of traditional utopian concepts in fully capturing the feminist-utopian dimension. Recognizing this gap, feminist theorists have criticized the limited scope of utopian research and have proposed an explicitly feminist theoretical framework that conceptualizes utopia as a practical approach to societal argumentation. By adopting this perspective, the article closely examines the Frankfurt Women's Manifesto and elucidates key elements of feminist constitutional utopias.
Keywords: Utopia, Women's Rights, Feminist Constitutions, Constitutional Law, Legal Gender Studies, Frankfurt Women's Manifesto

1 Einleitung

Am 29. September 1990 fand in der Frankfurter Paulskirche der Kongress „Frauen für eine neue Verfassung" statt, der den Entwurf für ein bemerkenswertes „Frauenmanifest" diskutierte.[1] Zuvor hatten verschiedene – westdeutsche[2] – Initiativen und Frau-

---

1 Für eine ausführliche Dokumentation siehe das Sonderheft der Zeitschrift Feministische Studien extra (1991), passim.

2 Das Frankfurter Frauenmanifest ist weitgehend ohne Beteiligung ostdeutscher Frauen und ohne Einbeziehung ihrer Perspektiven entstanden. Zu den Visionen ostdeutscher Frauen siehe Lembke, Ulrike (2022): „Visionen als feministisches Erbe? Zwischen universellem Repräsentationsanspruch, neoliberaler Alternativlosigkeit und den Un/Möglichkeiten feministischer politischer Praxis". In: Aleksander, Karin / Auga, Ulrike E. / Dvorakk, Elisavate / Heft, Kathleen / Jähnert, Gabriele / Schimkat, Heike (Hg.): Feministische Vi-

engruppen ihre Visionen für eine feministische Verfassung für das wiedervereinigte Deutschland zu Papier gebracht.[3] Die unterschiedlichen Entwürfe waren ebenso wie der Verfassungsentwurf des Runden Tisches[4] Grundlage für die „vorläufigen" Vorschläge für eine neue Verfassung, die in der Frankfurter Paulskirche diskutiert wurden. Das Frankfurter Frauenmanifest orientierte sich dabei an Aufbau und Text des Grundgesetzes.[5] Teilweise sah es Klarstellungen und Konkretisierungen bestehender Artikel vor, beispielsweise des Art. 3 GG. Das Manifest nahm aber auch ausdrücklich neue Verbürgungen auf, etwa das Recht jeder Frau, zu entscheiden, ob sie eine Schwangerschaft austrägt oder nicht, sowie den Anspruch auf gleichen Lohn für gleiche und gleichwertige Arbeit.

Das Frankfurter Frauenmanifest ist keine singuläre Erscheinung. Es finden sich einige Beispiele für Verfassungsutopien, die von Frauenrechtlerinnen, aus emanzipatorischen Bewegungen heraus, entwickelt wurden. Die – mittlerweile – wohl bekannteste europäische feministische Verfassungsutopie ist die Erklärung der Rechte der Frau und Bürgerin (*Déclaration des droits de la Femme et de la Citoyenne*), welche die Frauenrechtlerin *Olympe de Gouges* im Jahr 1791 als Gegenentwurf zur französischen Erklärung der Menschen- und Bürgerrechte verfasste.[6] Sie sah u. a. die Teilhabe von Frauen an der Volksvertretung und ihre Zulassung zu allen öffentlichen Ämtern vor. Jüngstes Beispiel für feministische Verfassungsutopien ist das (gescheiterte) Verfassungsreferendum in Chile 2022, das durch eine intensive gesellschaftliche Debatte begleitet wurde, in deren Mittelpunkt auch die feministische Ausrichtung der Verfassung stand. Feministische Aktivist*innen hatten konkrete Forderungen zum Verfassungstext angebracht, u. a. die Verankerung der gleichberechtigten politischen Teilhabe von Frauen, sexueller und reproduktiver Rechte, den Schutz und die Anerkennung der geschlechtlichen Identität, die Achtung und Anerkennung des überlieferten Wissens indigener Frauen sowie einen Anspruch auf staatliche Bildung frei von Sexismus.[7]

---

sionen vor und nach 1989. Geschlecht, Medien und Aktivismen in der DDR, BRD und im östlichen Europa. Opladen, Berlin, Toronto: Verlag Barbara Budrich, 39–65; Mittrop, Johanna (2023): „Vom Runden Tisch zur Gemeinsamen Verfassungskommission? Beitrag ostdeutscher Frauen* zur vereinigungsbedingten Erneuerung' des Art. 3 Abs. 2 GG". In: Dux, Elisabeth / Groß, Johanna / Kraft, Julia / Militz, Rebecca / Ness, Sina (Hg.): FRAU.MACHT.RECHT. 100 Jahre Frauen in juristischen Berufen. Baden-Baden: Nomos, 51, 63 f.

3 Siehe u. a. Hering, Heide / von Paczensky, Susanne / Sadrozinski, Renate (1990): „Frauen in bester Verfassung". In: STREIT 1990 (4), 118 f. und Breitling, Gisela (1991): „Feministisches Manifest". In: Feministische Studien extra 9 (s1), 102–107. DOI: 10.1515/fs-1991-s124; Stand: 30.06.2024.

4 Dokumentation „Entwurf eines Frankfurter Frauenmanifests. Frauen für eine neue Verfassung" (1991). In: Feministische Studien extra 9 (s1), 107, 108. DOI: 10.1515/fs-1991-s125; Stand: 30.06.2024.

5 Teilweise wurde dieser „Pragmatismus" auch kritisch gesehen, vgl. Platt, Sabine (1991): „Bemerkungen zur Diskussion". In: Feministische Studien extra 9 (s1), 46, 48. DOI: 10.1515/fs-1991-s110; Stand: 30.06.2024.

6 Gerhard, Ute (1987): „Menschenrechte auch für Frauen. Der Entwurf der Olympe de Gouges". In: Kritische Justiz 20 (1), 127–149. https://www.jstor.org/stable/23996421; Stand: 30.06.2024.

7 Brito, Sofía Esther (Hg.): Por una constitución feminista (2020). Santiago de Chile: Libros del Pez Espiral.

Der nachfolgende Beitrag beleuchtet das Feministisch-Utopische der Arbeit am und mit dem Verfassungstext. Den tatsächlichen Ausgangspunkt der nachstehenden Überlegungen bilden feministische Utopien im Allgemeinen und Verfassungen als Gegenstand dieser Utopien im Besonderen. In der modernen Utopieforschung spielen solche feministische Verfassungsutopien bislang noch eine untergeordnete Rolle. Dies mag damit zusammenhängen, dass zentrale Utopiebegriffe – sowohl der sogenannte klassische Utopiebegriff als auch *Ernst Blochs* Begriff der konkreten Utopie – nur eingeschränkt geeignet sind, um das Feministisch-Utopische zu fassen. Dieser blinde Fleck der Utopieforschung ist von feministischen Theoretikerinnen zurecht bemängelt und ein explizit feministisch-demokratietheoretischer Zugriff entwickelt worden, um „das ‚Utopische' ganz praktisch als gesellschaftliche Argumentationsweise zu begreifen".[8] Aus einer solchen Perspektive nimmt dieser Beitrag das Frankfurter Frauenmanifest näher in den Blick und arbeitet einige zentrale Elemente feministischer Verfassungsutopien heraus.

2 Feministische Utopien und Verfassungen

2.1 Feministisch-utopische Literatur

Zentraler Gegenstand der Utopieforschung sind literarische Werke, die Utopien (oder Dystopien) entwerfen. Es gibt unzählige Werke, vorwiegend von Autorinnen, die dem Geschlechterverhältnis gewidmet sind und Visionen einer geschlechtergerechteren Zukunft entwerfen. Sie skizzieren Frauengesellschaften, die gänzlich ohne Männer leben[9], Gesellschaften, in denen es kein Geschlecht gibt oder es einem steten Wandel unterliegt, Welten, in denen Frauen besonders mächtige Fähigkeiten haben.[10]

Die erste feministische Utopie erschien bereits 1405 – und damit über 100 Jahre vor dem Roman *Utopia* von *Thomas Morus*, der als prägend für den Begriff der Utopie gilt.[11] *Das Buch der Stadt der Frauen* von *Christine de Pizan* behandelt den Bau einer

8 Dierkes, Mirjam (2013): „Plädoyer für eine utopietheoretische Erweiterung feministischer Gesellschaftskritik". In: Femina Politica. Zeitschrift für feministische Politikwissenschaft 22 (1), 68, 71. https://nbn-resolving.org/urn:nbn:de:0168-ssoar-445531; Stand: 30.06.2024.

9 Bekannt ist insbesondere der utopische Roman *Herland* von Charlotte Perkins Gilman (1918).

10 Für weitere Beispiele siehe etwa Hauer, Gudrun (2000): „Schöne neue Frauenwelten? Feministische Utopien in der Literatur des 20. Jahrhunderts". In: Österreichische Zeitschrift für Politikwissenschaft 29 (1), 59–73. https://nbn-resolving.org/urn:nbn:de:0168-ssoar-59387; Stand: 30.06.2024; Stalfort, Anne (1998): „Literarische Utopien von Frauen in der deutschen und US-amerikanischen Literatur des 20. Jahrhunderts". In: Freiburger FrauenStudien. Zeitschrift für interdisziplinäre Frauenforschung 4 (2), 59–76. https://nbn-resolving.org/urn:nbn:de:0168-ssoar-319563; Stand 30.06.2024.

11 Darauf verweist Schröder, Hannelore (2005): „Sechshundert Jahre feministische Utopien von und für Frauen. Gegen die Beschränktheiten ‚des klassischen Utopiebegriffs'". In: Erwägen Wissen Ethik 16 (3), 333, 334.

Stadt, die Frauen Schutz vor Männern bieten soll, durch die Erzählerin, der die personifizierte Vernunft, die Rechtschaffenheit und die Gerechtigkeit begegnen, um sie bei dem Bau der Stadt der Frauen zu unterstützen.

Zentrales Element feministisch-utopischer Literatur ist nach *Barbara Holland-Cunz* die politische Organisation des Staates mit Partizipationsmöglichkeiten für Frauen (häufig in basisdemokratischer, „rätedemokratischer" Form).[12] Wiederkehrende Motive sind auch das gleichberechtigte Zusammenleben als Familie und Gesellschaft mit neuen Möglichkeiten der (Erwerbs- und Care-)Arbeitsteilung, wobei die Frage der Reproduktion in vielen Werken eine Rolle spielt und nicht selten mit medizinisch-technischen Innovationen beantwortet wird. Schließlich prägt feministisch-utopische Literatur ein kollektives Geschichtsbewusstsein oder eine Revolutionsgeschichte, die zur Utopie geführt hat und das Denken der Menschen in der Utopie prägt.[13]

Ein eher unbekannteres Beispiel für eine solche utopische Erzählung ist die kurze Novelle „Vor der Gründung des Frauenstaats" von *Magda E. Trott*. Die Novelle erschien 1914 in der Zeitung „Frauenkapital – eine werdende Macht".[14] Sie handelt von einer Versammlung von Frauen, vor der die Rednerin „Fräulein Dr. Möller" leidenschaftlich für die Gründung eines Frauenstaats als Bundesstaat des Deutschen Reiches in der Lüneburger Heide eintritt. Die Versammlung findet in einer Nachkriegssituation in der Zukunft statt. Es ist eine Gesellschaft, in der Frauen das aktive und passive Wahlrecht errungen haben und das Recht auf Selbstbestimmung. Eine Gesellschaft, in der die gut betuchten Frauen, „die Glücklicheren, die nicht den Verlust des Lebensgefährten beklagen mussten, oder die mit Glücksgütern gesegnet" sind, ihre Mittel in eine genossenschaftliche Frauenbank fließen lassen, um den solidarischen Frauenstaat zu ermöglichen und die Lüneburger Heide für diese Sache zu erwerben. Dort wollen sie leben, wirtschaften und sich durch Ackerbau und Viehzucht selbst versorgen. Ein freiwilliges Dienstjahr aller jungen Frauen nach Vollendung des 20. Lebensjahres soll hierzu beitragen. Die Novelle endet damit, dass ein Abgesandter die Versammlung betritt und die Botschaft überbringt, dass die Reichsregierung die Gründung des Frauenstaats billigt und zu Verhandlungen lädt. Die versammelten Frauen brechen in Jubelstimmung aus.

Die Novelle skizziert die mögliche (politische) Organisation des Frauenstaats recht konkret und benennt auch einzelne Rechte (und Pflichten) der Menschen der utopischen Gesellschaft. Auffällig ist der Novelle eine reichtreue Haltung, der Frauenstaat wird als Teil des Deutschen Reiches erdacht, die Loyalität der Frauen zum Deutschen

---

12 Holland-Cunz, Barbara (1986): „Politische Struktur und Machtverhältnisse in der feministischen Utopie". In: dies. (Hg.): Feministische Utopien. Aufbruch in die postpatriarchale Gesellschaft. Meitingen: Corian-Verlag Wimmer, 61, 72 ff.

13 Ebd., 61, 87 ff.

14 Trott, Magda E. (1914): „Vor der Gründung des Frauenstaates. Eine utopische Novelle". In: Frauenkapital – eine werdende Macht, 14–16.

Reich mehrfach betont. Auch ist die Selbstverortung der Autorin der bürgerlichen Frauenbewegung deutlich erkennbar. So wird betont, dass der erdachte Frauenstaat und die Frauenbewegung nichts gemein habe mit dem „hypermodernen Feminismus" der Suffragetten in England.[15] Es zeigt sich bei dieser utopischen Novelle eine enge Verzahnung des Utopischen mit einer bestimmten Frauenbewegung, ein prägendes Kollektivbewusstsein, gespeist aus der gemeinsamen Kriegserfahrung.

Das Beispiel illustriert, wie feministisch-utopische Texte „ganz spezielle Verbindungen zwischen dem Gegenwärtigen und dem Zukünftigen" aufzeigen, wie sie „unsere Vorstellungskraft an[regen], das heute noch nicht Mögliche zu denken und unser politisches Handeln auch darauf auszurichten; sie ermutigen uns letztlich, uns aus der Sackgasse politischer Resignation herauszubewegen und als politisch(-feministisch) Handelnde nicht länger Selbstbegrenzung zu üben".[16] Hieraus erklärt sich der Reiz von Utopien für emanzipatorische Bewegungen, die Kritik an bestehenden Ungleichheiten und Diskriminierungen üben, sowie eine gesellschaftliche Transformation zu einer gerechteren Gesellschaft fordern.

2.2 Verfassungen als Hoffnungsträgerinnen emanzipatorischer Bewegungen

Die besondere Form von feministischen Utopien in Gestalt konkreter Verfassungstextarbeit steht bislang weder im Fokus der Utopieforschung noch der feministischen Verfassungsrechtswissenschaft. Dementsprechend können über die Motivation für die Praxis, einen Verfassungstext zu erarbeiten bzw. mit einem bestehenden Verfassungstext zu arbeiten, nur erste Thesen aufgestellt werden, die noch eingehender Untersuchung bedürfen.

Die besondere Anziehungskraft von Verfassungen als Folien für die Entwicklung konkreter feministischer Visionen dürfte sich aus der Funktion von Recht als Machtinstrument speisen, verbunden mit der Hoffnung auf das transformatorische Potential von Recht. Das U.S.-amerikanische *Feminist Utopia Project*, das verschiedene Vorschläge und Interventionen aus der feministischen Praxis und Theorie – auch konkrete Utopien einer feministischen Verfassung – bündelt, betont die Hoffnung auf die Transformationskraft von Verfassungen für emanzipatorische Bewegungen: „Law […] bespeaks the society we wish to be. We are the law, and the law is us."[17] Auch die Frauenrechtlerin *Anita Augspurg* wusste bereits im Kampf um die Einführung des Frauenwahlrechts in Deutschland im Jahr 1895: „Die Frauenfrage ist […] in allererster

15 Vgl. ebd.
16 Hauer (2000), 59.
17 Cross, Katherine (2015): „Feminist Constitution". In: Brodsky, Alexandra / Kauder Nalebuff, Rachel (Hg.): The Feminist Utopia Project. Fifty-Seven Visions of a Wildly Better Future. New York: The Feminist Press at the City University of New York, 62.

Linie […] Rechtsfrage, weil nur von der Grundlage verbürgter Rechte, nicht idealer (welche beiden Eigenschaften des Rechtes sich leider nicht immer decken), an ihre sichere Lösung überhaupt gedacht werden kann".[18] Die Hoffnung auf die Transformationskraft von Recht klingt hierin leiser an, betont wird vielmehr die Bedeutung von Recht als Grundlage für emanzipatorische Bewegungen, als „point of no return", von dem aus weitergehende Forderungen und Visionen erst entwickelt werden können.

Verfassungen bilden zudem den Konsens über die organisatorischen Eckpfeiler und grundlegenden Versprechen einer Gesellschaft ab, der sich aus der Aufarbeitung von Vergangenem speist und dem vor dem Hintergrund des Gegenwärtigen ein Blick in die Zukunft immanent ist. Anlässlich der Verfassungsreform nach der deutschen Wiedervereinigung beschrieb *Jutta Limbach* Verfassungen als Antworten auf die gesellschaftlichen Herausforderungen ihrer Zeit:[19]

> Was sind Verfassungen anderes als Antworten auf die Herausforderungen ihrer Zeit? Insbesondere die Formulierung von Grund- und Menschenrechten ist eine intellektuelle Weise, eine kritikwürdige Vergangenheit aufzuarbeiten und gegenwärtig Erreichtes festzuschreiben. Vor allem aber ist das Bekenntnis zu Grundrechten ein Versuch, das künftige Zusammenleben von Menschen gerechter und humaner zu gestalten. Das schließt nicht aus, sondern fordert geradezu dazu heraus, den Grundrechtskatalog unserer Verfassung neu durchzumustern und daraufhin zu befragen, ob sie dem Wandel unseres gesellschaftlichen Denkens und Wissens ausreichend gerecht wird.

Die Historikerin *Ute Gerhard*, die maßgeblich an dem Frankfurter Frauenkongress beteiligt war, stellte den „einklagbare[n] Wertekanon" der Verfassung heraus.[20] Eine Verfassung setzt – so auch *Andrea Maihofer* in der Dokumentation zum Frankfurter Frauenkongress – „die Eckpfeiler fest für die künftige Entwicklung einer Gesellschaft":[21]

> Sie beeinflußt, welche künftigen gesellschaftlichen Interessen, ökonomischen Fehlentwicklungen und ökologischen Probleme künftig überhaupt wahrgenommen und nach welchen Kriterien sie beurteilt werden. Ebenso präjudiziert sie, welche politischen Forderungen künftig zugelassen und damit Chancen auf gesellschaftliche Verwirklichung haben. […] Überhaupt erweist sich das Grundgesetz bei näherer Betrachtung als patriarchal-hegemoniale Verallgemeinerung der Lebens- und Denkweisen des westlichen bürgerlichen Mannes. Die Frau als eigenständiges gesellschaftliches Subjekt ist in ihm bislang

---

18 Zitiert nach Widerhofer, Laura (2018): „Die Frauenfrage als Rechtsfrage. Eine Entdeckung der weiblichen Rechtssubjektivität". In: Forum Recht 2018 (3), 73. https://forum-recht-online.de/wp/wp-content/uploads/2019/07/01FoR_3_18_Die-Frauenfrage.pdf; Stand: 30.06.2024.

19 Limbach, Jutta (1991): „Zur Rechtsstellung von Eltern und Kindern". In: Feministische Studien extra 9 (s1), 51. DOI: 10.1515/fs-1991-s111; Stand: 30.06.2024.

20 Gerhard, Ute (1991a): „Maßstäbe einer Verfassung auch für Frauen. Eine andere Freiheit, Gleichheit, Würde". In: Feministische Studien extra 9 (s1), 11, 13. DOI: 10.1515/fs-1991-s104; Stand: 30.06.2024.

21 Maihofer, Andrea (1991): „Eine notwendige Ergänzung des Gleichberechtigungsartikels". In: Feministische Studien extra 9 (s1), 38, 39. DOI: 10.1515/fs-1991-s109; Stand: 30.06.2024.

> nicht repräsentiert. Schon allein, sich hierüber klar zu werden und sich über Alternativen auseinanderzusetzen (auch wenn deren Verwirklichung derzeit vielleicht recht unwahrscheinlich erscheinen mag), könnte ein wichtiger Gewinn einer Verfassungsdebatte für uns Frauen sein.

Es verwundert vor dem Hintergrund dieser Schilderungen nicht, dass es in Situationen gesellschaftlicher und politischer Umbrüche immer wieder Frauen und feministische Bewegungen sind, die ihre Forderungen für eine gerechtere Zukunft mit der Vision einer feministischen Verfassung verbinden. Das Feministisch-Utopische geht dabei über eine Kritik bestehender Verhältnisse hinaus und findet in der Verfassung eine sehr konkrete und hinsichtlich der möglichen Realisierung vielversprechende Hoffnungsträgerin. Dabei wird Recht nicht zuvörderst als Unterdrückungs- und Machtinstrument kritisiert, sondern sein Transformationspotential in expliziten Verfassungsversprechen manifestiert. (Verfassungs-)Recht ist Bezugspunkt der Reflexion über ungleiche Gesellschaftsverhältnisse und bildet zugleich den Fluchtpunkt des Feministisch-Utopischen.

3 Utopieforschung

Die Utopieforschung ist geprägt durch zwei zentrale Utopiebegriffe – den sogenannten „klassischen" Utopiebegriff und den Utopiebegriff nach *Ernst Bloch*. Sie sind durch feministisch-theoretische Ansätze ergänzt bzw. modifiziert worden, die hier herangezogen werden, um das Feministisch-Utopische zu konzeptualisieren.

3.1 *Thomas Morus* und der „klassische" Utopiebegriff

Der als „klassisch" bezeichnete Utopiebegriff wird auf *Thomas Morus* zurückgeführt, der mit seinem Roman *Utopia* aus dem Jahr 1516 den Begriff der Utopie geprägt hat. Im Sinne der *Thomas Morus*-Weise sind Utopien – so fasst es der Utopieforscher *Richard Saage* zusammen – „Fiktionen innerweltlicher Gesellschaften, die, staatsfrei oder staatlich verfaßt, sich entweder zu einem Wunsch- oder Furchtbild verdichten, das auf Fehlentwicklungen der eigenen Gesellschaft reagiert".[22] Dieser weite Utopiebegriff erstreckt sich letztlich auf jede Vision gesellschaftlichen Zusammenlebens und stellt als einziges eingrenzendes Element den Bezug zum Staat bzw. der Staatsorganisation heraus.

---

22 Saage, Richard (2005): „Plädoyer für den klassischen Utopiebegriff". In: Erwägen Wissen Ethik 16 (3), 291.

Der „klassische“ Utopiebegriff wurde – insbesondere von *Ernst Bloch* – dafür kritisiert, einerseits zu eng auf den Staatsroman begrenzt zu sein und andererseits in seinem „überindividuellen Anspruch“ ohne Element historischer Selbstreflexion zu abstrakt zu sein. Von feministischer Seite ist er kritisiert worden, weil er beschränkt sei auf – so die Politikwissenschaftlerin *Hannelore Schröder* – „Utopien von Männern, deren Protagonisten Männer sind, die ‚Fehlentwicklungen‘ nur Männer betreffend kritisieren, Zukunftspläne für Männer entwerfen, die Männer realisieren, worin männliche Forscher kein Problem sehen.“[23]

Trotz dieser Kritik wird der „klassische“ Begriff auch heute noch in der Utopieforschung vertreten, u. a. *Richard Saage* will diesen als Idealtypus verwenden, um einerseits die Utopie von anderen geistesgeschichtlichen Phänomenen präzise abgrenzen zu können und andererseits Mischformen identifizieren zu können, die die Utopie mit anderen Konzeptionen eingegangen ist.[24]

3.2 *Ernst Blochs* konkreter Utopiebegriff

Ernst Bloch setzte hingegen auf einen enger gefassten Utopiebegriff, den er maßgeblich im *Prinzip Hoffnung* entwickelte. Die *konkrete Utopie* zeichnet sich nach *Bloch* dadurch aus, dass sie „ein Noch-Nicht-Sein erwartbarer Art für sich hat, das heißt, nicht in einem Leer-Möglichen herumspielt und abirrt, sondern ein Real-Mögliches psychisch vorausnimmt“.[25] Sie braucht den „Bezug aufs Real-Mögliche“,[26] den „mit Hoffnung geladene[n], de[n] phantasievolle[n] Blick der utopischen Funktion“, der durch das „Reelle[n] in der Antizipation selbst“ berichtigt wird. Erforderlich ist nach *Bloch* zudem ein „solide[s] Subjekt dahinter“,[27] das für sozialistische Gesellschaftsutopien durch das proletarische Klassenbewusstsein getragen werde.[28] Zu diesem „subjektiven Faktor“ des Utopischen schreibt *Bloch*: „[O]hne Kraft eines Ich und Wir dahinter wird selbst das Hoffen fade.“[29] Der Utopiebegriff nach *Bloch* betont also das individuelle Moment im Zusammentreffen mit dem reellen Moment, den angelegten Tendenzen der Zeit, ihre Wirkung zu entfalten.[30]

---

23 Schröder (2005), 333.
24 Saage (2005), 291, 292.
25 Bloch, Ernst (1959): Das Prinzip Hoffnung, 3 Bde. Frankfurt am Main: Suhrkamp. Bd. 1, 164.
26 Vgl. ebd.
27 Ebd., 165.
28 Ebd., 168.
29 Ebd., 167.
30 Vgl. Dierkes, Mirjam (2012): „Von der (ausgegrenzten) Erfahrung zum ‚Noch-Nicht‘. Emanzipation als Theorie und Praxis feministischer Herrschafts(verschleierungs)kritik“. In: Birkle, Carmen / Kahl, Ramona / Ludwig, Gundula / Maurer, Susanne (Hg.): Emanzipation und feministische Politiken. Verwicklungen, Verwerfungen, Verwandlungen. Sulzbach: Ulrike Helmer Verlag, 69, 72.

Am Ende des 36. Kapitels im 4. Teil zu den Sozialutopien geht *Bloch* auf Utopien der Frauenbewegung ein. Unter der Unter-Überschrift „Aktueller Rest: bürgerliche Gruppenutopien" zählt er diese zu den „ganz späte[n] Sozialutopien". *Bloch* erkennt sie jedoch nicht als „reife Utopien" an; sie hätten etwas „Spezialisiert-Kurzsichtige[s]".[31] Ihnen fehle der „Wille zum *Umbau der gesamten Gesellschaft*; wie dies in den großen Sozialutopien üblich" sei.[32] Utopien aus der Frauenbewegung beschränkten sich auf „die Befreiung vom Korsett und das Recht zu rauchen, zu wählen und zu studieren".[33] *Bloch* attestiert den Frauenbewegungen zudem ein „Inhaltsproblem", das darin bestünde, Geschlecht nicht vollständig überwinden zu wollen.[34] Am Beispiel der Utopien der Frauenbewegungen unterstreicht *Bloch* ein besonderes Element konkreter Utopien: Sie müssen sich in einer umfassenden Weise gegen die bestehende Gesellschaftsordnung auflehnen. Die Aufhebung der Geschlechterordnung als Vision lässt *Boch* hierfür nicht genügen. Er hält den Utopien der Frauenbewegungen zudem vor, keine Utopie für das Geschlecht selbst, kein utopisches Selbstbild für die Frau entworfen zu haben. Diese Sichtweise offenbart *Bloch*s mangelndes Verständnis sowohl für das Ausmaß der strukturellen Benachteiligung aufgrund des Geschlechts als auch das Selbstbild des Lebens als Frau in einer gleichberechtigten Gesellschaft, das Frauenbewegungen entwerfen und als Ziel verfolgen. Die Markierung feministischer Utopien als „Partialutopien"[35] folgt einer Strategie, die aus feministischer Perspektive immer wieder kritisiert worden ist. *Catharine MacKinnon* hat sich dem Vorwurf des Partikularismus etwa in Bezug auf die feministische Rechtsforschung entgegengestellt.[36] Aus diesem Grund und wegen *Bloch*s abwertender Darstellung von Frauen innerhalb der Frauenbewegung als entweder das „freie Mädchen", das zu uninspiriert lediglich auf gleiche Rechte für sich selbst beharre, oder „die Männliche", „die Führende", „die beginnende Stimmrechtlerin", der ein „unleugbarer Männerhaß" eigen sei,[37] ist *Bloch*s Utopiebegriff jedenfalls mit Vorurteilen belastet, die für eine Anwendung auf feministische Verfassungsutopien zu überwinden wären.

---

31 Bloch, Ernst (1959): Das Prinzip Hoffnung, 3 Bde. Frankfurt am Main: Suhrkamp. Bd. 2, 681.
32 Vgl. ebd.
33 Ebd., 689.
34 Ebd., 694 f.
35 Ebd., 683.
36 Feminist Jurisprudence wird stigmatisiert als „particularized and protectionist in male eyes", und zwar von linken wie liberalen Männern. Siehe MacKinnon, Catharine A. (1989): Toward a Feminist Theory of the State. Cambridge, London: Harvard University Press, 249.
37 Bloch (1959), Bd. 2, 687 f.

3.3 Feministisch-theoretische Annäherung an den Utopiebegriff

Feministische Stimmen im utopietheoretischen Feld schlagen – wie *Barbara Holland-Cunz* – zum Teil einen versöhnlichen Umgang mit der Bloch versus Morus-Polarität vor. Sie plädiert dafür, die Gegenüberstellung der Utopiebegriffe aufzugeben und die Ansätze nebeneinander zu stellen: *„Morus plus Bloch"*.[38] Einen Ansatz, der den konkreten Utopieansatz *Blochs* so weiterdenkt, dass er auch die Betrachtung feministischer Verfassungsutopien erlaubt, entwickelt *Mirjam Dierkes*. Sie fragt danach, „ob, und vor allem *wie*, Utopie aktuell überhaupt als Kategorie für die gesellschaftliche Analyse und normative Theorieentwicklung gedacht werden kann und soll".[39] Die Inhalte feministische Utopien seien vor allem dadurch gekennzeichnet, dass sie auf die Veränderung der gesellschaftlich-ökonomischen Grundlagen gerichtet seien. Sie schlägt vor, „das ‚Utopische' ganz praktisch als gesellschaftliche Artikulationsweise zu begreifen"[40]; und dafür eine demokratietheoretische Perspektive einzunehmen.[41] Und zwar nicht nur deshalb, weil regelmäßig die Gestaltung der Demokratie zentraler Inhalt von Utopien ist, sondern auch, weil Demokratie „als stets weiterzuentwickelnde, gesellschaftliche (Selbst)Verständigungsweise [...] als konkrete, prozessuale Utopie verstanden werden" kann.[42]

Das Utopische entsteht so besehen als Möglichkeit eines Anderen auf der Suche nach Alternativen, „in der Praxis der Artikulation und Re-Artikulation von Kritik, [...] der Gestaltung und Um-Gestaltung der eigenen Lebensverhältnisse".[43] Eine solche Perspektive nimmt auch das Subjekt in den Fokus. Das Utopische lässt sich konkret im „Selbst-Erfahrenen" bzw. „Selbst-Empfundenen" ausmachen, von dem aus die „Fluchtlinien der Sehnsucht" entworfen werden.[44]

Dieser Ansatz eröffnet eine analytische Perspektive auf das Feministisch-Utopische, auf die Hoffnung in die Transformationskraft von Verfassungen, und das vor dem Hintergrund der Selbsterfahrung (von Frauen, von marginalisierten Personen), die in emanzipatorischen Bewegungen kollektiv artikuliert wird. Es wird so mögliche, feministische Verfassungsutopien auch als feministische Praxis zu begreifen und nachzuzeichnen, inwiefern sie auf Grundlage der Reflexion über Leerstellen und blinde

---

38 Holland-Cunz, Barbara (2005): „Bloch versus Morus. Eine Diskurs-Konstruktion der Utopieforschung". In: Erwägen Wissen Ethik 16 (3), 305 f.
39 Dierkes (2013), 68, 69.
40 Ebd., 68, 71.
41 Ebd., 68, 72.
42 Ebd., 68, 73.
43 Maurer, Susanne (2012): „Utopisches Denken statt Utopie? Gedankenexperiment und (unbestimmte) Grenzüberschreitung als feministische Politik". In: Birkle, Carmen / Kahl, Ramona / Ludwig, Gundula / Maurer, Susanne (Hg.): Emanzipation und feministische Politiken. Verwicklungen, Verwerfungen, Verwandlungen. Sulzbach: Ulrike Helmer Verlag, 75, 83.
44 Dierkes (2013), 68, 77 unter Bezugnahme auf Maurer (2012), 75, 83.

Flecke des Verfassungsrechts als konkrete Visionen eines „Noch-Nicht" entworfen werden.

4 Verfassungsutopie als feministische Praxis: Das Frankfurter Frauenmanifest

Aus dieser Perspektive wird nun das Frankfurter Frauenmanifest in den Blick genommen, um das Feministisch-Utopische entlang einiger zentraler Elemente – der Versuch einer Typologie feministischer Verfassungsutopien – zu untersuchen.

4.1 Die Verfassungsutopie als Gesellschaftskritik

Die Verfassungsutopie stellt eine spezifische Form der Kritik an der Gesellschaft und ihrer staatlichen Ordnung dar. Der konkreten Arbeit mit dem Verfassungstext ist diese Kritik immanent. Die Utopie für eine andere, gerechtere Gesellschaft wird von ihr getragen, Recht als „feministischer Möglichkeitsraum in der Verfassungsdiskussion"[45] genutzt. In der Einleitung zur Dokumentation des Frankfurter Frauenkongresses bringt *Ute Gerhard* das Umschlagen von der theoretischen und feministischen Kritik in die konkrete feministische Praxis der Verfassungsutopie zum Ausdruck:[46]

> [N]un ging es ganz und gar nicht mehr nur um die wissenschaftliche oder feministische Kontroverse um Gleichheit und/oder Differenz, vielmehr wurde es ernst mit der Notwendigkeit, theoretische Erkenntnis umzusetzen in politische Praxis, in diesem Fall, in die Formulierung eines Verfassungstextes, der ein Instrument politischer Auseinandersetzung und der Durchsetzung von Fraueninteressen werden sollte.

Das Frankfurter Frauenmanifest orientiert sich – für Verfassungsutopien nicht unüblich – „zur besseren Vergleichbarkeit"[47] an dem Wortlaut und der Anordnung des Grundgesetzes und zeigt die Visionen des Frauenkongresses durch Hervorhebung der Änderungen und Ergänzungen des Grundgesetzes in einer Synopse auf. Dabei reichen die Änderungen und Ergänzungen von lediglich punktuellen Ergänzungen mit dem Ziel der Sichtbarkeit von Frauen und marginalisierten Personen bis zur ex-

---

45 Siehe zu dieser Formulierung, allerdings im Kontext des Engagements ostdeutscher Feminist*innen: Fehrs, Kristiane / Nagel, Klara / Paulson, Joy-Robin / Ramm, Ronda (2022): „Möglichkeitsräume im Umbruch. Ein postsozialistischer Blick auf das feministische Potential der Verfassungsdiskussion der Wendezeit". In: Berliner Blätter 85, 61, 69. DOI: 10.18452/24004; Stand: 30.06.2024.

46 Gerhard, Ute (1991b): „Einleitung". In: Feministische Studien extra 9 (s1), 3, 4. DOI: 10.1515/fs-1991-s102; Stand: 30.06.2024.

47 Dokumentation „Entwurf eines Frankfurter Frauenmanifests. Frauen für eine neue Verfassung" (1991), 107, 108.

pliziten Formulierung neuer Rechte. Das „Konkret-Reelle“ im *Bloch*schen Sinn wird in der niedergeschriebenen Verfassungsutopie nahezu idealtypisch visualisiert. In der synoptischen Darstellung treten Kritik und Utopie, das „Noch-Nicht“ und die „konkret-reelle“ Vision, in einen unmittelbaren Dialog.

4.2 Die Wiedervereinigung als Entstehungskontext

Das Moment für die Entstehung emanzipatorischer Verfassungsutopien liegt in einer Situation des gesellschaftlichen und/oder politischen Um- bzw. Aufbruchs.[48] In der Um- bzw. Aufbruchssituation suchen emanzipatorische Bewegungen nach Möglichkeiten der gesellschaftlichen und politischen Neugestaltung und können diese in Verfassungsutopien konkret werden lassen. Für den Frankfurter Frauenkongress und das Frauenmanifest bildet die deutsch-deutsche Wiedervereinigung dieses Moment.

Das Frankfurter Frauenmanifest stützte sich ausdrücklich auch auf den Verfassungsentwurf des Zentralen Runden Tisches der DDR,[49] ohne jedoch im unmittelbaren Zusammenwirken mit ostdeutschen Frauen entstanden zu sein.[50]

4.3 Die „Kraft eines Ich und Wir“: der Frauenkongress und der Bezug zur Frauenbewegung

Feministische Verfassungsutopien entstehen in enger Verbindung zu oder aus Frauenbewegungen heraus. Das Frankfurter Frauenmanifest nimmt in seiner Einleitung Bezug auf die Frauenbewegung der 1970er Jahre („[n]ach mehr als zwanzig Jahren neuer Frauenbewegung“) und greift zentrale Forderungen dieser Bewegung auf – es geht um die (sexuelle) Selbstbestimmung von Frauen, den Schutz vor (sexualisierter) Gewalt, das Recht auf Schwangerschaftsabbruch, sowie die Forderung nach materieller Gleichberechtigung und ökonomischer Absicherung von Frauen und Familien.

Der subjektive Faktor der Verfassungsutopie, die „Kraft eines Ich und Wir“, liegt darin, dass feministische Bewegungen „*Kritik an Herrschaft und deren Verdeckungszusammenhängen* [betreiben]“ und dabei „ihren utopischen Impuls […] aus der ständigen Reflektion des historischen und des eigenen ‚Gewordenseins‘, der eigenen Erfahrung“

---

48 Holland-Cunz (1986), 61: „Aufbruchszeiten waren immer Zeiten der Formulierung utopischer Entwürfe; eine konsolidierte Bewegung wendet sich dann Fragen kurzfristiger Strategien und theoretischer Analyse zu.“

49 Gerhard (1991b), 3, 4; Dokumentation „Entwurf eines Frankfurter Frauenmanifests. Frauen für eine neue Verfassung“ (1991), 107, 108.

50 Vgl. Mittrop (2023), 51, 63 f.; zum feministischen Potential der Verfassungsdiskussion des Zentralen Runden Tisches des sowie insbesondere der Arbeit des Unabhängigen Frauenverbands siehe Fehrs/Nagel/Paulson/Ramm (2022), 61–74.

beziehen.[51] Dafür müssen und können Frauen nicht genau wissen, wie die geschlechtergerechte Welt aussehen würde, weil sie – so bringt es die feministische Rechtswissenschaftlerin *Catharine A. MacKinnon* auf den Punkt – nie in ihr gelebt haben.[52] Sie speisen vielmehr nicht nur ihre gemeinsame Kritik, sondern auch die gemeinsame Utopie aus der Erfahrung der Ungleichheit, aus dem Erleben rechtlicher und sozialer Benachteiligungen.

Dabei zeigt sich als eine weitere Besonderheit feministischer Utopien, dass „[d]as Utopische [...] in feministischer Perspektive eher im Kontext von Streit, Widerspruch und Konflikten zu suchen [ist] als in Praxen scheinbar ‚heiler Welt'".[53] Was hiermit gemeint ist, wird am Frankfurter Frauenmanifest besonders deutlich. Entstanden ist es auf Initiative des Frauenreferats der Stadt Frankfurt und der Frauenforschung an der Universität Frankfurt (insbesondere *Ute Gerhard*) unter Beteiligung von Frauen aus der autonomen Bewegung, aus institutionalisierten Bereichen von Politik und Wissenschaft, darunter auch Juristinnen – letztere in interessanter Rolle. Die Dokumentation zum Frankfurter Frauenmanifest spricht hier von einem „spannenden und produktiven Lernprozeß. Insbesondere zwischen Juristinnen, die das Realitätsprinzip ‚herrschender Juristenmeinung' zu berücksichtigen wußten, und Feministinnen, die ihre Utopie von einer anderen besseren Gesellschaft verteidigten".[54]

Die Notwendigkeit einer breiten Diskussion frauenpolitisch Engagierter wird auch in den Beiträgen zur Dokumentation des Frauenkongresses angesprochen: Verfassungsentwürfe können „nicht das Ergebnis des Nachdenkens einzelner Frauen sein. Im Gegenteil, dazu ist eine breite Diskussion unter Frauen nötig. Nur so können Formulierungen gefunden werden, die den Differenzen auch unter uns Frauen gerecht werden."[55] Uneinigkeit und Widerspruch, die streitigen Diskussionen, sind schon im Textentwurf für eine neue Verfassung selbst dokumentiert. Dies wird in der Einleitung zum Manifest auch angekündigt: „Kontroverse Punkte oder alternative Vorschläge sind eckig eingeklammert."[56] Es sind jene Vorschläge, auf die sich nicht ohne Widerspruch geeinigt werden konnte. Solche Vorschläge finden sich etwa bei den Erweiterungen des Art. 3 Abs. 2 GG. Zudem hält die Dokumentation in den Bemerkungen

---

51 Dierkes (2012), 69, 73.

52 MacKinnon (1989), 241: „Women are not permitted fully to know what sex equality would look like, because they have never lived in it. It is idealist, hence elitist, to hold that they do. But they do not need to. They know inequality because they have lived it, so they know what removing barriers to equality would be. Many of these barriers are legal; many of them are social; most of them exist at an inferface between law and society."

53 Dierkes (2013), 68, 76 f.

54 Gerhard (1991b), 3, 4.

55 Maihofer (1991), 38, 45.

56 Dokumentation „Entwurf eines Frankfurter Frauenmanifests. Frauen für eine neue Verfassung" (1991), 107, 108.

zur Diskussion auf dem Frauenkongress fest, welche Vorschläge aus dem Frankfurter Frauenmanifest mehrheitlich Zustimmung oder Ablehnung erfuhren.

4.4 Ausgewählte Inhalte des Frankfurter Frauenmanifestes

Die „Fluchtpunkte der Sehnsucht"[57] feministisch-utopischen Denkens in Verfassungstext drücken sich in den normativen Bezugspunkten der Gleichheit, Freiheit und Menschenwürde aus. Gleichheit wird feministisch-utopisch als materielle, substantielle Gleichheit erdacht, die über die rein formale Rechtsgleichheit hinausreicht. Freiheitsrechte werden aus einer feministischen Perspektive spezifisch ergänzt um Freiheitsrechte, die Frauen besonders betreffen, z. B. das Recht auf reproduktive und sexuelle Selbstbestimmung. Es wird aber auch eine geschlechtersensible und diskriminierungsfreie sowie verantwortungsvolle[58] Inanspruchnahme aller Freiheitsrechte verlangt. Die Trias wird komplettiert durch die Menschenwürde, die ausdrückliche Anerkennung der Würde der Frau. Darüber hinaus entwirft das Frankfurter Frauenmanifest auch Visionen zur Stärkung der direkten Demokratie und der politischen Partizipation von Frauen. Getragen wird das Frankfurter Frauenmanifest zudem durch das Streben nach Frieden und Freundschaft zu den anderen europäischen Staaten, die Vision einer solidarischen und verantwortungsbewussten Ausübung von Freiheitsrechten sowie das Bewusstsein der Verantwortung für die dauerhafte Erhaltung der natürlichen Lebensgrundlagen einschließlich der Natur und das verantwortungsvolle Handeln im Bewusstsein der Lehren aus Ausschwitz. Diese Aspekte werden bereits in der Präambel hervorgehoben. Einige Vorschläge des Frankfurter Frauenmanifestes sollen exemplarisch das zugrunde liegende feministisch-utopische Denken, auch in der Auseinandersetzung über diese Vorschläge, illustrieren. Sie entwerfen die Vision eines eigenständigen feministischen Subjekts und zeugen zugleich von der feministischen Kritik an der dem Grundgesetz zugrunde gelegten patriarchal-hegemonialen Sicht- und Denkweise.

4.4.1 Die Würde der Frau und die selbstbestimmte Entscheidung über den Schwangerschaftsabbruch

Die Würde der Frau wird in dem Frankfurter Frauenmanifest mehrfach explizit hervorgehoben, zunächst prominent in Art. 1 Abs. 1: „Die Würde von Frau, Mann und

57 Maurer (2012), 75, 87.

58 Insoweit bezieht sich das Frankfurter Frauenmanifest auf den Verfassungsentwurf des Zentralen Runden Tisches, die Möglichkeit zu selbstbestimmtem verantwortlichem Handeln als höchste Freiheit beschrieb, vgl. Gerhard (1991a), 11, 16.

Kind ist unantastbar. Sie zu achten und zu schützen ist Pflicht des Staates, der Gesellschaft sowie jeder und jedes Einzelnen." Aber auch die Meinungsfreiheit erfährt in Art. 5 Abs. 2 S. 2 GG eine Ergänzung mit Bezug zur Menschenwürde der Frau: „Das Recht der freien Meinungsäußerung findet seine Grenzen insbesondere dort, wo die Würde der Frau verletzt wird."

Die Hervorhebung der Würde der Frau erfolgte unter Bezugnahme auf die Ungleichheitserfahrung von Frauen, u. a. im Zusammenhang mit der (verunmöglichten) Selbstbestimmung über ihren Körper und ihre Sexualität, auf die Erfahrung, dass die Würde der Frau tatsächlich „angetastet" wurde und wird.[59] Immanent ist der Anerkennung der Frau als Rechtsubjekt mit Würde die Kritik an dem männlichen Subjekt als idealisierte Referenz des Grundgesetzes. Der Beeinträchtigung der Selbstbestimmung setzt das Frankfurter Frauenmanifest insbesondere ein explizites Recht auf Schwangerschaftsabbruch entgegen. Verankert bei der Religions- und Gewissensfreiheit sieht Art. 4 Abs. 4 vor: „Jede Frau hat das Recht, [nach ihrem Gewissen] zu entscheiden, ob sie eine Schwangerschaft austrägt oder nicht." Einigkeit bestand sowohl beim Verfassen des Frankfurter Frauenmanifestes als auch dem Frauenkongress darüber, das Recht auf Schwangerschaftsabbruch als zentrale Forderung zu formulieren. Uneinigkeit herrschte hingegen über die Markierung der Entscheidung als Gewissensentscheidung[60] oder Ausdruck der Persönlichkeitsentfaltung sowie über den Standort der Regelung.[61] In der Diskussion über das Frankfurter Frauenmanifest sprachen sich die Teilnehmerinnen mehrheitlich dafür aus, das Recht auf Schwangerschaftsabbruch beim Gleichberechtigungsgrundsatz des Art. 3 GG zu verankern.[62]

4.4.2 Die Gleichberechtigung der Geschlechter

Intensiv diskutiert wurde zudem über den Vorschlag zur Ergänzung und Konkretisierung von Art. 3 Abs. 2 GG. Das Frankfurter Frauenmanifest enthält folgende Formulierungen:

> Frauen und Männer sind gleichberechtigt. [Gleichberechtigung heißt auch Gleichheit und Anerkennung von Verschiedenheit.] Der Staat garantiert die gleichberechtigte Teilhabe der Geschlechter in allen gesellschaftlichen Bereichen [insbesondere in Politik,

59 Gerhard (1991a), 11, 17 f.

60 Dafür, unter Betonung, das Anliegen könne sich nur als Gewissensfrage in der juristischen und verfassungsrechtlichen Arena behaupten: Frommel, Monika (1991): „Schwangerschaftsabbruch ist eine Gewissensfrage". In: Feministische Studien extra 9 (s1), 59–64. DOI: 10.1515/fs-1991-s114; Stand: 30.06.2024.

61 Für einen eigenständigen Artikel: Sadrozinski, Renate (1991): „Das Recht auf Schwangerschaftsabbruch in der Verfassung verankern!". In: Feministische Studien extra 9 (s1), 56, 58. DOI: 10.1515/fs-1991-s113; Stand: 30.06.2024.

62 Burgsmüller, Claudia (1991): „Bemerkungen zur Diskussion". In: Feministische Studien extra 9 (s1), 71, 72. DOI: 10.1515/fs-1991-s116; Stand: 30.06.2024.

> Arbeitsleben und Familie]. Die gleichberechtigte Partizipation der Frau ist insbesondere durch Quotierung und andere geeignete Maßnahmen herzustellen. [Es ist die Aufgabe des Staates, durch Schaffung geeigneter Rahmenbedingungen auf tatsächliche Gleichstellung von Frauen in allen gesellschaftlichen Bereichen hinzuwirken.]

Umstritten war zunächst, ob es einer positiven Anerkennung der Geschlechterdifferenz durch die „Anerkennung der Frau als gleichberechtigtes eigenständiges gesellschaftliches Subjekt mit eigener Geschichte und eigener Identität und Würde" bedurfte.[63] Dagegen wurde in der Diskussion die Gefahr einer biologistischen und die geschlechtsspezifische Arbeitsteilung perpetuierenden Auslegung des Begriffs der Verschiedenheit angebracht. Befürwortend wurde darauf verwiesen, mit der Formulierung auch die Lebensrealität von Frauen abzusichern, die entsprechend tradierter Rollenverteilungen lebten.[64] Zentraler Gegenstand der Diskussion war zudem die Aufnahme von Quotierungsinstrumenten in die Verfassung. Dabei waren sich die Teilnehmerinnen einig hinsichtlich des Nutzens von Frauenquoten, aber uneinig, ob die Quotierung ausdrücklich in der Verfassung genannt werden sollte.[65] *Heide Pfarr* brachte schließlich mit dem letzten Klammerzusatz einen Alternativvorschlag ein, der den Staat über bloß formale Gleichstellung hinaus verpflichten sollte.

An anderer Stelle war die Aufnahme einer Quotierung wohl weniger umstritten: Das Frankfurter Frauenmanifest unterlegte die politische Partizipation von Frauen mit dem Grundsatz der Parité in Art. 38 Abs. 1. Dort sollte es heißen: „[Die Abgeordneten des Deutschen Bundestages] müssen mindestens zur Hälfte Frauen sein." Die Aufnahme der Quote für den Bundestag ist Zeugnis der Kritik an der unzureichenden politischen Repräsentation und Teilhabe von Frauen. Sie zeigt auf, dass rein formal bestehenden Zugangschancen nicht ausreichen, um das Ziel materieller Gleichberechtigung zu erreichen. Strukturelle Hürden bauen sich jedoch nicht von selbst ab, dies erfordert aktives Handeln von Staat und Parteien. Auch die Bundesregierung sollte nach der Vorstellung des Frankfurter Frauenmanifestes paritätisch besetzt sein (Vorschlag zur Ergänzung von Art. 62 GG). Die Utopie einer gleichberechtigten Demokratie sah zudem die Stärkung direktdemokratischer Elemente vor. So enthielt das Frankfurter Frauenmanifest eine Regelung für Volksbegehren und Volksentscheide auf Bundes- und Landesebene. Zudem sah der (neu vorgeschlagene) Art. 21a GG vor, dass BürgerInnenbewegungen in ihrem Engagement unter den Schutz der Verfassung zu stellen und mit besonderen Rechten hinsichtlich der Befassung des Bundestages mit von ihnen aufgebrachten Themen auszustatten seien.

Auch die Lohngleichheit wurde im Frankfurter Frauenmanifest verankert, in Art. 12 Abs. 1 S. 3: „Für gleiche und gleichwertige Arbeit besteht Anspruch auf gleichen Lohn."

---

63 Dafür Maihofer (1991), 38, 45.
64 Vgl. Platt (1991), 46, 47.
65 Ebd., 46.

Zugleich wurden die Fragen aufgeworfen, ob es nicht eines umfassenden Gleichstellungsgesetzes für die Privatwirtschaft bedürfe, ob Verbandsklagen zum Abbau der Lohndiskriminierung einzuführen seien und wie ein Maßnahmenpaket aussehen könnte, das eine geschlechtergerechte Gestaltung der Arbeitszeit und Arbeitsorganisation erwirken könnte und den Erwerbs- und Lebensbiografien von Frauen gerecht würde.[66]

4.4.3 Umweltschutz

Stellvertretend für viele weitere inhaltliche Vorschläge des Frankfurter Frauenmanifestes soll hier abschließend der Vorschlag für eine Aufnahme des Umweltschutzes in enger Nähe zu den Staatsstrukturprinzipien genannt werden, der in der Dokumentation zum Frauenkongress nur eine untergeordnete Rolle einnahm. Die Verantwortung für den Erhalt der natürlichen Lebensgrundlagen fand nicht nur in der Präambel, sondern in einer Ergänzung des Art. 20 Abs. 1 S. 2 GG Ausdruck, die lauten sollte: „Die natürliche Umwelt steht als Lebensgrundlage des Menschen um ihrer selbst willen unter dem besonderen Schutz des Staates. Bei Konflikten zwischen ökologischer Belastbarkeit und ökonomischen Erfordernissen ist den ökologischen Belangen Vorrang einzuräumen, wenn anderenfalls eine erhebliche Beeinträchtigung der natürlichen Umwelt droht." Diesem Vorschlag liegt die Kritik an unzureichenden staatlichen Aktivitäten des Umweltschutzes zugrunde und zugleich die Kritik an der Priorisierung ökonomischer Gesichtspunkte gegenüber ökologischen Belangen.

5 Fazit

Der Einblick in das Frankfurter Frauenmanifest und die Diskussionen auf den Frauenkongress in der Paulskirche zeigt auf, wie feministische Verfassungsutopien im Austausch, auch: Widerspruch, verhandelt werden, und welchen Einfluss geschlechtertheoretische Erkenntnisse und Forderungen der Frauenbewegungen nehmen können. Die Vorschläge des Frankfurter Frauenmanifestes betreffen auch nach wie vor aktuelle feministische Anliegen; die Erinnerung an die feministische Arbeit des Frankfurter Frauenkongresses dient auch dazu, die Diskussionen und Vorschläge in aktuellen Diskursen zu berücksichtigen: So sind Diskussionen um die Verankerung von Paritätsregelungen im Wahlrecht (vgl. den Vorschlag zur Ergänzung von Art. 38 Abs. 1 GG)

66 Vogelheim, Elisabeth (1991): „Lohnungleichheit. ‚Verfassungsbruch in Permanenz'". In: Feministische Studien extra 9 (s1), 34, 37. DOI: 10.1515/fs-1991-s108; Stand: 30.06.2024.

ebenso aktuell wie die Problematik der sogenannten *Hatespeech*, insbesondere zu Lasten von Frauen (vgl. den Vorschlag zur Ergänzung von Art. 5 Abs. 2 GG).

Feministische Verfassungsutopien stellen eine vielschichtige feministische Praxis dar. Sie vereinen Gesellschafts- und Herrschaftskritik mit einem transformatorischen Anspruch an das Recht. Sie lassen „konkret-reell" werden, wie das rechtliche Fundament einer geschlechtergerechten Gesellschaft aussehen könnte und verwenden eine Form, die anschlussfähig für die verfassungsrechtliche und -politische Diskussion ist. Ihnen liegt dabei eine scharfe Kritik an den vorherrschenden Gesellschaftsverhältnissen zugrunde, sie wenden sich gegen „patriarchalische Gewaltverhältnisse, Sexismus, Macht aufgrund des Geschlechts und gegen Unterdrückung".[67] Feministische Verfassungsutopien speisen sich aus dem Selbst-Erfahrenen und sie speisen sich aus der artikulierten Kritik. Dabei beziehen sie ihre emanzipatorische Ausrichtung aus der kritischen Bearbeitung des Vergangenen[68] – bis zum Gegenwärtigen. Die Kritik bildet die Realitätsverankerung durch die Aufarbeitung struktureller Defizite in der Vergangenheit, die in der Utopie vermieden werden bzw. zu denen ein Gegenbild entworfen wird.[69] Dabei fordert das feministisch-utopische Denken „mit neuen Themen und unbequemen Fragen heraus, will politische Auseinandersetzungen initiieren" und hierfür neue Formen („[f]eministisches Netzwerk, Gebärstreik, organisierter Widerstand, Formen anarchistischer Organisation etc.") erproben.[70]

Feministische Verfassungsutopien enden schließlich nicht mit dem Entwurf eines Verfassungstextes. Auch das wird deutlich, wenn man sie als feministische Praxis betrachtet. Sie entwickeln Verfassungstext als Fundament für eine gleichberechtigte Gesellschaft, für andere gesellschaftliche Verhältnisse.[71] Ganz deutlich stellt dies *Ute Gerhard* fest, die maßgeblich am Frankfurter Frauenmanifest mitgewirkt hat: „[Wir] haben […] ganz ausdrücklich nicht nur die Durchsetzung und Verbesserung von Frauenrechten im Sinn […]; vielmehr zielt unser Unternehmen auf's Ganze, auf alle Bereiche der Gesellschaft und ihrer Verfassung, auf das zur Geltungbringen weiblicher Erfahrungen und Wertmaßstäbe, ja, auf die Einsicht, daß Frauenfragen immer auch gleichzeitig Männerfragen sind, weil Geschlechterpolitik in der Geschichte des Kapitalismus wie des jetzt unrealen Sozialismus das Fundament gesellschaftlicher Ungleichheit war und ist."[72] Dafür sei „die Verfassungsdiskussion nicht nur Mittel zum Zweck eines irgendwann zu verabschiedenden Verfassungstextes, sondern als politische Bewegung bereits Politik und Ziel".[73] Feministische Verfassungsutopien vereinen

---

67 Holland-Cunz (1986), 7, 9.
68 Vgl. Dierkes (2012), 69, 71.
69 Vgl. Saage (2005), 291, 294.
70 Holland-Cunz (1986), 61, 98.
71 Vgl. hierzu Böttger, Barbara (1991): „Gleichberechtigung. Ein uneingelöstes Versprechen". In: Feministische Studien extra 9 (s1), 25, 26. DOI: 10.1515/fs-1991-s105; Stand: 30.06.2024.
72 Gerhard (1991a), 11, 13.
73 Gerhard (1991b), 3, 4.

konkrete Verfassungsvisionen und Herrschaftskritik mit einen praktisch-politischen Impuls. Sie schaffen Bewusstsein für Diskriminierung und Ungleichbehandlung, und fragen nach Intervention.

Zur Person: Dana-Sophia Valentiner ist Juniorprofessorin für Öffentliches Recht an der Universität Rostock.

Prof. Dr. Dana-Sophia Valentiner
Universität Rostock, Juristische Fakultät, Ulmenstraße 69, 18057 Rostock, Deutschland,
Dana-Sophia.Valentiner@uni-rostock.de.

Un/Mögliche Gerechtigkeit

Alternativen zu strafrechtlichen Verfahren bei sexualisierter Gewalt

SIMONE KREUTZ

Im/Possible Justice

Alternatives to Criminal Proceedings in Cases of Sexualized Violence

Abstract: Sexualized violence is widespread. Besides its high occurrence, victims seem to face a justice gap that cannot be closed with conventional legal instruments. However, the question of the effectiveness of conventional legal instruments arises fundamentally and not only with regard to prospects of success. The paper examines the extent to which alternative legal practices like transformative justice can provide a remedy. To this end, the paper first considers the question of justice through a notion of multidimensional or queer justice. It then turns to the question of responsibility and the demand for collective responsibility that arises from the changed understanding of justice. Finally, it outlines some challenges as well as the utopian potential of alternative legal practices.

Keywords: Justice, Justice Gap, Collective Responsibility, Sexual Criminal Law, Sexualized Violence, Transformative Justice

1 Einleitung

Genaue Zahlen zum Ausmaß sexualisierter Gewalt liegen nicht vor. Das Bundeskriminalamt verzeichnet allein für das Jahr 2022 11.896 Fälle von Vergewaltigungen, sexuellen Nötigungen und sexuellen Übergriffen.[1] Doch stellt dies lediglich das „Hellfeld"

---

1 Vgl. Bundeskriminalamt (2023): „T01 Grundtabelle – Fälle (V1.0)". In: PKS 2022 Bund – Falltabellen. [online] https://www.bka.de/SharedDocs/Downloads/DE/Publikationen/PolizeilicheKriminalstatistik/2022/Bund/Faelle/BU-F-01-T01-Faelle_xls.xlsx?__blob=publicationFile&v=3; Stand: 08.06.2023. Die Fälle umfassen nur Straftaten nach §§ 177, 178 StGB. Insgesamt wurden 118.196 Straftaten gegen die sexuelle Selbstbestimmung erfasst, dies entspricht allen Straftaten des dreizehnten Abschnitts des StGB (§§ 174–184l StGB).

dar – nur schätzungsweise 7,5 Prozent der Gewalterfahrungen werden bei der Polizei angezeigt.[2] Hochgerechnet entspräche dies also fast 160.000 Fällen pro Jahr, d. h. mehr als 430 Fällen pro Tag.[3] Strafrechtliche Konsequenzen erfolgen dabei nur für einen Bruchteil der angezeigten Fälle, denn aufgrund der zumeist komplizierten Beweislage werden die Verfahren überwiegend eingestellt. Daran hat auch die Reform des Sexualstrafrechts aus dem Jahr 2016 bisher kaum etwas geändert.[4] Anja Kruber et al. zeigen zwar auf, dass es im Generationenvergleich durchaus Verbesserungen im Umgang mit sexualisierter Gewalt gibt, was sich bspw. an einer gestiegenen Sensibilisierung bezüglich unterschiedlicher Gewaltformen oder einer abnehmenden Stigmatisierung bezüglich des Sprechens über Gewalterfahrungen zeigt. Dennoch bleibt die Zahl derer, die sexualisierte Gewalt erfahren, weiterhin hoch und die Zahl derer, die Anzeige diesbezüglich erstatten, weiterhin verschwindend gering.[5] Das lässt die Annahme zu, dass ein Großteil der Betroffenen von sexualisierter Gewalt im Rahmen der konventionellen Rechtspraktik, genauer gesagt im Strafrecht, keinen Raum zur Aufarbeitung der erfahrenden Gewalt vorfinden. Sie auf diesem Wege keine Gerechtigkeit erfahren.

---

2 Vgl. Kruber, Anja / Weller, Konrad / Bathke, Gustav-Wilhelm / Voss, Heinz-Jürgen (2021): PARTNER 5 Erwachsene 2020. Primärbericht. Sexuelle Grenzverletzungen und sexualisierte Gewalt. Merseburg: Hochschule Merseburg, 38 f. Bei der Höhe des Hellfeldes wurde sich an Kruber et al. (2021) orientiert, andere Quellen zeichnen ein Hellfeld zwischen 5 und 15 Prozent, vgl. Schwarz, Carolina (2020): „Kaum Verurteilungen von Tätern". In: taz, 24.11.2020. [online] https://taz.de/Sexualisierte-Gewalt-in-Deutschland/!5727344/; Stand: 08.06.2023. Als „Hellfeld" werden alle polizeilich bekannten Straftaten bezeichnet. Das „Dunkelfeld" bezeichnet demnach alle stattgefundenen, aber nicht polizeilich bekannt gewordenen Straftaten. Zur Frage warum das „Hellfeld" bei Fällen sexualisierter Gewalt so klein ist, vgl. Kubitza, Eva (2023): Warum sexualisierte Gewalt nicht angezeigt wird. Eine kognitionspsychologische Untersuchung. Gießen: Psychosozial-Verlag.

3 Studien haben ergeben, dass jede siebte Frau in Deutschland in ihrem Leben sexualisierte Gewalt erfährt. Diese Zahl umfasst jedoch lediglich jene Fälle, die vor der Reform des Sexualstrafrechts im Jahr 2016 juristisch als sexualisierte Gewalt galten, vgl. Müller, Ursula / Schröttle, Monika (2004): Lebenssituation, Sicherheit und Gesundheit von Frauen in Deutschland. Eine repräsentative Untersuchung zu Gewalt gegen Frauen in Deutschland. Berlin: Bundesministerium für Familie, Senioren, Frauen und Jugend, 30. Durch die Reform des Sexualstrafrechts am 07. Juli 2016 wurde durch eine Neuregelung des Paragrafen 177 StGB der Grundsatz „Nein heißt Nein" ins Strafgesetzbuch aufgenommen. Hierdurch soll jede sexuelle Handlung an einer Person, die gegen deren „erkennbaren Willen" stattfindet, unter Strafe gestellt werden. Vor der Reform des Paragrafens war hierfür die Anwendung von oder Drohung mit Gewalt bzw. das Ausnutzen einer „schutzlosen Lage" notwendig, um den Straftatbestand zu erfüllen. Zudem wurden neue Straftatbestände zu sexueller Belästigung (§ 184i StGB) und zu sexuellen Übergriffen aus Gruppen (§ 184j StGB) eingeführt, vgl. Bundestag (2016): Bundestag entscheidet „Nein heißt Nein". https://www.bundestag.de/webarchiv/textarchiv/2016/kw27-de-selbstbestimmung-434214; Stand: 08.06.2023.

4 Das Kriminologische Forschungsinstitut Niedersachsen ermittelte für das Jahr 2012, dass nur 8,4 Prozent aller angezeigten Vergewaltigungen zu einer Verurteilung führten, vgl. dpa (2014): „Chancen auf Verurteilung nach Vergewaltigung gesunken". In: Zeit Online, 17.04.2014. [online] https://www.zeit.de/gesellschaft/zeitgeschehen/2014-04/studie-vergewaltigung-anzeige-verurteilung; Stand: 08.06.2023. Zur Wirkkraft der Sexualstrafrechtsreform 2016, vgl. Grimm, Ronska / Lean, Anya (2021): „Kollektive Verantwortungsübernahme und transformative Gerechtigkeit. Alternativen zum Rechtssystem?". In: Feministischer InfoBrief, 121. [online] https://www.rav.de/publikationen/rav-infobriefe/feministischer-infobrief-121-2021/kollektive-verantwortungsuebernahme-und-transformative-gerechtigkeit; Stand: 08.06.2023.

5 Vgl. Kruber et al. (2021), 10, 38.

Allein mit Blick auf die Anzeigestatistik und die gerichtlichen Erfolgsaussichten, stellt sich somit die Frage nach der Wirkmächtigkeit strafrechtlicher Verfahren bei Fällen sexualisierter Gewalt. Für Betroffene scheint regelrecht eine Art „justice gap“[6] zu bestehen, welches im Rahmen der konventionellen Rechtspraktik nicht zu schließen zu sein scheint.

Alternative Rechtspraktiken, welche vorrangig unter den Begriffen *restorative justice* (dt. „restaurative Gerechtigkeit“), *transformative justice* (dt. „transformative Gerechtigkeit“) oder *community accountability* (dt. „kollektive Verantwortungsübernahme“) gefasst werden, versprechen eine andere Umgangsweise mit sexualisierter Gewalt und eine bessere Chance auf Gerechtigkeit.[7] *Restorative justice* stellt dabei die am weitesten verbreitete Alternative dar. Sie unterscheidet sich insbesondere durch die Loslösung von der Dyade bestehend aus Täter*in und Betroffene*r und einer aktiven Einbeziehung des sozialen Umfelds von konventionellen Rechtspraktiken. Die praktische Umsetzung erfolgt dabei vorrangig in Form von *restorative circles* (dt. „Gesprächskreise“, alternativ „Mediation“), wobei das Ziel die Restauration des sozialen Miteinanders unter Reintegration aller Beteiligten ist.[8] Trotz des Anspruchs eine Alternative zu konventionellen Rechtspraktiken darzustellen, bleibt *restorative justice* in der Regel an staatliche Strukturen gebunden bzw. findet innerhalb dieser statt und fungiert somit vielmehr als Ergänzung statt als Alternative.[9] In Abgrenzung hierzu entwickelten sich

---

6 McGlynn, Clare / Westmarland, Nicole (2019): „Kaleidoscopic Justice. Sexual Violence and Victim-Survivors' Perceptions of Justice“. In: Social & Legal Studies 28 (2), 179–201. DOI: 10.1177/0964663918761200, 180.

7 Vgl. Daly, Kathleen (2015): „What is Restorative Justice? Fresh Answers to a Vexed Question“. In: Victims & Offenders 11 (1), 9–29. DOI: 10.1080/15564886.2015.1107797; Kim, Mimi E. (2019): „Anti-Carceral Feminism. The Contradictions of Progress and the Possibilities of Counter-Hegemonic Struggle“. In: Affilia. Journal of Women and Social Work, 1–18. DOI: 10.1177/0886109919878276. Während diese Praktiken u. a. in den USA, in Australien und in Großbritannien seit mehreren Jahrzehnten insbesondere durch marginalisierte Gesellschaftsgruppen angewandt und im wissenschaftlichen Diskurs reflektiert werden, ist die Verbreitung im deutschsprachigen Raum vor allem auf (radikal-)linke Räume begrenzt. Hier gab und gibt es einzelne Gruppen, welche bei *transformative justice/community accountability* begleiten, wozu u. a. *ask gerd_a*, das *Transformative Justice Kollektive Berlin* und die *Unterstützer_innengruppe DEFMA* zählen. Als staatlich anerkannte (Teil-)Alternative zum Strafrechtssystem gibt es in Deutschland seit Mitte der 1980er Jahre die Möglichkeit des Täter-Opfer-Ausgleichs, welcher seit 1992 durch das TOA-Servicebüro als überregionale Zentralstelle koordiniert wird und in § 46a StGB verankert ist. Eine wissenschaftliche Auseinandersetzung mit kollektiver Verantwortung bei sexualisierter Gewalt findet in Deutschland – abseits von Schutzdebatten bei intergenerationaler Gewalt – bisher kaum statt, vgl. u. a. Brazzell, Melanie (2017): Was macht uns wirklich sicher? Toolkit für Aktivist_innen. https://www.transformativejustice.eu/wp-content/uploads/2017/07/toolkit-finished-1.pdf; Stand: 08.06.2023; Grimm/Lean (2021); Schwerdtner, Lilian (2021): Sprechen und Schweigen über sexualisierte Gewalt. Ein Plädoyer für Kollektivität und Selbstbestimmung. Münster: edition assemblage.

8 Vgl. Armatta, Judith (2018): „Ending Sexual Violence Through Transformative Justice“. In: Interdisciplinary Journal of Partnership Studies 5 (1), 1–38. DOI: 10.24926/ijps.v5i1.915, 12.

9 Vgl. Kim, Mimi E. (2018): „From Carceral Feminism to Transformative Justice. Women-of-Color Feminism and Alternatives to Incarceration“. In: Journal of Ethic & Cultural Diversity in Social Work 27 (3), 219–233. DOI: 10.1080/15313204.2018.1474827, 226.

Praktiken der *transformative justice* und *community accountability*, wobei beide nicht klar voneinander abgrenzbar sind, weshalb ich diese im Folgenden gemeinsam adressiere. *Transformative justice/community accountability* stehen in enger Verbindung zu abolitionistischen Kämpfen, grenzen sich vom bestehenden Rechtssystem ab und finden in informellen, nicht-institutionalisierten Räumen statt.[10] Die Abgrenzung zu *restorative justice* resultiert vorrangig daraus, dass neben der interpersonellen Gewalt auch die strukturelle Gewalt adressiert wird, welche im Rahmen von konventioneller Rechtspraktik und *restorative justice* nicht bzw. nicht genug thematisiert würde, was zu deren (Re-)Produktion beitrage.[11] Mimi E. Kim führt diesbezüglich aus: „Transformation, as opposed to restoration, also explicitly recognizes that interpersonal forms of violence take place within the context of structural conditions including poverty, racism, sexism, homophobia, ableism, and other systemic forms of violence".[12] Statt einer Restauration des sozialen Miteinanders, quasi einem Zurück zum Status quo nach der interpersonellen Gewalterfahrung, streben *transformative justice/community accountability* somit die Veränderung der zugrundeliegenden Macht- und Unterdrückungsstrukturen an, welche die interpersonelle Gewalt bedingen. Diese Loslösung von der rein interpersonellen Ebene drückt sich dabei vor allem im Begriff der *community accountability* aus, wobei die Verantwortung für die Ursachen der Gewalt als auch für die Aufarbeitung dieser kollektiv verstanden wird statt sie allein im Individuum zu verorten. *Transformative justice/community accountability* verfügen dabei über kein feststehendes „Instrumentarium", sondern die Gruppen, welche *transformative justice/community accountability* umsetzen, nutzen je spezifische Methoden für verschiedene „Arbeitsfelder", worunter die Unterstützung und Ermächtigung der betroffenen Person, die Verantwortungsübernahme und Transformation der gewaltausübenden Person, die Veränderung kollektiver Werte und Praktiken sowie die Transformation der zugrundeliegenden strukturellen Ursachen fällt.[13]

---

10 Vgl. ebd., 227.

11 Vgl. Armatta (2018), 13. Für eine grundlegende Kritik an strafrechtlichen Verfahren bzw. an staatlichen Strafinstanzen vgl. u. a. Davis, Angela Y. (2003): Are Prisons Obsolete?. New York, NY: Seven Stories Press; Duff, Koshka (Hg.) (2021): Abolishing the Police. London: Dog Section Press; Gilmore, Ruth Wilson (2007): Golden Gulag. Prisons, Surplus, Crisis, and Opposition in Globalizing California. Berkeley, CA: University of California Press; Loick, Daniel / Thompson, Vanessa E. (Hg.) (2022): Abolitionismus. Ein Reader. Berlin: Suhrkamp Verlag; Stanley, Eric A. / Smith, Nat / McDonald, Cece (Hg.) (2015): Captive Genders. Trans Embodiment and the Prison Industrial Complex. Edinburgh/Chico/Baltimore: AK Press.

12 Kim (2018), 227.

13 Vgl. INCITE! Women of Color Against Violence (2008): Law Enforcement Violence Against Women of Color and Trans People of Color. A Critical Intersection of Gender Violence and State Violence. An Organizer's Resource and Toolkit. Redmond, WA: INCITE! Women of Color Against Violence, 69. Obwohl es keine feststehenden Instrumentarien und Methoden gibt, existieren verschiedene „Toolboxes", welche als Orientierung genutzt werden können, vgl. Creative Interventions (2012): Creative Interventions Toolkit. A Practical Guide to Stop Interpersonal Violence. https://www.creative-interventions.org/wp-content/uploads/2020/10/CI-Toolkit-Final-ENTIRE-Aug-2020-new-cover.pdf, Stand: 08.06.2023.

Im Folgenden wende ich mich der Frage zu, inwiefern in alternativen Rechtspraktiken der *transformative justice/community accountability* eine Lösung für das bestehende „justice gap" der konventionellen Rechtspraktik liegen kann. Hierfür werde ich mich zuerst dem diesem Beitrag zugrundeliegenden Gerechtigkeitsbegriff anhand einer Vorstellung von multidimensionaler bzw. queerer Gerechtigkeit zuwenden. Daraufhin widme ich mich der Frage der Verantwortung und der sich aus dem veränderten Gerechtigkeitsverständnis ergebenden Forderung nach kollektiver Verantwortungsübernahme. Abschließend skizziere ich – unterschiedlichen Herausforderungen zum Trotz – das utopische Potenzial, welches in *transformative justice/community accountability* liegt.

2 Eine neue Perspektive auf Gerechtigkeit: queer statt linear

Gerechtigkeit zu erfahren, ist zentral für den Heilungsprozess vieler von Gewalt Betroffener. Keine Gerechtigkeit zu erfahren – wobei hierbei offen ist, wie Gerechtigkeit konkret verstanden wird – kann die Heilung langfristig verhindern.[14] Das Mittel, um nach Gewalterfahrungen Gerechtigkeit zu erhalten, wird gemeinhin im Rechtssystem und den dort festgelegten Strafen verortet.[15] Keine Strafe bedeutet demnach auch keine Gerechtigkeit, keine Anerkennung der erfahrenen Gewalt und letztendlich auch keine Heilung für die Betroffenen. Von diesem Gerechtigkeitsverständnis ausgehend und mit Blick auf die anfangs genannten Zahlen bezüglich der Anzeigestatistik und den gerichtlichen Erfolgsaussichten bei sexualisierter Gewalt, mag es wenig überraschen, dass eine Gruppe von Feminist*innen ihre Bestrebungen auf eine Ausweitung und Verschärfung des Sexualstrafrechts ausrichtet. Dieser, unter dem Begriff *carceral feminism* (dt. „Strafrechtsfeminismus")[16] zusammengefasste Strang des Feminismus, sieht dabei im Sexualstrafrecht eine Antwort auf und Lösung für sexualisierte Gewalt. Johanna Nickels und Christine Morgenstern erklären dies damit, „dass in der Kriminalisierung bzw. Vertiefung strafrechtlicher Sanktionen auch immer eine gesellschaft-

14 Vgl. Jülich, Shirley / Thorburn, Natalie (2017): „Sexual Violence and Substantive Equality. Can Restorative Justice Deliver?". In: J. Hum. Rights Soc. Work 2, 34–44. DOI: 10.1007/s41134-017-0029-0, 36.

15 Dabei werden im Kontext von Strafrechtstheorien die Ziele des Strafens jedoch nur selten mit Gerechtigkeit begründet, sondern vielmehr im Bereich der Prävention verordnet, sowohl mit Blick auf den*die Täter*in als auch mit Blick auf die Gesellschaft, vgl. Günther, Klaus (2022): „Kritik der Strafe". In: Loick, Daniel / Thompson, Vanessa E. (Hg.): Abolitionismus. Ein Reader. Berlin: Suhrkamp, 140–159, 143 f.

16 Der Begriff *carceral feminism* (dt. „Strafrechtsfeminismus") wurde ursprünglich von Elisabeth Bernstein im Rahmen ihrer Arbeiten zu US-amerikanischen Debatten zu Sexarbeit geprägt. *Carceral feminism* zeichnet sich dabei durch „the commitment of […] feminist activists to a law and order agenda and […] a drift from the welfare state to the carceral state as the enforcement apparatus for feminist goals" aus, Bernstein, Elisabeth (2007): „The Sexual Politics of the ‚New Abolitionism". In: differences. A Journal of Feminist Cultural Studies 18 (3), 128–151. DOI: 10.1215/10407391-2007-013, 143.

liche Anerkennung eines Übels [wie bspw. sexualisierter Gewalt; SK] liegt, die kaum durch andere Maßnahmen geleistet werden kann".[17]

Die Vorstellung des *carceral feminism* durch eine Ausweitung und Verschärfung des Sexualstrafrechts eine Antwort auf und Lösung für sexualisierte Gewalt finden zu können, wird durch den Strang des abolitionistischen Feminismus kritisiert.[18] Dabei begründet sich die Kritik in der Feststellung der Gruppen *Critical Resistance* und *INCITE! Women of Color Against Violence*, dass „staatsgewaltbasierte Ansätze gegen Gewalt gegen Frauen [...] geeignet sein [können], einige Gewalttaten kurzfristig aufzuhalten. Als eine allgemeine Strategie zur Überwindung von Gewalt hat Kriminalisierung jedoch nicht funktioniert".[19] Dies liege im Falle von sexualisierter Gewalt u. a. an dem eindimensionalen Verständnis von sexualisierter Gewalt. Dieses begrenzt sexualisierte Gewalt einerseits auf die geschlechtliche Dimension, wodurch vorrangig die bürgerliche, *weiße*, heterosexuelle cis-Frau als Betroffene erkannt werde, wohingegen Studien zeigen, dass insbesondere (mehrfach) marginalisierte Personen eine erhöhte Vulnerabilität aufweisen. Andererseits wird sexualisierte Gewalt allein auf der interpersonellen Ebene verortet, wodurch staatliche Gewalt ausgeblendet und an den „beschützenden" Staat appelliert wird, obwohl dieser nur für einen sehr kleinen Kreis an Betroffenen überhaupt und auch hier nur in begrenztem Umfang in dieser Rolle auftritt.[20] Im Folgenden werde ich jedoch weniger auf die Frage eingehen, ob in staatsgewaltbasierten Ansätzen eine Antwort auf sexualisierte Gewalt liegen kann, sondern einen Schritt zurückgehen und mich der Frage widmen, ob das Problem nicht bereits

---

17 Nickels, Johanna / Morgenstern, Christine (2022): „'Carceral Feminism'? Feministische Positionen in der deutschen Kriminalpolitik". In: Bartsch, Tillmann / Krieg, Yvonne / Schuchmann, Inga / Schüttler, Helena / Steinl, Leonie / Werner, Maja / Zietlow, Bettina (Hg.): Gender & Crime. Geschlechteraspekte in Kriminologie und Strafrechtswissenschaft. Baden-Baden: Nomos, 97–107, 100 f.

18 Vgl. Gruber, Aya (2020): The Feminist War on Crime. The Unexpected Role of Women's Liberation in Mass Incarceration. Oakland, CA: University of California Press; Kim (2019); Terwiel, Anna (2020): „What Is Carceral Feminism?". In: Political Theory 48 (4), 421–442. DOI: 10.1177/0090591719889946; Whalley, Elizabeth / Hackett, Colleen (2017): „Carceral Feminisms. The Abolitionist Project and Undoing Dominant Feminisms". In: Contemporary Justice Review 20 (4), 456–473. DOI: 10.1080/10282580.2017.1383762.

19 Critical Resistance / Incite! Women of Color Against Violence (2018): „Statement zu vergeschlechtlichter Gewalt und dem Prison-Industrial-Complex". In: Loick, Daniel (Hg.): Kritik der Polizei. Frankfurt/New York: Campus Verlag, 267–278, 270. Dabei stellt sich die Frage, inwiefern durch Kriminalisierung und Strafrecht überhaupt ein Ende der Gewalt erreicht werden soll. Christoph Willms schreibt diesbezüglich: „Der soziale Prozess von der Normsetzung und Kriminalisierung entsteht durch komplexe Interaktions- und Bewertungsprozesse, die untrennbar von der jeweiligen Politik und Struktur einer Gesellschaft sind. Das Strafrecht ist Ausdruck der politischen »Darstellung von Ordnung« und der »Demonstration von Herrschaft«", Willms, Christoph (2019): „«Kriminalität» und kriminologische Wissensproduktion im Wandel von Zeit und Moral". In: Malzahn, Rezi (Hg.): Strafe und Gefängnis. Theorie, Kritik, Alternativen. Eine Einführung. Stuttgart: Schmetterling Verlag, 43–64, 44.

20 Vgl. Armstrong, Elizabeth A. / Gleckman-Knut, Miriam / Johnson, Lanora (2018): „Silence, Power, and Inequality. An Intersectional Approach to Sexual Violence". In: Annu. Rev. Sociol. 44, 99–122. DOI: 10.1146/annurev-soc-073117-041410; Critical Resistance/INCITE! Women of Color Against Violence (2018), 270 f.; Phipps, Alison (2020): Me, Not You. The Trouble With Mainstream Feminism. Manchester: Manchester University Press, 45, 58.

in dem Gerechtigkeitsverständnis liegt, welches der konventionellen Rechtspraktik zugrunde liegt und welche Veränderungen diesbezüglich nötig wären. Die Beantwortung dieser Frage gibt dabei zwar auch Rückschlüsse hinsichtlich der Lösungsfunktion staatsgewaltbasierter Ansätze, geht aber darüber hinaus.

Clare McGlynn und Nicole Westmarland beschreiben das konventionelle Gerechtigkeitsverständnis als das Ergebnis eines linear ablaufenden und temporär begrenzten Dreischritts aus Tat, Verfahren und Urteil. Dieses fußt auf einem dichotomen Verständnis von Gerechtigkeit, getreu dem Motto: „You either get it or you don't; a conviction or not".[21] Der individuelle Gewaltakt wird dabei von seinen gesellschaftlichen Relationen abstrahiert und in Form von Geld- oder Haftstrafen generalisier- und messbar gemacht. Durch diese Generalisier- und Messbarmachung bleibt „die Verhältnismäßigkeit der Strafe zu den Straftaten […] letztendlich ungewiss, da sie weder die Opfer entschädigt noch die Übernahme von Verantwortung verlangt noch die Folgen des Verhaltens des Täters auf das von ihm verursachte Leid abstimmt".[22]

Der Kern der Kritik von McGlynn und Westmarland liegt dabei in der Perspektive begründet, von welcher aus Gerechtigkeit definiert wird. Dem linearen und dichotomen Verständnis von Gerechtigkeit, welches durch das Strafrecht bzw. durch vermeintlich neutrale Instanzen in Form von Gerichten bestimmt wird, stellen sie eine Betroffenenperspektive auf Gerechtigkeit entgegen, welche sie als *kaleidoscopic justice* bezeichnen:

> Often produced as a children's toy, a kaleidoscope is an optical instrument with two or more reflecting surfaces (usually mirrors) inclined to each other in an angle. Rotation of the kaleidoscope produces an ever-changing viewed pattern; each viewing being unpredictable in outcome.[23]

Gerechtigkeit ist dabei kein lineares, klar definiertes Ergebnis mehr, sondern wird zu einem vielschichtigen, sich kontinuierlich wandelnden Prozess. Gerechtigkeit löst sich in diesem Verständnis von einer abstrakten, klar definierten Wesensform und tritt in einen Zustand der Kontingenz und Vielschichtigkeit ein. Diese Vielschichtigkeit setzt sich dabei aus verschiedenen Elementen zusammen, wobei (strafrechtliche) Konsequenzen nur ein Element neben vielen – wie „recognition, voice, dignity, prevention and connectedness"[24] – darstellen (können).[25] Ähnlich wie die unterschiedlichen

---

21 McGlynn/Westmarland (2019), 181.

22 McLeod, Allegra M. (2022): „Abolitionistische Demokratien entwerfen". In: Loick, Daniel / Thompson, Vanessa E. (Hg.): Abolitionismus. Ein Reader. Berlin: Suhrkamp, 556–608, 596.

23 McGlynn/Westmarland (2019), 185.

24 Ebd., 186.

25 Forschung zur Perspektive von Betroffenen von sexualisierter Gewalt ist bisher nur in limitiertem Umfang vorhanden und basiert primär auf Arbeiten aus Australien, Neuseeland und Großbritannien. Für weitere empirische Arbeiten zu Betroffenengerechtigkeit, vgl. u. a. Clark, Haley (2015): „A Fair Way to Go. Justice for Victim-Survivors of Sexual Violence". In: Powell, Anastasia / Henry, Nicole / Flynn, Asher (Hg.):

Farbpartikel eines Kaleidoskops verändern auch die verschiedenen Gerechtigkeitselemente stetig ihr Verhältnis zueinander, mag das Bild im einen Moment noch von dem Wunsch nach Anerkennung dominiert sein, kann mit der nächsten Umdrehung schon der Wunsch nach Prävention im Mittelpunkt stehen, wobei weder die zeitliche Dimension des Wandels noch die konkrete Ausgestaltung kommender Gerechtigkeitsvorstellungen vorher absehbar ist. Die Vorstellung von einer linearen und eindimensionalen Gerechtigkeit wird durch ein multidimensionales Gerechtigkeitsverständnis ersetzt.[26] Diese Multidimensionalität führt dazu, dass Gerechtigkeit nicht allein aus juristischer Perspektive, nicht allein in Form juristischer Konsequenzen, bestimmt werden kann, sondern insbesondere in ihren affektiven und relationalen Dimensionen greifbar werden muss. Denn:

> Gerechtigkeit, die in einer Sorge darum verankert ist, wie Wiedergutmachung erlebt wird, zielt auch darauf ab, die bestehende Welt zu verändern, um Betroffenen mehr Möglichkeiten zur Heilung einzuräumen und um die Wahrscheinlichkeit zu reduzieren, dass anderen in Zukunft Schaden zugefügt wird.[27]

Das Konzept der *kaleidoscopic justice* beruht dabei auf einem Verständnis menschlichen Lebens, welches sich durch Nicht-Linearität und Unbestimmtheit auszeichnet und somit in seinen Folgen nicht bzw. nur begrenzt abschätzbar ist. Avery F. Gordon schreibt diesbezüglich: „That life is complicated may seem a banal formulation of the obvious, but I think it's actually a significant theory".[28] Auf dieser banal erscheinenden Tatsache basiert ihre Annahme, dass Gerechtigkeit kein *a priori* feststehender Begriff ist, nicht objektiv ist, sondern zu einem gewissen Grad immer eine subjektiv gebundene Beurteilung bleibt.[29] Aus ähnlichen Motiven heraus argumentiert auch Allegra M. McLeod für ein Konzept einer „grounded justice"[30], im Sinne eines stets unvollendeten und erfahrungsbasierten Gerechtigkeitsverständnisses. Hierdurch soll es ermöglicht werden, nicht nur den konkreten Erfahrungen gerecht zu werden, sondern auch offen für die sich wandelnden Bedürfnisse zu bleiben.[31]

Rape Justice. Beyond the Criminal Law. Basingstoke: Palgrave Macmillan, 18–35; Daly, Kathleen (2017): „Sexual Violence and Victims' Justice Interests". In: Zinsstag, Estelle / Keenen, Marie (Hg.): Restorative Responses to Sexual Violence. Legal, Social and Therapeutic Dimensions. Oxford: Routledge, 108–139; Holder, Robyn (2015): „Satisfied? Exploring Victims' Justice Judgements". In: Wilson, Dean / Ross, Stuart (Hg.): Crime, Victims and Police. International Contexts, Local Experiences. Basingstoke: Palgrave Macmillan, 184–213.

26 Vgl. McGlynn/Westmarland (2019), 180 ff.

27 McLeod (2022), 604.

28 Gordon, Avery F. (2004): Keeping Good Time. Reflections on Knowledge, Power and People. London: Routledge, 99 f.

29 Vgl. ebd., 99.

30 McLeod (2022), 604.

31 Vgl. ebd., 561, 606.

Durch den Perspektivwechsel hin zu einer multidimensionalen Gerechtigkeit, wird Gerechtigkeit nicht mehr als individuelles Verhältnis gefasst, welches allein zwischen Bürger*in und Staat oder zwischen Täter*in und Betroffene*r existiert, sondern wird kollektiviert.[32] Während Gerechtigkeit in Form von strafrechtlichen Konsequenzen lediglich eine*n Täter*in als Bezugspunkt braucht, benötigen andere Gerechtigkeitsdimensionen – wie „recognition, voice, dignity, prevention and connectedness"[33] – explizit das Kollektiv als Bezugsrahmen. Gerechtigkeit wird somit Teil einer kollektiven Beziehungsweise[34], wird in die sozialen Strukturen eingebettet, wodurch Gerechtigkeit letztendlich auch nur in dieser Kollektivität in ihrer ganzen Multidimensionalität gefunden werden kann und somit auch das Kollektiv als Ganzes miteinbeziehen muss.

Um die bisherigen Überlegungen zum Gerechtigkeitsverständnis zusammenzufassen und um herauszustellen was dies konkret für das Gerechtigkeitsverständnis der drei Rechtspraktiken – in Form von konventioneller Rechtspraktik, *restorative justice* und *transformative justice/community accountability* – bedeutet, nehme ich Bezug auf die Ausführungen von Melanie Brazzell und Daniel Loick bezüglich eines negativen, positiven und queeren Sicherheitsbegriffs.[35] Dabei geht es mir nicht darum eine Sicherheitsdimension in die bisherigen Überlegungen einzuziehen, sondern darum eine ähnlich gelagerte Konzeptionierung von Gerechtigkeit im Sinne von negativer, positiver und queerer Gerechtigkeit vorzuschlagen. Eine Adaption der von Brazzell und Loick vorgenommenen Dreiteilung erscheint dabei nicht nur aufgrund der Nähe von Un/Sicherheit und Un/Gerechtigkeit produktiv, stellt die Suche nach Gerechtigkeit doch oftmals eine Reaktion auf erfahrene Unsicherheit dar, sondern weisen beide Konzepte auch starke Überschneidung hinsichtlich ihres Verhältnisses zum Staat und zum Status quo, zum Individuum-Kollektiv-Komplex und zur Frage von Zeitlichkeit

---

32 Vgl. McGlynn/Westmarland (2019), 182, 189.

33 Ebd., 186.

34 Adamczak, Bini (2017): Beziehungsweise Revolution. 1917, 1968 und kommende. Berlin: Suhrkamp Verlag.

35 Vgl. Brazzell, Melanie (2021b): „Von negativer/strafrechtsfeministischer zu positiver/abolitionistischer Sicherheit. Transformative Gerechtigkeit für Betroffene von geschlechtsbasierter Gewalt". In: Laufenberg, Mike / Thompson, Vanessa E. (Hg.): Sicherheit. Rassismuskritische und feministische Debatten. Forum Frauen- und Geschlechterforschung Band 49. Münster: Verlag Westfälisches Dampfboot, 328–363; Loick, Daniel (2021): „Das Grundgefühl der Ordnung, das alle haben. Für einen queeren Begriff von Sicherheit". In: Laufenberg, Mike / Thompson, Vanessa E. (Hg.): Sicherheit. Rassismuskritische und feministische Debatten. Forum Frauen- und Geschlechterforschung Bd. 49. Münster: Verlag Westfälisches Dampfboot, 266–286. Brazzell entwickelt das Konzept von einem positiven und negativen Sicherheitsbegriff in Anlehnung an Isaiah Berlin, der zwischen einem positiven und negativen Freiheitsbegriff unterschieden hat, vgl. Berlin, Isaiah (1969): „Two Concepts of Liberty". In: Ders.: Four Essays on Liberty. Oxford, UK: Oxford Paperbacks, 118–172. Loick erweitert diese Einteilung um das Konzept der queeren Sicherheit anschließend an die Überlegungen von Christoph Menke und Juliane Rebentisch, die den ästhetischen Freiheitsbegriff begründet haben, vgl. Menke, Christoph (2013): Die Kraft der Kunst. Berlin: Suhrkamp; Rebentisch, Juliane (2013): Die Kunst der Freiheit. Zur Dialektik demokratischer Existenz. Berlin: Suhrkamp. Brazzell betrachtet die Erweiterung des Sicherheitsbegriffs um eine queere Dimension als nicht notwendig, sondern sieht die Elemente dessen bereits im positiven Sicherheitsbegriff enthalten, vgl. Brazzell (2021b), 354 f.

auf. Um auf Basis der vorangegangenen Überlegungen zur Gerechtigkeit eine Konzeption von negativer, positiver und queerer Gerechtigkeit vornehmen zu können, werde ich in einem kurzen Exkurs die drei Sicherheitsbegriffe skizzieren.

Loick schreibt bezüglich negativer und positiver Sicherheit:

> Während negative Sicherheitsbegriffe auf die Abwehr externer Bedrohungen zielen (Sicherheit *vor*, im Englischen *security*) und ein asymmetrisches Verständnis von Beschützenden und Zu-Schützenden zugrunde legen, zielen positive Sicherheitsbegriffe auf die Entfaltung kollektiver Handlungsfähigkeit (Sicherheit *zu*, im Englischen *safety*) und sind in Interdependenz und Gemeinschaftlichkeit verankert.[36]

Der negative Sicherheitsbegriff zielt dabei auf das Individuum ab, für das Sicherheit den Status quo, den Normalzustand, darstellt, welcher lediglich durch singuläre Gewaltereignisse gestört wird.[37] Durch den Zustand der Vereinzelung ist das Individuum auf den Staat als Sicherheitsgaranten angewiesen, wobei die Fokussierung auf die Sicherheit des Individuums zur Folge hat, dass die Sicherheit der einen zumeist nur auf Kosten von anderen erreicht werden kann, ihr also ein exkludierendes Element innewohnt.[38] Der positive Sicherheitsbegriff richtet sich hingegen an das Kollektiv, doch auch hier wird Unsicherheit primär als Störung eines sicheren Normalzustands verstanden. Im Gegensatz zum negativen Sicherheitsbegriff wird die Aufgabe der Aufrechterhaltung und Wiederherstellung von Sicherheit jedoch nicht an Dritte bzw. den Staat delegiert, sondern erfolgt aus dem Kollektiv heraus auf Basis von kollektiver Widerstandsfähigkeit, Solidarität und Interdependenz.[39] Doch auch der positive Sicherheitsbegriff birgt Loick zu Folge das Risiko der Externalisierung in sich, indem die Interdependenz und Gemeinschaftlichkeit zu einer Negation und eines Ausschlusses von allem Dekonstruktiven und Unproduktiven führen kann.[40] Das Problem beider Sicherheitsbegriffe liegt dabei in der Vorstellung verhaftet, dass ein Zustand umfassender Sicherheit möglich sei. Loick stellt sich gegen diese Vorstellung, indem er für die Akzeptanz der Permanenz von Unsicherheit wirbt, indem er fordert, *„dass man sich der Unsicherheit aussetzt.* Damit wir die Dichotomie von Sicherheit und Risiko dekonstruieren: Die Unmöglichkeit von Sicherheit ist zugleich die Bedingung ihrer Möglichkeit".[41] Diese Vorstellung von Sicherheit, welche immer auch die Unsicherheit in sich trägt, bezeichnet er als queere Sicherheit. Queer im Sinne queerer Sicherheit bzw. der nachfolgenden queeren Gerechtigkeit fungiert dabei nicht als Synonym für LGBTQIA*, sondern wird angelehnt an die Tradition der *Queer Theory* verwendet,

36 Loick (2021), 267, Herv. i. O.
37 Vgl. Brazzell (2021b), 336.
38 Vgl. Loick (2021), 271.
39 Vgl. Brazzell (2021b), 336.
40 Vgl. Loick (2021), 276.
41 Ebd., 280, Herv. i. O.

wobei queer als dekonstruktives Element verstanden wird, welches gesellschaftliche Gegebenheiten als diskursive Produkte versteht und denaturalisiert. Zentral ist dabei die kritische Infragestellung und Loslösung von Dichotomien, Normierungen und dem Status quo.[42]

Übertragen auf das Verständnis von Gerechtigkeit bzw. das Gerechtigkeitsverständnis der drei Rechtspraktiken – in Form von konventioneller Rechtspraktik, *restorative justice* und *transformative justice/community accountability* – erscheint die Dreiteilung in negative, positive und queere Gerechtigkeit nun folgendermaßen:

Negative Gerechtigkeit stellt das Gerechtigkeitsverständnis der konventionellen Rechtspraktik dar, sie ist ein durch staatliche Instanzen definierter, objektiver Begriff, dem eine Dichotomie von Gerechtigkeit und Ungerechtigkeit gemessen an Verurteilung und Strafe zugrunde liegt. Negative Gerechtigkeit erscheint als linear, ist allein auf Individuen (insbesondere den*die Täter*in) ausgerichtet und am Status quo orientiert.

Als positive Gerechtigkeit ist das Gerechtigkeitsverständnis von *restorative justice* zu verstehen. Positive Gerechtigkeit ist dabei teilweise staatlich definiert, wird jedoch ergänzt um einen kollektiven Prozess, der an den spezifischen Umständen orientiert ist, wodurch Gerechtigkeit zweidimensional wird und eine Kollektivierung für den Zeitabschnitt nach der Gewalterfahrung stattfindet. Allerdings findet nur eine Teil-Kollektivierung statt, da Gewalt nur als interpersonell verstanden und das Kollektiv nur in den Heilungs-, jedoch nicht in den Tatprozess einbezogen wird. Es bleibt eine lineare Ausrichtung erhalten, da *restorative justice* am Status quo ausgerichtet bzw. um die Wiederherstellung von diesem bemüht ist.

Eine queere Gerechtigkeit stellt letztendlich das Gerechtigkeitsverständnis von *transformative justice/community accountability* dar. Es löst sich von den staatlichen Strukturen und wird in einen kollektiven Prozess überführt, wodurch Gerechtigkeit multidimensional greifbar wird. Durch die Loslösung von der Vorstellung eines idealen Status quo und der Orientierung an Bedürfnissen und Erfahrungen wird queere Gerechtigkeit auch in einen Zustand der Offenheit überführt. Mit der Akzeptanz, dass sich Bedürfnisse konstant ändern, geht einher, dass Gerechtigkeit auch ein stetig offener Prozess ohne vorab bestimmbares Ergebnis ist. Doch gerade in der Anerkennung, dass Gerechtigkeit keinem linearen und dichotomen Verständnis folgt, liegt die Möglichkeit einer multidimensionalen Gerechtigkeit in der Form einer permanenten Suchbewegung. Wie bei queerer Sicherheit, gilt auch für queere Gerechtigkeit: Erst durch die Anerkennung der Unmöglichkeit von Gerechtigkeit, kann Gerechtigkeit gefunden werden. Zwar nie absolut und endgültig, aber situativ und im Moment befindlich.

---

42 Vgl. Cossman, Brenda (2019): „Queering Queer Legal Studies: An Unreconstructed Ode to Eve Sedgwick (and Others)". In: Critical Analysis of Law 6 (1), 23–38. https://papers.ssrn.com/sol3/papers.cfm?abstract_id=3437290; Stand: 08.06.2023, 25 f., 30.

3 Verantwortung anders denken: von der individuellen Zuschreibung zur kollektiven Übernahme

Anschließend an die vorangegangenen Überlegungen wende ich mich nun der Frage der Verantwortung im Zuge von Gerechtigkeitsprozessen zu, um mich hierdurch insbesondere der notwendigen Adressierung und Einbindung des Kollektivs im Rahmen einer queeren Form von Gerechtigkeit weiter anzunähern.

Im Rahmen konventioneller Rechtspraktik wird Verantwortung für gewöhnlich im Individuum verortet und allein auf die Vergangenheit bzw. vergangenes Handeln ausgerichtet (*backward looking responsibility*). Iris Marion Young bezeichnet diese Form von Verantwortung als *liability model*. Verantwortung beruht dabei auf drei Konditionen: der Kondition der Kausalität, der Freiwilligkeit und der Informiertheit. Das Erfüllen dieser Konditionen ist Voraussetzung für Verantwortung.[43] Die konventionelle Rechtspraktik stellt somit einen Akt der *Verantwortungszuschreibung* dar. Durch den Aspekt der Zuschreibung wird Verantwortung einerseits zu einem temporär eingegrenzten Ereignis dichotomer Ausprägung. Genau wie Gerechtigkeit wird sie zu einem Entweder/Oder – entweder liegt Verantwortung für eine spezifische Handlung vor oder nicht. Andererseits wird Verantwortung durch diese Zuschreibung zu einem Akt der Passivität, der das Individuum nur als Objekt der Zuschreibung betrachtet, statt dieses aktiv in die Verantwortung zu nehmen. Im passiven Akt der Verantwortungszuschreibung wird Verantwortung zugleich auf diese Zuschreibung begrenzt.

Das fiktive Subjekt einer solchen Verantwortung ist das kantische Ideal eines autonomen und selbstbestimmten Individuums, welches allein aus sich heraus und losgelöst von sozialen Strukturen agiert.[44] Die Rückbindung an die Gesellschaft erfolgt dabei allein über die Moral, indem die Gesellschaft zur moralischen Folie für das individuelle Handeln wird, an welcher dieses gemessen wird. Das in diesem Sinne verantwortliche Individuum wird somit zum moralischen Individuum, Verantwortung zu einer Frage der Moral. Die Moral wird dabei in der Gesellschaft naturalisiert. Das für den Schaden verantwortliche Subjekt wird somit externalisiert, steht im Kontrast zur Moral einer idealisierten Gesellschaft. Brazzell argumentiert, dass Verantwortung über die Moralisierung affektiv aufgeladen wird, wodurch Verantwortung ausschließlich negativ assoziiert wird und in einen Zustand der Handlungsunfähigkeit führen kann.[45] Es mag mit Blick auf die Moral deshalb auch angemessener erscheinen beim *liability model* eher den Begriff der Schuld, statt den der Verantwortung zu verwenden.

---

43 Vgl. Young, Iris Marion (2011): Responsibility for Justice. New York, NY: Oxford University Press, 97.
44 Vgl. Lotter, Maria-Sibylla (2017): „Verantwortung und Schuld". In: Heidbrink, Ludger / Langbehn, Claus / Loh, Janina (Hg.): Handbuch Verantwortung. Wiesbaden: Springer VS, 1–14, 8 f.
45 Vgl. Brazzell, Melanie (2021a): „Theorizing Transformative Justice. Comparing Carceral and Abolitionist Selves, Agencies, and Responsibilities". In: Duff, Koshka (Hg.): Abolishing the Police. London: Dog Section Press, 161–177, 173.

Eine Aufrechterhaltung dieser individualisierten Vorstellung von Verantwortung ist jedoch nur möglich, wenn auch alles Handeln und somit auch alles gewalttätige Handeln, als grundsätzlich autonom und selbstbestimmt verstanden wird. (Gewalttätiges) Handeln wäre demnach ein rein singuläres Ereignis. Doch die Vorstellung des kantischen Ideals existiert lediglich in der Theorie. Denn das Individuum existiert nicht außerhalb von sozialen Strukturen, sondern steht stets in einem reziproken Verhältnis zu seiner Umwelt durch welche es stetig geformt wird. Dies passiert dabei in durch Intimität, Anerkennung und Sorge geprägten Beziehungen, ebenso wie durch Macht-, Gewalt- und Unterdrückungsverhältnisse.[46] Sexualisierte Gewalt sowie andere Formen der Gewalt lassen sich deshalb auch nicht allein als individueller Gewaltakt verstehen, sondern müssen als Teil von bzw. in einem reziproken Verhältnis zu gesellschaftlichen Macht- und Herrschaftsverhältnissen verstanden werden. Sexualisierte Gewalt wird einerseits durch diese (re-)produziert und trägt andererseits zur (Re-)Produktion dieser bei.[47] Während diese Annahme einem Großteil feministischer Analysen von sexualisierter Gewalt zugrunde liegt und sich im Begriff der *rape culture* (dt. „Vergewaltigungskultur") widerspiegelt, wird sexualisierte Gewalt im breiten gesellschaftlichen Diskurs sowie in der konventionellen Rechtspraktik nach wie vor oft als individuelle Handlung und folglich als individuelle Verantwortung für einen singulären Akt aufgefasst.[48] Liz Kelly beschreibt sexualisierter Gewalt hingegen als auf einem Kontinuum liegend. Unter Kontinuum versteht sie einerseits einen gemeinsam geteilten Charakter, der unterschiedlichen Ereignissen zugrunde liegt, sowie andererseits eine Abfolge von Ereignissen, welche kontinuierliche ineinander übergehen und nicht klar voneinander abgrenzbar sind.[49] Dadurch, dass sexualisierte Gewalt nicht

---

46 Vgl. ebd., 169.

47 Vgl. Butler, Judith (2021): „Bodies That Still Matter". In: Halsema, Annemie / Kwastek, Katja / van den Oever, Roel (Hg.): Bodies That Still Matter. Resonances of the Work of Judith Butler. Amsterdam: Amsterdam University Press, 177–193; Holzleithner, Elisabeth (2017): „Sexuelle Selbstbestimmung als Individualrecht und als Rechtsgut". In: Lembke, Ulrike (Hg.): Regulierungen des Intimen. Sexualität und Recht im modernen Staat. Wiesbaden: Springer, 31–50; Rojas, Clarissa / Kim, Mimi E. / Bierria, Alisa (2011): „Community Accountability. Emerging Movements to Transform Violence". In: Social Justice 37 (4), 1–12. ; Stand 29.04.2023.

48 Auch wenn innerhalb feministischer Analysen weitestgehend Einigkeit über die Relevanz gesellschaftlicher Machtverhältnisse besteht, gibt es dennoch Unterschiede bezüglich der Frage wie sich diese konkret ausgestalten, vgl. Whisnant, Rebecca (2021): „Feminist Perspectives on Rape". In: Stanford Encyclopedia of Philosophy. https://plato.stanford.edu/entries/feminism-rape/; Stand: 08.06.2023. Dies spiegelt sich auch in den Begrifflichkeiten „sexualisierte Gewalt" und „sexuelle Gewalt" wider, wobei der erste Begriff den Fokus auf (vergeschlechtlichte) Machtverhältnisse legt und somit die Gewalt nicht als sexuellen Akt, sondern als Machtakt versteht, während der zweite Begriff nicht (komplett) die Bedeutung von sexuellem Verlangen/Trieben ablehnt. Insofern in Rahmen konventioneller Rechtspraktik und im gesellschaftlichen Diskurs über Verantwortung abseits von der gewalttätigen Person diskutiert wird, geht es unter Bezugnahme auf Vergewaltigungsmythen, zumeist nur um die Betroffenen selbst, vgl. Bohner, Gerd (1998): Vergewaltigungsmythen. Sozialpsychologische Untersuchungen über täterentlastende und opferfeindliche Überzeugungen im Bereich sexueller Gewalt. Landau in der Pfalz: Verl. Empirische Pädagogik.

49 Vgl. Kelly, Liz (1988): Surviving Sexual Violence. Cambridge: Polity, 76.

mehr als isolierter Akt, sondern als Teil eines sozialen Gefüges betrachtet wird, treten auch die Macht- und Herrschaftsverhältnisse hervor, die ansonsten oftmals normalisiert und ignoriert werden.[50]

Wenn sexualisierte Gewalt jedoch nicht mehr als individueller Akt, nicht mehr eindimensional auf Ebene des Individuums gedacht wird, kann auch nicht mehr allein von einer individuellen oder auch eindimensionalen Verantwortung im Sinne von Youngs *liability model* ausgegangen werden.[51] Young versucht diese Leerstelle des *liability models* auszugleichen, indem sie es um die Dimension des *social connection model* ergänzt:

> All those who contribute by their actions to structural processes with some unjust outcomes share responsibility for the injustice. [...] Being responsible in relation to structural injustice means that one has an obligation to join with others who share that responsibility in order to transform the structural processes to make their outcomes less unjust.[52]

Young entlässt hierdurch nicht das Individuum aus der Verantwortung, sondern ergänzt die Mikroebene des Individuums um die Makroebene der Struktur. Obwohl Young dieses Model, wie der Name sagt, in den sozialen Verbindungen begründet, wendet sie sich diesen nur abstrakt in einem strukturellen Sinne zu. Eine detaillierte Betrachtung der sozialen Verbindungen erfolgt nicht; die Mesoebene – im Sinne von Beziehungsweisen – bleibt unberücksichtigt.[53] Im Gegensatz zum Konzept der individuellen Verantwortung, welche auf die Vergangenheit ausgerichtet ist, orientiert sich das *social connection model* an der Zukunft (*forward looking responsibility*) und zielt auf eine *indirekte* Verantwortungsübernahme statt auf eine Verantwortungszuschreibung wie im *liability model* ab. *Indirekt* dadurch, dass Young in ihrem Model die Makroebene adressiert, welche durch den Grad ihrer Abstraktheit jedoch keine *direkte* Verantwortungsübernahme in spezifischen Fällen zulässt. Durch ihr rein zweidimensionales Verständnis von Verantwortung hält Young eine Trennung zwischen individueller und struktureller Ebene aufrecht, die auf theoretischer Ebene Sinn ergibt, aber gerade mit Blick auf eine direkte Verantwortungsübernahme nicht sinnvoll erscheint. Um von einer *direkten* Verantwortungsübernahme sprechen zu können, bedarf es deshalb einer Berücksichtigung der Mesoebene, die ich als Ebene der kollektiven Verantwortung

---

50 Vgl. Brazzell, Melanie (2015): „Responsibility for Sexual Violence. Dialogues with I. M. Young & the Community Accountability Movement". In: Feminism and (Political) Progress. Fifth Oxford Graduate Political Theory Conference (May 13–14, 2015, University of Oxford), 12.

51 Youngs Vorstellung vom *social connection model* können dabei auch in ein Verhältnis zu Karl Jaspers Konzept einer metaphysischen Schuld gesetzt werden, die sich nicht aus einer Handlung, sondern aus der Verpflichtung zur Solidarität zwischen den Menschen ableitet: „Metaphysical guilt is based not on a narrow construal of what one does, but rather on the wider concept of who one chooses to be", May (1991), 241, zit. nach Lotter (2017), 13.

52 Young (2011), 97.

53 Vgl. Brazzell (2015), 7.

bezeichne. Als Akteur*innen der Mesoebene, der Beziehungsweisen, verstehe ich dabei Gruppen, Kollektive und dergleichen im Rahmen derer Individuen handeln und in Beziehung zueinanderstehen. Auch Maura Bairley argumentiert für eine Berücksichtigung der Mesoebene bei Fragen der Verantwortung:

> A group behaves as a whole, and within a group individuals will enact things on behalf of the whole. […] So, that's the lens that I'm thinking about that enables us to hold both an individual and a group level perspective. Yes, there are individuals who are making choices about violence […]. And, at the same time, I think that we can hold the idea that socially, that on a community level, we use violence instrumentally, and we draft and invite and seduce people into committing violence on all of our behalves.[54]

Bairley sieht eine geteilte Verantwortung für Gewalt und gewalttätiges Handeln auf der Mesoebene. Auch wenn die situative Entscheidung für gewalttätiges Handeln beim Individuum liegt, bildet das Umfeld den Rahmen für dieses Handeln, macht es erst möglich und trägt somit ebenfalls Verantwortung. Kollektive Verantwortung verstehe ich dabei nicht kausal, im Sinne einer linearen Handlungskette singulärer Ereignisse, sondern vielmehr in der Permanenz sozialer Verhältnisse verortet. Im Gegensatz zu Bairley spreche ich jedoch nicht von einem rein instrumentellen Verhältnis von Gruppen zu Gewalthandlungen ihrer individuellen Mitglieder. Dies könnte zu der Annahme verleiten, dass das Handeln von Gruppen stets bewusst und vorsätzlich stattfindet. Wenn jedoch ein kantisches Ideal des autonomen und selbstbestimmten Individuums abgelehnt wird, so muss dies auch für Gruppen gelten. Ein rein instrumentelles Verständnis von Gewalt würde vielmehr subtilere Formen und Prozesse der Verantwortung sowie die strukturelle Bedingtheit von individuellem sowie kollektivem Handeln verschleiern. Die kollektive Verantwortung ist dabei sowohl rückwärtsgewandt als auch zukunftsorientiert, was bedeutet, dass sie einerseits die kollektive Rolle im spezifischen Gewaltprozess reflektiert (*backward looking*) und andererseits die kollektiven Begebenheiten insofern verändert, dass sich die Gewalt nicht wiederholen kann (*forward looking*). Wobei sich hierin zeigt, dass die Trennung beider Perspektiven auf Verantwortung grundsätzlich nur begrenzt möglich ist, da die Auseinandersetzung mit bzw. Aufarbeitung von sexualisierter Gewalt selbst Auswirkungen auf Ursprünge und Bedingungen zukünftiger Gewalt hat und vice versa.

Nickels und Morgenstern erklären die fortbestehende Fokussierung der konventionellen Rechtspraktik auf die individuelle Verantwortung damit, dass dies „die vielschichtige[n] und komplexe[n] Probleme individuell und damit im öffentlichen Diskurs leichter adressier- und handhabbar erscheinen lässt".[55] Ein Verständnis von queerer Gerechtigkeit und kollektiver Verantwortungsübernahme vereinfacht die Pro-

---

54 Brazzell (2015), 1.
55 Nickels/Morgenstern (2022), 101.

zesse sicherlich nicht, doch liegt hierin neben bestehenden Herausforderungen auch ein utopisches Potenzial, da sie ein Möglichkeitsfenster öffnen für ein anderes Denken über Gerechtigkeit und Verantwortung und somit letztendlich auch für (andere) Handlungsmöglichkeiten. Dies gilt ganz konkret mit Blick auf das „justice gap" bei sexualisierter Gewalt, aber auch hierüber hinaus.

4 Alternative Rechtspraktiken: von der Herausforderung zum utopischen Potenzial

Das grundlegende Problem von *transformative justice/community accountability* liegt in der Frage, wer überhaupt die Mesoebene darstellt, wer also zueinander in Beziehung steht, wer die Beziehungsweisen ausbildet und somit letztendlich Akteur*in kollektiver Verantwortungsübernahme ist. Die Individualisierung, die sich im Rahmen konventioneller Rechtspraktik zeigt, spiegelt sich auch in der Wahrnehmung der neoliberalen Gesellschaft als Ganzes wieder. Die Vorstellung einer *community*, wie sie dem Konzept der *community accountability* zugrunde liegt, erscheint im Globalen Norden, wenn überhaupt, nur für wenige Teile der Gesellschaft zu gelten. Bisher finden *transformative justice/community accountability* deshalb auch primär innerhalb relativ klar definierter Gruppen statt, welche bereits über eine Art Kollektivbewusstsein verfügen.[56] Eine Möglichkeit für die Definition des Kollektivs abseits relativ klar definierter Gruppen bietet Mia Mingus, welche den Begriff *pod* im Gegensatz zu *community* verwendet. Dabei löst Mingus sich von der Vorstellung klar abgrenzbarer Entitäten, wie politischen Gruppen, kulturellen Vereine, etc., als (einzige) Akteur*innen der Mesoebene, sondern denkt diese von den Beziehungsweisen her. Dabei ergibt sich für jede Person ein ganz individueller *pod* basierend auf den je individuellen Beziehungen.[57]

Doch selbst wenn relativ klar definierte Gruppen vorliegen, sind diese nicht automatisch als Akteur*innen der kollektiven Verantwortungsübernahme geeignet. Die abolitionistische Kritik am Staat, welche diesen als unfähig beschreibt gleichen Schutz für alle zu garantieren, da dieser alle Arten von Diskriminierung in sich selbst eingeschrieben hat und nie frei von diesen handelt, kann ebenfalls gegenüber anderen so-

---

56 Vgl. Communities Against Rape and Abuse (2008): „Taking Risks. Implementing Grassroots Community Accountability Strategies". In: Chen, Ching-In / Dulani, Jai / Piepzna-Samarasinha, Leah Lakshmi (Hg.): The Revolution Starts at Home. Confronting Partner Abuse in Activist Communities, 64–79. http://criticalresistance.org/wp-content/uploads/2014/05/Revolution-starts-at-home-zine.pdf; Stand: 08.06.2023. Besonders deutlich wird dies auch im Zuge sexualisierter Gewalt innerhalb linker Bewegungen, ein Beispiel hierfür stellt die sexualisierte Gewalt auf dem linken Festival Monis Rache dar, vgl. gruppe mora (Hg.): Piss on Patriarchy. Eine Auseinandersetzung mit der sexualisierten Gewalt auf dem Festival Monis Rache. Münster: edition assemblage.

57 Vgl. Mingus, Mia (2016): „Pods and Pod Mapping Worksheet". In: Bay Area Transformative Justice Collective. https://batjc.wordpress.com/resources/pods-and-pod-mapping-worksheet/; Stand: 08.06.2023.

zialen Entitäten angebracht werden.[58] Diese sind ebenso das Produkt gesellschaftlicher Prozesse und (re-)produzieren somit auch immer gesellschaftliche Macht- und Herrschaftsverhältnisse. Akteur*innen der Mesoebene sind keine neutralen Instanzen; eine Annahme dessen käme einer Romantisierung gleich. Die Gefahr einer solchen zeigt sich gerade auch im Moment der Gewaltkonfrontation, der nicht gerade wenige Gruppen vor tiefgreifende Probleme stellt und zum Moment der Enttäuschung über die eigene Verfasstheit wird.[59] Anstelle einer kollektiven Verantwortungsübernahme zeigen sich oftmals gegenläufige Verhaltensweisen – von der Normalisierung des gewalttätigen Verhaltens bis hin zum aktiven Nicht-Handeln bei der Wahrnehmung sexualisierter Gewalt, welches sich insbesondere im Moment des Schweigens ausdrückt.[60] Eine Hinwendung zum Kollektiv im Moment der Verletzung und Enttäuschung erscheint dabei geradezu kontraintuitiv, doch kann gerade hierin eine Chance der gemeinsamen Entwicklung und Veränderung liegen.[61] Denn die Fähigkeit der kollektiven, ebenso wie der individuellen Verantwortungsübernahme ist keine natürlich gegebene Fähigkeit, sondern das Ergebnis eines bewussten und aktiven Lernprozesses.[62] Dabei kann die Vorstellung des Lernprozesses durchaus kritisch betrachtet werden, setzt diese doch eine notwendig positiv verlaufende Entwicklung von diesem und somit auch ein positives Menschenbild voraus. Dies wirft die Frage nach normativen Leitlinien oder anderweitig ausgestalteten Prozessen auf, die eine emanzipatorische Entwicklung des Lernprozesses sicherstellen.

Zentral für diesen Lernprozess ist das Verständnis von Gewalt bzw. die Art sich zu dieser in ein Verhältnis zu setzen. Während der direkte Akt der sexualisierten Gewalt in gewisser Weise greifbar ist, ist dies für die kollektive Teilhabe an der Gewalt zumeist nicht (direkt) der Fall. Der Großteil dieser Handlungen wird vielmehr gar nicht als potenziell gewaltvoll wahrgenommen, da diese durch den Prozess der Normalisierung als alltäglich erscheinen.[63] Doch es geht nicht nur darum, dass die Gruppe die eigenen Handlungen in ein Verhältnis zum Akt der Gewalt setzt und als Teil dessen anerkennt,

---

58 Vgl. Whalley/Hackett (2017), 459.
59 Vgl. Brazzell (2021a), 176.
60 Vgl. Fanghanel, Alexandra (2020): „Asking for it. BDSM Sexual Practice and the Trouble of Consent". In: Sexualities 23 (3), 269–286. DOI: 10.1177/1363460719828933, 277; Hess, Jacob Z. / Allen, Nicole E. / Todd, Nathan R. (2011): „Interpreting Community Accountability. Citizen View of Responding to Domestic Violence (or not)". In: The Qualitative Report 16 (4), 1096–1123. DOI: 10.46743/2160–3715/2011.1123.
61 Vgl. Brazzell (2021a), 168.
62 Vgl. Burke, Connie (2011): „Think. Re-Think. Accountable Communitie". In: Chen, Ching-In / Dulani, Jai / Piepzna-Samarasinha, Leah Lakshmi (Hg.): The Revolution Starts at Home. Confronting Intimate Violence Within Activist Communities, Edinburgh/Chico/Baltimore: AK Press, 264–279, 266 f. Eine mögliche Herangehensweise stellt dabei das von Mimi E. Kim entwickelte *community engagement continuum* dar, welches vier Ebenen kollektiven Handelns identifiziert: 1) *outreach and education*, 2) *mobiliziation*, 3) *organizing* und 4) *accountability*, vgl. Kim, Mimi E. (2005): The Community Engagement Continuum. Outreach, Mobilization, Organizing and Accountability to Address Violence Against Women in Asian and Pacific Islander Communities. Oakland, CA: Asian & Pacific Islander Institute of Domestic Violence, 10–13.
63 Vgl. Young (2011), 90.

sondern auch darum, die individuelle Gewalterfahrung als kollektive Verletzung wahrzunehmen.[64] Sich also nicht nur in ein Verhältnis zur gewalttätigen, sondern auch in ein Verhältnis zur betroffenen Person zu setzen. Dabei ist die Betroffenheit keine direkte, individuelle Betroffenheit, sondern eine Betroffenheit, die über die Beziehungsweisen stattfindet. Wenn jedes Individuum als in einem Netz aus Beziehungsweisen eingebettet wahrgenommen wird, dann hat die Gewalterfahrung von Personen zu denen dieses in einer Beziehung steht Auswirkungen auf dieses selbst, da die Gewalterfahrung die bestehende Form der Beziehungsweise verändert. Dies führt zu einem veränderten Verhältnis zur Gewalt: „Rather than a ‚vicitim's problem' or ‚someone else's responsibility,' surrounding friends and family may come to see violence as *their problem* and *their responsibility*".[65] Daraus ergibt sich, dass Aspekte in den Fokus geraten, die im Rahmen konventioneller Rechtspraktik keinen Raum finden, wie Fragen der Sorge, der Solidarität und der gegenseitigen Unterstützung (*mutual aid*).

Sara Kershner et al. betonen deshalb, dass in der kollektiven Verantwortungsübernahme nicht nur die Möglichkeit auf Gerechtigkeit für das Individuum besteht, sondern, dass hierin auch die Chance für eine kollektive Befreiung durch die Transformation der Beziehungsweisen, für eine Loslösung aus gesellschaftlichen Macht- und Herrschaftsstrukturen liegt.[66] Die Möglichkeit, dass über den Weg der kollektiven Verantwortungsübernahme eine kollektive Befreiung möglich ist, mag irritieren oder gar irrational erscheinen, enthält es aber doch ein utopisches Potenzial. Das utopische Potenzial liegt für Harsha Walia dabei in der Bedeutung dieser Prozesse als Präfigurationen der kollektiven Befreiung; im Prozess der kollektiven Verantwortungsübernahme zeigt sich die kommende Welt, die es schrittweise zu erreichen gilt. Denn wie Walia betont:

> Es geht auch darum, sich alternative Institutionen und Beziehungen auszudenken und zu schaffen. [...] Gesellschaften zu schaffen, die auf Gleichheit, gegenseitiger Hilfe und Selbstbestimmung beruhen [...], einer grundlegenden Neuausrichtung von uns selbst, unseren Bewegungen und unseren Gemeinschaften.[67]

Diese präfigurativen Räume als Räume des Ausprobierens und Erprobens sind dabei essentiell, da durch die Auslagerung sexualisierter Gewalt an strafrechtliche Institutionen es auf der Mesoebene an Wissen und Praktiken im Umgang mit dieser fehlt.[68] Mol-

64 Vgl. Rojas et al. (2011), 3.
65 Hess et al. (2011), 1119, Herv. i. O.
66 Vgl. Kershnar, Sara / Haines, Staci / Harkins, Gillian / Greig, Alan / Wiesner, Cindy / Levy, Mich / Shah, Palak / Kim, Mimi / Carr, Jesse (2007): Toward Transformative Justice A Liberatory. Approach to Child Sexual Abuse and other forms of Intimate and Community Violence. A Call to Action for the Left and the Sexual and Domestic Violence Sectors, https://criticalresistance.org/wp-content/uploads/2020/05/G5_Toward_Transformative_Justice-Document.pdf; Stand: 08.06.2023, 5.
67 Walia (2013), 249, zit. nach McLeod (2022), 570.
68 Vgl. Rojas et al. (2011), 3.

ly Ackhurst appelliert deshalb für ein Engagement innerhalb der vielfältigen Möglichkeiten alltäglichen Handelns, da alle Bemühungen ansonsten auf einer rein diskursiven Ebene verbleiben ohne sich in wirklichen Transformationen zu materialisieren.[69] Wie bereits gesagt: Kollektive Verantwortungsübernahme ist keine natürlich gegebene Fähigkeit, sondern muss erlernt werden und dieses Erlernen braucht Räume. *Transformative justice/community accountability* können als diese Räume fungieren und dabei auch das bestehende „justice gap" der konventionellen Rechtspraktik schließen, indem sie Gerechtigkeit und Verantwortung neudenken in Form von queerer Gerechtigkeit und kollektiver Verantwortungsübernahme. Dabei sind *transformative justice/community accountability* bei Weitem nicht ideal, sondern oftmals auch enttäuschend und ohne Erfolg, doch liegt in ihnen das Potenzial nicht nur andere Antworten auf sexualisierte Gewalt zu finden, sondern hierdurch unsere Beziehungsweisen grundlegend zu verändern.

Zur Person: Simone Kreutz ist wissenschaftliche Mitarbeiterin an der Humboldt-Universität zu Berlin. Sie studierte Staatswissenschaften und Politikwissenschaft in Passau, Cardiff und Berlin und promoviert zur Frage der kollektiven Verantwortung für sexualisierte Gewalt im Rahmen von hierarchiekritischen Kollektivzusammenhängen. Ihre Interessenschwerpunkte umfassen Abolitionismus und transformative Gerechtigkeitstheorien, feministische und kritische Theorien sowie kritische Gewaltforschung, mit einem Schwerpunkt auf sexualisierter Gewalt.

Simone Kreutz, M. A.
Humboldt-Universität zu Berlin, Lehrstuhl für Öffentliches Recht und Geschlechterstudien,
Unter den Linden 11, 10117 Berlin, Deutschland, simone.kreutz@hu-berlin.de.

69 Vgl. Ackhurst, Molly (2019): „Everyday Moments of Disruption. Navigating Towards Utopia". In: Studies in Arts and Humanities 5 (1), 115–128. https://eprints.bbk.ac.uk/id/eprint/40962/; Stand: 08.06.2023, 120.

Ziviler Ungehorsam

Alternative zum Recht oder alternative rechtliche Praxis?

SEBASTIAN TOBER

Civil Disobedience

An Alternative to Law or an Alternative Legal Practice?

Abstract: Judicial decisions and prevailing opinion consider the legal justification of civil disobedience to be inherently contradictory. This view will be critically examined. To this end, the concept of civil disobedience will be connected to the notion of a breach of conduct-regulating norms. It will be demonstrated that civil disobedience can indeed be conceptualized as a legal practice.
Keywords: civil disobedience, legal justifiability, norm theory, breach of conduct-regulating norms

1 Einleitung

In der rechtlichen Diskussion über die Aktionen der Aktivist*innen des sog. „Aufstands der letzten Generation" (kurz „Letzte Generation") firmiert der Begriff des zivilen Ungehorsams. Einige verwenden ihn als argumentative Stütze, um eine strafrechtliche Rechtfertigung zu begründen[1] oder diese jedenfalls zu erörtern.[2] Andere halten den Begriff dagegen für ungeeignet, eine Rechtfertigung für Klimaaktivist*innen her-

---

1 Bönte, Mathis (2021): „Ziviler Ungehorsam im Klimanotstand". In: Onlinezeitschrift für Höchstrichterliche Rechtsprechung zum Strafrecht 22 (3), 164–172; wohl Leitmeier, Lorenz (2023): „Ziviler Ungehorsam und autoritärer Legalismus?". In: Onlinezeitschrift für Höchstrichterliche Rechtsprechung zum Strafrecht 24 (3), 70–73; wohl Wolf, Jana (2022): „Klimaschutz als rechtfertigender Notstand". In: VerfBlog 14.11.2022 (unpag.). https://verfassungsblog.de/klimaschutz-als-rechtfertigender-notstand/ (Stand: 07.06.2024).

2 Wolf, Jana/Wenglarczyk, Fynn (2023): „Klima-Proteste: Ziviler Ungehorsam zwischen demokratischen Grenzen und grenzenloser Rechtfertigung". In: JuWissBlog 03.02.2023 (unpag.). https://www.juwiss.de/2-2023/ (Stand: 07.06.2024); Bayer, Daria (2022): „Auto fahren oder Klima retten?". In: VerfBlog 06.10.2022 (unpag.). https://verfassungsblog.de/auto-fahren-oder-klima-retten/ (Stand: 07.06.2024) spricht von „zivilem Widerstand".

zuleiten.[3] Die Rechtsprechung[4] und die herrschende Lehre[5] gehen bislang davon aus, dass der Begriff für eine *rechtliche* Rechtfertigung *prinzipiell* ungeeignet ist, da diese „logisch widersprüchlich“ sei. Wer Aktionen des zivilen Ungehorsams der *Möglichkeit* einer rechtlichen Rechtfertigung zuführen will, muss sich insoweit einem Einwand stellen, der als das „logische Argument“ bezeichnet werden kann. Dieses Argument soll in diesem Beitrag auf seine Schlüssigkeit untersucht werden. Es geht damit nicht darum, ob einige Aktionen der Letzten Generation gerechtfertigt sein könnten, son-

3 So Effer-Uhe, Daniel (2023): „Zivilrechtliche und strafrechtliche Notwehr gegen Nötigungshandlungen trotz fehlender Verwerflichkeit? Zum Rechtswidrigkeitsbegriff in § 240 II StGB einerseits und in § 32 StGB / § 227 BGB andererseits“. In: Neue Juristische Online-Zeitschrift 23 (20), 576–582, 580; Eidam, Lutz (2023): „Klimaschutz und ziviler Ungehorsam“. In: JuristenZeitung 78 (6), 224–230, 229; Mitsch, Wolfgang (2023): „Autofahrer vs. Klimaretter – Wer ist gerechtfertigt?“. In: Deutsches Autorecht, 93 (4), 234–237, 235; Rönnau, Thomas (2023): „Grundwissen – Strafrecht: Klimaaktivismus und ziviler Ungehorsam“. In: Juristische Schulung 63 (2), 112–115, 113 f.; Rönnau, Thomas / Saathoff, Jonas (2023): „Referendarexamensklausur – Strafrecht: Grenzen von Klimaprotesten“. In: Juristische Schulung 63 (5), 439–447, 442 f.; Schwarz, Kyrill-Alexander (2023): „Rechtsstaat und ziviler Ungehorsam“. In: Neue Juristische Wochenschrift 76 (5), 275–280; Zieschang, Frank (2023): „Klimaschutz als rechtfertigender Notstand bei Hausfriedensbruch?“. In: Juristische Rundschau 2023 (3), 136–147, 146; Zimmermann, Till / Griesar, Fabio (2023): „Die Strafbarkeit von Straßenblockaden durch Klimaaktivisten gem. § 240 StGB“. In: Juristische Schulung 63 (5), 401–408, 403; zweifelnd Satzger, Helmut / v. Maltitz, Nicolai (2021): „Das Klimastrafrecht – ein Rechtsbegriff der Zukunft“. In: Zeitschrift für die gesamte Strafrechtswissenschaft, 133 (1), 1–34, 30–32.

4 BVerfGE 73, 206, 252; BayObLG BeckRS 2023, 8998 Rn. 52; OLG Celle, BeckRS 2022, 21494 Rn. 8–12.

5 Botta, Jonas (2023): „Klimaaktivismus im demokratischen Rechtsstaat“. In: Verwaltungsarchiv 114 (2), 206–242, 233 f.; Cohen, Carl (1966): „Civil Disobedience and the Law“. In: Rutgers Law Review, 21 (1), 1–42, 7; Geis, Max-Emanuel (2021): „Ziviler Ungehorsam“. In: Hilgendorf, Eric / Joerden, Jan (Hg.), Handbuch Rechtsphilosophie, 2. Auf., Berlin: J. B. Metzler, 534–538, 537; Homann, Vanessa (2023): „Heiligt der Zweck alle Mittel? – Die Strafbarkeit der ‚Letzten Generation‘ im Rahmen ihrer Klimaproteste – Teil II: Mögliche Rechtfertigungsgründe“. In: Juristische Arbeitsblätter 55 (8), 649–654, 654; Kienzerle, Andrea (2022): „Keine Rechtfertigung einer Sachbeschädigung wegen zivilen Ungehorsams aus Klimaschutzgründen“. In: Fachdienst Strafrecht 2022 (19), 451633; Rönnau (2023), 114; Rönnau, Thomas (2021). In: Cirener, Gabriele / Radtke, Henning / Rissing-van Saan, Ruth / Rönnau, Thomas / Schluckebier, Wilhelm, Leipziger Kommentar zum Strafgesetzbuch (13. Auflage), Berlin: De Gruyter, Vor §§ 32 ff., Rn. 142; Zieschang, Frank (2023): „Klimaschutz als rechtfertigender Notstand bei Hausfriedensbruch?“. In: Juristische Rundschau 2023 (3), 146. Ähnlich Busche, Daniel (2023): „Verfassungsrechtliche Vorgaben für die strafrechtliche Bewertung der Sitzblockaden von Klimaaktivisten“. In: Klima und Recht 2 (4), 103–107, 107. Weitere Nachweise finden sich bei: Bönte (2021), 169 Fn. 38; Fleisch, Nico (1989), Ziviler Ungehorsam oder Gibt es ein Recht auf Widerstand im Schweizerischen Rechtsstaat?, Grüsch: Verlag Rüegger, 135; Laker, Thomas (1986): Ziviler Ungehorsam: Geschichte – Begriff – Rechtfertigung, Baden-Baden: Nomos, 163 Fn. 8 und 9. Kritisch Brockhaus, Robert (2023): Geheimnisschutz und Transparenz, Tübingen: Mohr Siebeck, 533–537; Dreier, Ralf (1983a): „Widerstandsrecht im Rechtsstaat? Bemerkungen zum zivilen Ungehorsam“. In: Achterberg, Werner / Krawietz, Dieter (Hg.), Recht und Staat im sozialen Wandel. Festschrift für Hans Ulrich Scupin zum 80. Geburtstag, Berlin: Duncker & Humblot, 573–599, 587–589; Eidam (2023), 228; Preuß, Tamina (2023): „Die strafrechtliche Bewertung der Sitzblockaden von Klimaaktivisten“. In: Neue Zeitschrift für Verkehrsrecht 36 (2), 60–74, 72 Fn. 159; Roxin, Claus (1993): „Strafrechtliche Bemerkungen zum zivilen Ungehorsam“. In: Albrecht, Peter-Alexis (Hg.), Festschrift für Horst Schüler-Springorum zum 65. Geburtstag, Köln (u. a.): Carl Heymanns Verlag, 441–457, 443.

dern – dieser Frage vorgelagert – darum, ob ziviler Ungehorsam überhaupt konsistent als rechtliche Praxis gedacht werden kann.[6]

2 Das logische Argument

In der Optik des logischen Arguments erscheint die rechtliche Rechtfertigung als Parasit auf dem Begriff des zivilen Ungehorsams: geht sie zu aggressiv vor, tötet sie ihren Wirt. Bei einer Rechtfertigung scheint vom zivilen Ungehorsam nichts mehr übrig zu bleiben. Das Argument lässt sich dabei auf begrifflicher und empirischer Ebene formulieren. Im Folgenden soll gezeigt werden, dass das Argument in beiden Fassungen nicht schlüssig ist.

2.1 Man kann das logische Problem auf begrifflicher Ebene formulieren. In diesem Sinn stellt etwa das Bundesverfassungsgericht fest, dass ziviler Ungehorsam „*per definitionem* Illegalität mit dem Risiko entsprechender Sanktionen einschließt"[7]; es sei daher „widersinnig, den Gesichtspunkt des zivilen Ungehorsams als Rechtfertigungsgrund" vorzubringen. Was ist davon zu halten?

2.1.1 Die Wendung „per defintionem" präsentiert die Rechtswidrigkeit (Illegalität) des zivilen Ungehorsams umstandslos als Bedeutung dieses Ausdrucks; sie wird als analytische Wahrheit behandelt. Dies setzt voraus, dass es extensional festgelegte, wenigstens paradigmatische Fälle des zivilen Ungehorsams gibt, die alle jedenfalls die Eigenschaft der Rechtswidrigkeit teilen. In Bezug auf die Aktionen von *Martin Luther King*, der in den 1950er und 1960er Jahren für die Veranstaltung diverser Aktionen im Rahmen des Civil Rights Movement verantwortlich zeichnete, erscheint dies aber zweifelhaft. Aufgrund der teilweise drastischen Reaktionen der staatlichen Behörden erlangten die Aktionen zwar große Aufmerksamkeit; jedenfalls die meisten Aktionen des Civil Rights Movement waren aber gar nicht rechtswidrig. In fast allen Fällen waren die Protestaktionen nach dem Bundesrecht legal.[8] Da *King* als „der wohl herausragendste Praktiker des zivilen Ungehorsams"[9] gilt, zeigt sich, dass sich keine feststehende bzw. allgemein anerkannte Extension des Ausdrucks „ziviler Ungehorsam" angeben lässt, aus der die Rechtswidrigkeit analytisch folgen würde.

---

6 Es geht dabei um sog. mittelbaren zivilen Ungehorsam, bei dem Protestgegenstand und -ziel auseinanderfallen, s. dazu 2.1.2.2.

7 BVerfGE 73, 206, 252, Kursive durch den Verfasser.

8 Schieder, Tobias (2018): Ethisch motivierter Rechtsungehorsam, Rechtsdebatten zu Widerstandsrecht, Gewissensfreiheit und zivilem Ungehorsam in der Bundesrepublik Deutschland 1949–1989, Tübingen: Mohr Siebeck, 197; Quint, Peter (2008): Civil Disobedience and the German Courts: The Pershing Missile Protests in Comparative Perspective, London (u. a.): Routledge Cavendish, 39.

9 Schieder (2018), 197.

2.1.2 Wenn man sich trotzdem darauf festlegen will, den Begriff des zivilen Ungehorsams für rechtswidrige Aktionen zu reservieren, lässt er sich zwar derart *stipulieren*. Doch wie überzeugend ist diese Begriffsbildung?

2.1.2.1 Zunächst scheint der Wortlaut für die Rechtswidrigkeit zu sprechen, wenn man „Ungehorsam" versteht als eine Negation der grundsätzlich bestehenden Gehorsamspflicht der Rechtspersonen. Nimmt man den Ausdruck so, meint er das „Nichtbefolgen von Anordnungen und Befehlen"[10]. Dafür spricht, sprachlich gesehen, dass das Präfix „un" in unzähligen Fällen zu einer Negation führt; doch findet sich auch eine Unmenge an Fällen, in denen die un-Präfigierung die Bedeutung eines Wortes nicht negiert, sondern verändert: So ist ein Unmensch auch ein Mensch, es sei denn, er ist untot (dann ist er ein Zombie), ein Unfall ist nicht das Gegenteil eines Falls, Unwetter ist auch Wetter und – wie diese Aufzählung zeigt – eine Unmenge auch eine Menge. Ungehorsam lässt sich daher im Verhältnis zum Gehorsam und seiner Negation als etwas Drittes verstehen[11]: als positiv affirmative Negation des Gehorsams. Was dies bedeutet, kann unter Rekurs auf die Urteilsformen bei *Immanuel Kant* angedeutet werden:

> *Der Qualität nach* sind die Urteile entweder *bejahende* oder *verneinende* oder *unendliche*. – Im *bejahenden* Urteile wird das Subjekt *unter* der Sphäre eines Prädikats gedacht, im *verneinenden* wird es *außer* der Sphäre des letztern gesetzt und im *unendlichen* wird es in die Sphäre eines Begriffs, die *außerhalb* der Sphäre eines andern liegt, gesetzt.[12]

Beim unendlichen Urteil wird also nicht die Kopula negiert („*ist nicht* gehorsam"); sondern es gehört die Negation logisch zum Prädikat („ist *ungehorsam*"). Anders als das verneinende Urteil spricht es dem Subjekt kein Prädikat ab; sondern es wird dem Subjekt die Negation als Prädikat *zugesprochen* bzw. es wird in den Umfang des Begriffs gesetzt. Legt man dem Begriff des Ungehorsams diese Unterscheidung von kopulativer und prädikativer Negation zugrunde, muss jemand, der sich ungehorsam verhält, nicht bloß *negativ* als unfähig verstanden werden, Befehlen zu gehorchen; vielmehr lässt sich dieser auch *positiv* als jemand begreifen, der die *Unmöglichkeit* von Gehorsam *affirmiert*. Das bedeutet, dass der Ungehorsame die Unmöglichkeit demonstriert, einer Organisation oder einer sonstigen Autorität, die Gehorsam von ihm verlangen, Unterstützung zu leisten. In diesem Verständnis des Ungehorsams ist eine Einsicht von *Hannah Arendt* aufgehoben. In dem postum veröffentlichten Essay „Was heißt persönliche Verantwortung in einer Diktatur?" beschäftigt sich *Arendt* mit der von ihr sogenannten Theorie des Rädchens im Getriebe. Diese Theorie ersetze die Verantwor-

---

10 Laker (1986), 131.

11 Ähnliche Überlegungen haben Hörster, Norbert (2006): Was ist Recht? Grundfragen der Rechtsphilosophie (1. Auflage), München: C. H. Beck, 83 und Staake, Marco (2018): Werte und Normen, Baden-Baden: Nomos, 366 zum Verhältnis von Recht und Unrecht angestellt; dort finden sich die Beispiele „Unmensch" bzw. „Unwetter".

12 Kant, Immanuel (1904): Logik: Ein Handbuch zu Vorlesungen (3. Auflage), Leipzig: Verlag der Dürr'schen Buchhandlung, 113.

tung des Einzelnen in bürokratischen Systemen durch kleine Rädchen, die das Ganze in Betrieb halten, ohne die also die Verwaltung nicht funktionieren würde, die für sich genommen aber ausgetauscht werden könnten, ohne dadurch das System selbst zu verändern. *Arendt* plädiert dafür, den Einzelnen nicht als ein solches auswechselbares Rädchen zu betrachten; das Funktionieren des Rädchens sei vielmehr als Unterstützung des Systems zu begreifen, anstatt dieses als „Gehorsam" gegenüber Vorgesetzen zu beschreiben. *Arendt* stellt damit die Bedeutung von zivilem Ungehorsam heraus; nicht nur für Diktaturen, sondern auch für andere Staatsformen, auch für Demokratien.[13] Nach *Arendt* ist das Befolgen von Gesetzen *immer* eine Unterstützung dieser Gesetze. Die entscheidende Frage sei danach nicht: „Warum hast du gehorcht?", sondern: „Warum hast du Unterstützung geleistet?"[14]. Sie schlägt daher vor, dass „wir das bösartige Wort ‚Gehorsam' aus dem Vokabular unseres moralischen und politischen Denkens streichen [sollten]"[15]. Denn „[n]ur ein Kind gehorcht; wenn ein Erwachsener „gehorcht", dann unterstützt er in Wirklichkeit die Organisation oder die Autorität oder das Gesetz, die ‚Gehorsam' verlangen"[16]. Die Rede vom „Gehorsam" ist daher mit *Arendt* für ein freiheitliches Rechtsverständnis als inadäquat zu kritisieren. Der Gehorsam entspringt dem Vokabular eines vormodernen obrigkeitsstaatlichen Rechtsverständnisses. Wenn man Ungehorsam als bloße Negation eines so verstandenen Gehorsams auffassen würde, affirmierte dieser selbst ein Rechtsverständnis, das die Rechtspersonen auf den Status des Befehlsempfängers reduzierte. Die Ungehorsamen wären dann wie ungezogene Kinder, die noch nicht gelernt haben, sich der staatlichen Autorität unterzuordnen. Der hiesige Vorschlag, Ungehorsam positiv als Affirmation der Unmöglichkeit von Gehorsam aufzufassen, vermeidet diese Konsequenz und ist insoweit vorzugswürdig. Das ist kein substanzielles Argument, sondern zeigt lediglich die Möglichkeit einer zweckmäßigen Verwendung des Ausdrucks „Ungehorsam", die die Frage seiner Rechtswidrigkeit nicht begrifflich vorentscheidet. Der Wortlaut ist verschiedenen Deutungen zugänglich.

2.1.2.2 Der Wirklichkeitsbezug der Begriffsbildung[17] könnte für die Rechtswidrigkeit des zivilen Ungehorsams sprechen. Bei der Begriffsbildung wird die Komplexität der Wirklichkeit im Hinblick auf relevante Eigenschaften reduziert. Ein hinreichender

---

13 Vgl. auch ihren späteren Text über zivilen Ungehorsam, Arendt, Hannah (1989): „Ziviler Ungehorsam". In: Knott, Marie (Hg.), Zur Zeit. Politische Essays, Hamburg: Rotbuch Verlag, 119–159; darin erhebt Arendt selbst einen Einwand gegen die rechtliche Rechtfertigung; dieser wird überzeugend entkräftet von Brockhaus (2023), 536 f.

14 Arendt, Hannah (2022): „Was heißt persönliche Verantwortung in einer Diktatur?". In: Knott, Marie (Hg.), Was heißt persönliche Verantwortung in einer Diktatur? (6. Auflage), München: Piper, 7–52, 52.

15 Arendt (2022), 52.

16 Arendt (2022), 49; vgl. auch Karpen, Ulrich (1984): „‚Ziviler Ungehorsam' im demokratischen Rechtsstaat". In: JuristenZeitung 39 (6), 249–262, 250.

17 S. zum Wirklichkeitsbezug der juristischen Begriffsbildung, Wank, Rolf (1985): Die juristische Begriffsbildung, München: C. H. Beck, 84 f.

Zusammenhang zwischen Wirklichkeit und Begriff des zivilen Ungehorsams besteht nur dann, wenn dieser alle *relevanten* Eigenschaften hinreichend isomorph modelliert. Handelt es sich bei der Rechtswidrigkeit um eine solche Eigenschaft? Ausgangspunkt dieser Überlegung muss der Normal- bzw. Durchschnittsfall sein, den man beim zivilen Ungehorsam vor Augen hat. Betrachtet man dafür die Klassiker wie *Henry David Thoreau, Mahatma Ghandi* und *Martin Luther King* stellt man fest, dass sie alle formell sanktioniert wurden. Wie bereits bemerkt, waren allerdings viele Aktionen des Civil Rights Movements nicht rechtswidrig. Dies kann an dieser Stelle aber nicht gegen das logische Argument vorgebracht werden. Es muss hier zwischen dem mittelbaren und unmittelbaren zivilen Ungehorsam unterschieden werden.[18] Viele Aktionen des Civil Rights Movement verstießen unmittelbar gegen diejenigen Normen, die auch das Ziel des Protests waren. Diese unmittelbare Variante des Ungehorsams kann offensichtlich rechtmäßig sein; Voraussetzung dafür ist, dass die verletzte Norm gegen eine höherrangige Norm, insbesondere die Verfassung verstößt. Das logische Argument kann sich aber nur auf den mittelbaren zivilen Ungehorsam beziehen, bei dem Protestgegenstand- und Ziel auseinanderfallen. Hier geht es darum, dass es entweder nicht sinnvoll oder schon gar nicht möglich ist, gegen diejenigen Normen zu verstoßen, die kritisiert (oder erstrebt) werden sollen. Gegen eine insuffiziente Klimaschutzpolitik kann man nicht verstoßen, weshalb die Aktivist*innen der Letzten Generation auf andere Normen, insbesondere solche des Straßenverkehrsrechts und des Versammlungsgesetzes ausweichen, um für effektive Klimaschutzpolitik zu demonstrieren. Dass mittelbarer ziviler Ungehorsam rechtlich gerechtfertigt werden kann, zeigt aber das Pätsch-Urteil[19] des Bundesgerichtshofs für Strafsachen (BGHSt). *Werner Pätsch*, ein ehemaliger Mitarbeiter des Bundesamtes für Verfassungsschutz (BfV) hatte Kenntnis von Abhörpraktiken des BfV erlangt, die er für illegal hielt, und machte diese Praktiken 1963 der Öffentlichkeit bekannt, indem er Informationen an einen Redakteur der Wochenzeitung *Die Zeit* übergab („Abhöraffäre“[20]). Er erfüllte die Tatbestände des fahrlässigen Landesverrats gem. § 110c Abs. 1 StGB a. F. und der vorsätzlichen Verletzung der Amtsverschwiegenheit nach § 353 b Abs. 1 Hs. 1 StGB. Der BGHSt musste sich zu der Frage des „illegalen Staatsgeheimnisses“ positionieren: Ist es strafbar, Geheimnisse über rechtswidrige, insbesondere verfassungswidrige, staatliche Praktiken öffentlich zu rügen? Das Gericht urteilte unter Rekurs auf die verfassungsrechtliche Wechselwirkungslehre, dass das Grundrecht der freien Meinungsäußerung nach Art. 5 Abs. 1 GG das Recht umfasst, Gesetzes- und Verfassungsverstöße von Behörden mit dem

---

18 S. nur Laker (1986), 164 f.

19 BGHSt 20, 342.

20 Darauf hat bereits Dreier, Ralf (1985a): „Rechtsgehorsam und Widerstandsrecht“. In: Broda, Christian u. a. (Hg.): Festschrift für Rudolf Wassermann zum sechzigsten Geburtstag, Darmstadt (u. a.): Hermann Luchterhand Verlag, 299–316, 310 hingewiesen. Der Fall Pätsch wird dargestellt bei Schieder (2018), 203–213; s. ferner Brockhaus (2023), 69 f., 103–108, 387–392, 399–403.

Ziel ihrer Abstellung zu rügen.[21] Soweit es sich nicht um einen schweren Verstoß gegen die verfassungsmäßige Ordnung handelt, sei die Rüge tatbestandsmäßig, aber die Rechtswidrigkeit aufgehoben.[22] Diese grundlegende Entscheidung des BGHSt prägt die Rechtslage zum sog. Whistleblowing bis heute, wobei die Rechtfertigung aktuell primär nach dem rechtfertigenden Notstand gem. § 34 StGB erörtert wird.[23] Die Frage der Anwendbarkeit ist gerichtlich zwar bislang nicht eindeutig entschieden; der Fall Pätsch zeigt aber, dass es jedenfalls in sehr engen Grenzen möglich ist, zivilen Ungehorsam zu leisten und rechtlich gerechtfertigt zu werden.[24] Dem logischen Argument wird man zugeben müssen, dass (mittelbarer) ziviler Ungehorsam im Regelfall rechtswidrig ist. Es kann jedoch auch Grenz- und Ausnahmefälle geben, in denen er rechtlich gerechtfertigt ist.[25]

2.1.2.3 Auch die philosophische Theoriebildung scheint für die Rechtswidrigkeit zu sprechen. So wird in juristischen Argumentationen der zivile Ungehorsam meist mit der berühmten Definition von *John Rawls* vorgestellt,[26] der diesen versteht als „public, nonviolent, conscientious yet political *act contrary to law* usually done with the aim of bringing about a change in the law or policies of the government“[27]. Allerdings können Fachbegriffe aus anderen Disziplinen nicht unvermittelt in die Rechtswissenschaft übernommen werden. Es ist eine Transferleistung erforderlich, da Begriffe ihren Sinn nur relativ zu einem Erkenntnisinteresse erhalten.[28] Der bloße Hinweis darauf, dass eine rechtliche Rechtfertigung nicht zur Idee des zivilen Ungehorsams passe oder seinen Sinn verfehlen würde,[29] greift daher für eine juristische Argumentation zu kurz;

---

21 BGHSt 20, 342, Ls. 1.

22 Ob bei einem schweren Verstoß eine Rechtfertigung oder ein Tatbestandsausschluss vorliegt, ließ das Gericht offen; heute gilt § 93 Abs. 2 StGB (Tatbestandsausschluss); der Tatbestandsausschluss führt nach dem hiesigen Vorschlag zum Prima-facie-Ungehorsam, s. u. 2.1.3.1.

23 s. Brockhaus (2023), 431–468; zwar trat § 34 StGB erst am 1.1.1975 in Kraft (2. Strafrechtsreformgesetz, BGBl. I. 1969, 717), doch war zum Zeitpunkt der BGHSt-Entscheidung der übergesetzliche Notstand allgemein anerkannt, sodass seine Prüfung auch im Fall Pätsch nahegelegen hätte.

24 Dreier, Ralf (1983b): „Widerstandsrecht und ziviler Ungehorsam im Rechtsstaat“. In: Glotz, Peter (Hg.), Ziviler Ungehorsam im Rechtsstaat (1. Auflage), 54–75, 71; Laker (1986), 309–313; Brockhaus (2023), 539; gegen die von Roxin (1993), 449 und Klein (1984): „Ziviler Ungehorsam im Rechtstaat?“. In: Rüthers, Bernd / Stern, Klaus (Hg.): Freiheit und Verantwortung im Verfassungsstaat, München: C. H. Beck, 177–197, 185–189 erhobenen Einwände lässt sich mit Laker (1986), 312 festhalten, dass es „einen rechtsdogmatisch gesicherten Bereich gerechtfertigten zivilen Ungehorsams gibt, der nicht auf fiktive Fälle unter unrealistischen Bedingungen beschränkt ist“.

25 Dreier, Ralf (1985b): „Der Rechtsstaat im Spannungsverhältnis zwischen Gesetz und Recht“. In: JuristenZeitung 40 (8), 353–359, 358.

26 Ähnlich Eidam (2023), 227: „Nahezu gleichlautend und stark angelehnt an die gerade referierten philosophischen Definitionsversuche (von Rawls, Dworkin und Arendt, S. T.) wird der zivile Ungehorsam im juristischen Schrifttum definiert“.

27 Rawls, John (1999): A Theory of Justice: Revised Edition, Cambridge: Harvard University Press, 320, Kursive durch den Verfasser.

28 Wank (1985), 141–143.

29 Vgl. aus rechtsphilosophischer Perspektive Frankenberg, Günter (1984): „Ziviler Ungehorsam und Rechtsstaatliche Demokratie“. In: JuristenZeitung 39 (6), 266–275, 268–270 und Geis (2021), 537.

kann die Idee des zivilen Ungehorsams oder sein Sinn doch juristisch nicht vorgefunden werden; vielmehr gilt es, eine *juristische* Idee zu *entwickeln*. Es ist an die Autonomie der rechtswissenschaftlichen Begriffsbildung zu erinnern.[30] Dies ist für den zivilen Ungehorsam essenziell, denn wenn seine „Rechtfertigung" in Rede steht, ist offen, ob damit seine Aktionen wirklich ins Recht gesetzt werden sollen, oder ob diese auf einer naturrechtlichen oder jedenfalls vorpositiven Ebene verhandelt wird.[31] *Rawls* versteht die Rechtfertigung vorpositiv, sodass es nicht Wunder nimmt, dass er zivilen Ungehorsam als Gesetzesverletzung definiert. Das philosophische Interesse am zivilen Ungehorsam bezieht sich vor allem auf eine Bestimmung des Verhältnisses von Bürger und Staat, in der wiederum eine Bestimmung über das Verhältnis von Recht und Moral verortet werden kann. Denn wäre das positive Recht immer normativ richtiges Recht, gäbe es keinen Anlass, dieses aus moralischen Gründen zu verletzen. Dafür muss man zivilen Ungehorsam aber notwendig als Rechtsverletzung auffassen. Dies zeigt nur, dass unterschiedliche Disziplinen verschiedene Erkenntnisinteressen verfolgen. Ein juristisches Konzept des zivilen Ungehorsams darf sich mit einer vorpositiven Betrachtung gerade nicht begnügen. Reale Aktionen des zivilen Ungehorsams erzeugen reale, juristische, d. h. vom Recht zu bewältigende Probleme: Es geht um ordnungsrechtliche und strafrechtliche Verantwortlichkeit, aber auch um zivilrechtliche Fragen, insbesondere stehen Schadensersatzansprüche im Raum.[32] Dafür kommt es darauf an, ob die Aktionen *rechtlich* gerechtfertigt sind.[33] Philosophische Arbeiten zum zivilen Ungehorsam können den juristischen Diskurs inspirieren (und das sollten sie auch), aber nicht argumentativ binden oder auf bestimmte Begriffe verpflichten.

2.1.2.4 Gegen das Merkmal der Rechtswidrigkeit spricht seine seltsame Konsequenz, dass Aktionen, die prima vista zum zivilen Ungehorsam zählen, durch einen gerichtlichen Freispruch secunda vista kein ziviler Ungehorsam sind.[34] Da die Feststellung der Rechtswidrigkeit einen komplexen Prüfungsprozess voraussetzt, würde dies den Begriff des zivilen Ungehorsams unpraktikabel machen.[35] Ob eine Aktion gerichtlich dem zivilen Ungehorsam zugeordnet wird, lässt sich im Zeitpunkt der Vor-

---

30 Demko, Daniela (2002): Zur „Relativität der Rechtsbegriffe" in strafrechtlichen Tatbeständen, Berlin: Duncker & Humblot, 70; Wank (1985), 79–82.

31 Vgl. Schieder (2018), 193; Hassemer, Winfried (1985): „Ziviler Ungehorsam – ein Rechtfertigungsgrund?". In: Festschrift für Rudolf Wassermann zum sechzigsten Geburtstag, Darmstadt (u. a.): Hermann Luchterhand Verlag, 325–349, 331.

32 Hassemer (1985), 332; zu zivilem Ungehorsam und Zivilrecht, s. nur Jacobs, Laura (2020): Ziviler Ungehorsam und Zivilrecht? Wem gehört der Protest?. In: Forum Recht 02/2020, 38–40.

33 Es ist nicht ausgemacht, ob diese Frage einheitlich zu beantworten ist, s. Brockhaus (2023), 273–276.

34 Vgl. das begriffliche Dilemma bei Vinthagen, Stellan (2015): A Theory of Nonviolent Action: How Civil Resistance Works, London: Zed Books, 72.

35 Eberl, Matthias (1994): „Ziviler Ungehorsam und Friedlicher Widerstand im demokratischen Verfassungsstaat: Wo liegen die Grenzen politischer Opposition in der rechtsstaatlichen Demokratie?". In: Zeitschrift für Politik 41 (4), 359–388, 364; Fleisch (1989), 136, 176; Laker (1986), 164.

nahme der Handlung nicht mit Sicherheit beantworten.[36] Wann wäre man also berechtigt, eine Aktion als zivilen Ungehorsam zu qualifizieren? Viele der diversen neuen Protestformen des radikalem Klimaaktivismus liegen in einer „juristischen Grauzone, deren gerichtliche Aufhellung Jahre beanspruchen kann“[37]. In der Zwischenzeit werden Staatsanwaltschaften und Verwaltungsbehörden die Aktionen sanktionieren. Es empfiehlt sich insofern ein Begriff des zivilen Ungehorsams, der ohne das Merkmal der Rechtswidrigkeit auskommt.

2.1.2.5 Wenn ziviler Ungehorsam notwendig rechtswidrig wäre, gäbe es außerdem keinen vor Gericht erfolgreichen zivilen Ungehorsam, womit der Begriff Aktionen des zivilen Ungehorsams ihre gerichtliche Wirksamkeit absprechen würde.[38] Nur warum sollten sich nicht auch Gerichte davon überzeugen lassen, dass die Klimakrise einige Aktionen der Letzten Generation rechtfertigt? Natürlich lässt sich argumentieren, dass Gerichte den Aktivist*innen die gerichtliche Anerkennung stets versagen müssen, weil bewusste Normverletzungen als Mittel, auf den öffentlichen Willensbildungsprozess einzuwirken, als mit den Grundprinzipien des demokratischen Rechtsstaates unvereinbar zu erkennen seien.[39] Dafür ist aber einiger argumentativer Aufwand erforderlich; denn diese demokratietheoretische Argumentation lässt sich auch bestreiten.[40] Dieses Aufwands kann man sich nicht einfach durch begriffliche Manöver entledigen.[41] Die juristisch interessanten Fragen, z. B. inwiefern ziviler Ungehorsam gegen die Mehrheitsregel verstößt,[42] würden aus dem Begriff so herausgekürzt.[43] Es müsste der aktuelle Diskurs über die Frage, inwiefern Aktionen der Letzen Generation gerechtfertigt sein könnten, ohne den Begriff des zivilen Ungehorsams stattfinden, da man sich damit zu

---

36 Laker (1986), 164.

37 Formulierung bei Laker (1986), 163 in Bezug auf die Straßenblockaden im Herbst 1983 aus Protest gegen den NATO-Doppelbeschluss.

38 Wenn man entgegen der hiesigen Argumentation das logische Argument auf den unmittelbaren zivilen Ungehorsam bezieht, ließe sich dieser im Erfolgsfall begrifflich nicht erklären, da in dieser Konstellation die Aktion gerade darauf abzielt, dass das Recht bzw. seine Anwendung so geändert werden, dass eine vermeintlich rechtswidrige Aktion nicht als rechtswidrig behandelt wird; vgl. Neubauer, Gerald (2016): Das Recht des Staates auf zivilen Ungehorsam, Baden-Baden: Nomos, 67.

39 So Perron, Walter (2019). In: Schönke, Adolf / Schröder, Horst (Begr.), Strafgesetzbuch Kommentar (30. Auflage), 2019, § 34 Rn. 41a.

40 S. etwa Bönte (2021); Wolf/Wenglarczyk (2023); diese Argumentation lässt sich überdies nur auf bestimmte Fallgestaltungen des zivilen Ungehorsams anwenden, aber z. B. nicht auf das Whistleblowing.

41 Wenn man etwa auf Basis der dargelegten Argumentation der Überzeugung ist, dass mittelbarer ziviler Ungehorsam nie rechtlich gerechtfertigt werden kann und deshalb die Rechtswidrigkeit in die Definition aufnimmt, verstieße man gegen das Definitionskriterium der Nichtredundanz.

42 S. dazu Hassemer (1985), 336 f.

43 Wozu eine Ansicht führt, die zivilen Ungehorsam uninformativ mit Rechtswidrigkeit gleichsetzt, hat jüngst Leitmeier (2023), 71 pointiert zum Ausdruck gebracht: „[D]iese Ansicht [beendet …] den demokratietheoretischen Diskurs über Rechtsstaat und zivilen Ungehorsam mit der eindimensionalen Formel: Sachbeschädigung ist Sachbeschädigung ist kriminell ist zu bestrafen“.

dieser Frage nicht sinnvoll äußern könnte.[44] Entweder sind einige Aktionen gerechtfertigt; dann sind sie kein ziviler Ungehorsam und der eigene Begriff sagt über sie gar nichts aus. Oder sie sind rechtswidrig und erfüllen damit zwar den Begriff; aber dann hätte er zu dieser Einsicht nichts beigetragen, da er die Rechtswidrigkeit stets voraussetzt, um überhaupt anwendbar zu sein. Die Rechtfertigbarkeit des zivilen Ungehorsams erweist sich damit als Adäquatheitsbedingung der juristischen Begriffsbildung.

2.1.3 Gesucht wird damit ein Begriff, der das provokative Moment des zivilen Ungehorsams hinreichend zum Ausdruck bringt, gleichzeitig aber die Rechtfertigung nicht begrifflich ausschließt.

2.1.3.1 Das provokative Element des zivilen Ungehorsams lässt sich so verständlich machen, dass sich darin eine gesellschaftliche Erwartung darüber ausdrückt, dass eine Aktion von staatlicher Seite als rechtswidrig *behandelt* werden wird.[45] Die Illegalität des zivilen Ungehorsams erschöpfte sich dann darin, dass er *mutmaßlich* rechtswidrig sein muss.[46] Wenn sich eine Aktion als rechtmäßig herausstellt, kann diese mit *Ralf Dreier* insoweit als „prima facie-Ungehorsam"[47] verstanden werden.[48] *Dreier* hat vorgeschlagen, zivilen Ungehorsam als *tatbestandliche* Normverletzung zu verstehen:[49] Die Normverletzung könne dann „durch höherrangige oder Ausnahmenormen rechtlich gerechtfertigt werden"[50]. Der Vorzug dieses Vorschlags besteht darin, dass er alle genannten Schwächen vermeidet, die das Merkmal der Rechtswidrigkeit mich sich bringen würde, aber dennoch dem Wirklichkeitsbezug der Begriffsbildung gerecht wird. Denn wenn man davon ausgeht, dass ziviler Ungehorsam im Regelfall rechtswidrige

---

44 Andernfalls drohen Fehlschlüsse, insb. in Form der quaternio terminorum, etwa: „Die Aktivist*innen der Letzten Generation berufen sich auf zivilen Ungehorsam. Ziviler Ungehorsam ist aber rechtswidrig. Die Aktivist*innen der letzten Generation handeln daher rechtswidrig"; zu diesem Fehlschluss, s. Wank (1985), 70.

45 S. aus soziologischer Perspektive, Vinthagen (2015), 72.

46 Neubauer (2016), 67; diese firmiert als „Prima-facie-Illegalität", s. Dreier (1985a), 307; Dreier (1985b), 358; so auch Laker (1986), 216; Spescha, Marc (1988): Rechtsbruch und sozialer Wandel: Über Ursachen und Wirkungen demonstrativer Normverletzungen im sozialen Konflikt und in gesellschaftlichen Veränderungsprozessen, Berlin: Duncker & Humblot, 187 f.; Remele, Kurt (1992): Ziviler Ungehorsam. Eine Untersuchung aus der Sicht christlicher Sozialethik, Münster: Aschendorff Verlag, 119; Kleger, Heinz (1993): Der neue Ungehorsam: Widerstände und politische Verpflichtung in einer lernfähigen Demokratie, Frankfurt (u. a.): Campus Verlag, 214; Brockhaus (2023), 534; ähnlich Rucht, Dieter: „Recht auf Widerstand? Aktualität, Legitimität und Grenzen ‚Ziviler Ungehorsams'". In: Guggenberger, Bernd / Offe, Claus (Hg.), An den Grenzen der Mehrheitsdemokratie: Politik und Soziologie der Mehrheitsregel, Opladen: Westdeutscher Verlag, 254–281, 278 Fn. 12.

47 Dreier (1983a), 588; Dreier (1983b), 61.

48 Der Prima-facie-Ungehorsam wird von Dreier jedoch übergeneralisiert, da tatbestandlich die prima facie-Illegalität ausreicht, wodurch dieser auf die Fälle reduziert wird, in denen wider Erwarten nicht einmal ein Verhaltensnormverstoß vorliegt. Dieser Fall trifft nach dem hiesigen Vorschlag auf viele Aktionen des Civil Rights Movement zu, insoweit als sie gegen verfassungswidriges Landesrecht verstießen, wenn man auf einen rechtlichen und nicht auf einen sozialen Geltungsbegriff abstellt.

49 Dreier (1983a), 588; Dreier (1983b), 56; ihm folgend Laker (1986), 162–164; Kleger (1993), 214 f.; Roxin (1993), 443, 447; Eberl (1994), 363 f.; Brockhaus (2023), 533 f.

50 Dreier (1983a), 593–596; Dreier (1983b), 64–69.

Aktionen beschreibt, aber ausnahmsweise gerechtfertigt werden kann, wird eben dieses Regel-Ausnahme-Verhältnis normativ nachgebildet, da die Tatbestandsmäßigkeit die Rechtswidrigkeit einer Aktion indiziert.[51]

2.1.3.2 Strafrechtlich entspricht der Vorschlag von *Dreier* dem dreigliedrigen Deliktsaufbau, der zwischen Tatbestandsmäßigkeit und Rechtswidrigkeit einer Handlung unterscheidet.[52] Dieser geht von der normentheoretischen Annahme aus, dass den Tatbeständen Verbots- und Gebotsnormen zugrunde liegen, die die rechtfertigenden Situationen nicht erfassen; stattdessen sollen den Erlaubnistatbeständen Erlaubnisnormen zugrunde liegen, die sich kategorial von den Verbots- und Gebotsnormen unterscheiden.[53] Es erscheint daher aussichtsreich, die mutmaßliche Rechtswidrigkeit durch einen Rekurs auf die Normentheorie näher aufzuklären, insbesondere um sich gegen argumentativen Widerstand, der sich strafrechtswissenschaftlich hinter der sog. Lehre von den negativen Tatbestandsmerkmalen[54] formiert, abzusichern. Denn wie der dreigliedrige Deliktsaufbau basiert auch die Lehre von den negativen Tatbestandsmerkmalen zwar auf der Idee, dass die Tatbestandsmäßigkeit und Rechtswidrigkeit das Unrecht einer Handlung bilden; sie formen aber einen *Gesamtunrechtstatbestand*, in dem Rechtfertigungsgründe als negative Tatbestandsmerkmale enthalten sein sollen. Nach dieser Lehre, wonach die *Normwidrigkeit* mit der *Rechtswidrigkeit* einer Handlung identisch ist, wäre der von *Dreier* vorgeschlagene zivile Ungehorsam ein „Unbegriff"[55]. Hier kann allerdings die Normentheorie – mit *Thomas Grosse-Wilde* gesprochen – dabei helfen, „eine implizite ‚Tiefengrammatik' und Struktur der Grundelemente einer Rechtsordnung zu erkennen"[56], und so das Verständnis des zivilen Ungehorsams als *Normungehorsam* plausibilisieren. Die Normentheorie basiert auf der Unterscheidung von primären Verhaltensnormen und sekundären Sanktionsnormen. Strafrechtlich folgt daraus, dass die Strafbarkeit einer Handlung den Verstoß gegen eine Verhaltensnorm voraussetzt, die durch eine kontradiktorische Reformulierung aus dem Tatbestand der Strafgesetze folgt.[57] Die Verhaltensnorm hat dabei eine vom

---

51 S. nur Fischer, Thomas (2024): Strafgesetzbuch mit Nebengesetzen (70. Auflage), München: C.H. Beck, Vor. § 13 Rn. 13, 46; zur Kritik an dieser Redeweise, s. Paeffgen, Hans-Ullrich / Zabel, Benno (2023). In: Kindhäuser, Urs / Neumann, Ulfried / Paeffgen Hans-Ullrich / Saliger, Frank (Hg.), Strafgesetzbuch, Band 1 (6. Auflage), Nomos, Baden-Baden, Vor. §§ 32–35, Rn. 15 Fn. 92 m. w. N.

52 Zum Deliktsaufbau, s. Kindhäuser, Urs / Hilgendorf, Eric (2022): In: Strafgesetzbuch. Lehr- und Praxiskommentar (9. Auflage), Baden-Baden: Nomos, Vor. § 13 Rn. 1–24.

53 Vgl. Schladitz, Pepe (2021): Normtheoretische Grundlagen der Lehre von der objektiven Zurechnung: Sicheres Fundament oder Achillesferse?, Tübingen: Mohr Siebeck, 213.

54 Zur Lehre von den negativen Tatbestandsmerkmalen, s. nur Paeffgen/Zabel (2023), Vor. §§ 32–35, Rn. 16–21.

55 Dreier (1983a), 588.

56 Grosse-Wilde, Thomas (2018): „Die Vielheit der Normen(-theorien) im englischsprachigen und deutschsprachigen Rechtsdiskurs". In: Schneider, Anne / Wagner, Markus (Hg.), Normentheorie und Strafrecht, Baden-Baden: Nomos, 215–243, 215.

57 Schladitz (2021), 236 Fn. 240 m. w. N.

Strafgesetz unabhängige normative Existenz. *Karl Binding*, auf den die Normentheorie in der deutschen Rechtswissenschaft zurückgeführt wird, hielt die Anerkennung primärer Normen für *logisch* zwingend, da sich der Rechtsverstoß strafrechtlich nicht mit einer Verletzung des Strafgesetzes begründen lässt; handelt der Täter doch gerade in Gemäßheit dieses Gesetzes: „Weit entfernt [...] dass der Verbrecher das Strafgesetz übertritt, nach welchem er beurteilt wird, muss er vielmehr immer, damit er bestraft werden könne, diesem Gesetze in seinem ersten Teile gemäss, in Einklang damit gehandelt haben"[58]. Es ist fraglich, wie überzeugend diese Begründung ist, scheint doch ein Fehlschluss vorzuliegen, der auf der Verwechslung von einer sprachlichen Analyse mit der Entdeckung von Elementen beruht, von denen angenommen wird, dass sich aus ihnen das ganze (Straf-)Recht aufbauen lasse. Der Schluss von einer unpräzisen façon de parler („Der Täter übertritt das Strafgesetz") auf die Existenz einer vom Strafgesetz unabhängigen Normenordnung, kann aber jedenfalls durch einen Hinweis auf den semantischen Normbegriff von *Robert Alexy* verständlich gemacht werden.[59] Danach ist zwischen Norm und Normsatz zu unterscheiden. Die Norm wird als Bedeutung des Normsatzes verstanden. Bereits *Pepe Schladitz* hat darauf hingewiesen, dass dieses Modell dabei helfen kann, den Begriff der Verhaltensnorm „zu erfassen", denn „nur weil die Verhaltensnorm im kodifizierten Strafgesetz [...] nicht unmittelbar Ausdruck gefunden hat, heißt das nicht, dass sie nicht normative Realität hat"[60]. Fraglich ist, ob sich normentheoretisch dann begründen lässt, dass auch den Erlaubnissätzen eigenständige Erlaubnisnormen zugrunde liegen, die sich von den Verhaltensnormen unterscheiden. Dafür könnte man argumentieren, dass es auf eine Imperativentheorie[61] hinauslaufen würde, wenn man die Existenz eigenständiger Erlaubnisnormen leugnen würde: die Rechtsordnung bestünde dann nur aus Befehlen, die Gehorsam verlangen.[62] Jedenfalls eine nähergehende Untersuchung sollte die genannten Schwierigkeiten für das Konzept des Normungehorsams überwinden können, zumal es sich nicht um logische oder begriffliche Probleme handelt. Im Vokabular der Normentheorie ließe sich die tatbestandliche Normverletzung dann als „Verhaltensnormverstoß" bezeichnen.[63] Der Begriff des zivilen Ungehorsams erweist sich somit als rechtfertigbar.[64]

---

58 Binding, Karl (1991): Die Normen und ihre Übertretung. Band 1 (Neudruck der 4. Auflage), Aalen: Scientia Verlag, 4.

59 Alexy, Robert (1994): Theorie der Grundrechte (1. Auflage), Frankfurt a. M.: Suhrkamp, 42–47.

60 Schladitz (2021), 376.

61 Zur Imperativentheorie und ihrer Kritik, s. Schladitz (2021), 227–229.

62 Zu diesem Argument, s. Schladitz (2021), 91 f.

63 Die Normentheorie darf nicht zur Unrechtslegitimation verwendet werden; der Inhalt der Norm muss mit der Einsicht des Einzelnen verbunden bleiben, s. Zaczyk, Rainer (2014): „Kritische Bemerkungen zum Begriff der Verhaltensnorm". In: Goltdammer's Archiv für Strafrecht 161, 73–90.

64 Es ließe sich einwenden, dass man begrifflich mit einer unvollständigen rechtlichen Prüfung operieren würde, da die Verhaltensnorm nur eine unvollständige Formulierung der konkreten Verhaltensanforderungen enthält; dieser Einwand lässt sich nicht isoliert entkräften, da sich die Vorzüge des zivilen Ungehorsams

2.2 Das logische Argument lässt sich auch auf empirischer Ebene formulieren. So könnte man einwenden, dass der zivile Ungehorsam seine Wirksamkeit verlöre, wenn er rechtlich gerechtfertigt wird. Diese ist für die Rechtfertigung aber erforderlich.[65] Um das Argument so zu formulieren, dass die Rechtfertigung von zivilem Ungehorsam auf einen Widerspruch führt, wäre man aber auf die Prämisse (P) angewiesen: „Ziviler Ungehorsam ist nur wirksam, wenn er auch rechtswidrig ist", die in dieser Form offensichtlich zu stark formuliert ist. Gegen sie spricht, dass rechtswidrige, insbesondere strafbare, Aktionen das eigene Anliegen sogar delegitimieren können. Dies berücksichtigt auch die Letzte Generation in ihrer kommunikativen Strategie. Während sie durch ihre Aktionen Normbrüche begehen, betonen sie gleichzeitig, dass ihre Aktionen aufgrund der mit der Klimakrise verbundenen Gefahrenlage gerechtfertigt sind.[66] Dies erscheint zunächst ambivalent, behaupten sie doch die Rechtmäßigkeit ihrer Aktionen im Medium des Normbruchs! Sie setzen einen Normbruch öffentlich in Szene, um ihn gleichzeitig zu bestreiten. Betrachtete man diesen Akt der Kommunikation so, erschiene er als performativer Selbstwiderspruch[67], da sein propositionaler Inhalt seinen eigenen Sinnbedingungen widerspräche. Dieser Selbstwiderspruch auf aktivistischer Ebene, so er denn vorläge, verwiese auf das logische Problem auf theoretischer Ebene. Doch der Widerspruch entsteht nur dann, wenn man nicht zwischen (verletzter) Verhaltensnorm und Erlaubnisnorm unterscheidet. Normbruch ist nicht gleich Rechtsbruch. Die Aktivist*innen entscheiden sich bewusst für ein Verhalten, von dem sie erwarten, dass die Behörden es als Straftat behandeln werden. Deshalb inszenieren

---

als Rechtsbegriff nur im Ganzen einer Theorie beurteilen lassen. Zur „Überflüssigkeitsthese" in Bezug auf zivilen Ungehorsam als Rechtsbegriff s. ferner Dreier (1983a), 596 f.; Dreier (1983b), 71.

65 Vgl. Botta (2023), 233 f., der die Anwendung des logischen Arguments auf § 34 StGB antizipiert: es sei widersprüchlich, die Erforderlichkeit mit dem Argument zu begründen, dass erst der Rechtsbruch für die notwendige Aufmerksamkeit für Klimaschutzbelange sorge; ähnlich Honer (2023): „Ziviler Ungehorsam in der freiheitlichen Demokratie des Grundgesetzes". In: Juristische Schulung 63 (5), 408–414, 413, der gegen zivilen Ungehorsam als Rechtfertigungsgrund anführt, er beziehe „seinen Reiz aus der Illegalität". Rönnau/Saathoff (2023), 443 verneinen die rechtfertigende Wirkung zivilen Ungehorsams mit dem Argument, dass Aktivisten strafrechtliche Sanktionen in Kauf nehmen, „um größtmögliche Aufmerksamkeit zu generieren. Bei einer legalen Protestform würde dieser Effekt verfehlt". Auch der von Botta zitierte Bönte (2021), 170, vermeidet einen Widerspruch, indem er zivilen Ungehorsam mit möglichen milderen Mitteln vergleicht, „die keinen Straftatbestand erfüllen", d. h. in hiesiger Diktion: keinen Verhaltensnormverstoß darstellen; anders aber Wolf (2022): „Kein milderes Mittel kann zudem ein Aktivismus ohne Ungehorsam darstellen. Der Rechtsbruch fungiert gerade als Katalysator für Aufmerksamkeit und Provokation: Ohne Gesetzesverletzung wäre der Klimaaktivismus als geeignetes Mittel zur Gefahrabwendung konterkariert."; nach Brockhaus (2023), 535 f.: würde es „einen strafrechtsdogmatischen Fehlschluss darstellen, eine Rechtfertigung abzulehnen, weil das Mittel bei Straffreiheit nicht geeignet wäre".

66 S. auch das auf der eigenen Website veröffentlichte Gutachten zu Straßenblockaden, online abrufbar unter: https://letztegeneration.de/wp-content/uploads/2022/03/Gutachten-Strassenblockade.pdf (Stand: 07.06.2024).

67 Zu diesem Widerspruch, s. Habermas, Jürgen (1983): Moralbewußtsein und kommunikatives Handeln (1. Auflage), Frankfurt a. M.: Suhrkamp, 90 f.; Alexy, Robert (1992): Begriff und Geltung des Rechts (1. Auflage), Freiburg (u. a.): Karl Alber, 67–69.

sie einen Verhaltensnormverstoß, um dadurch eine Erlaubnisnorm (vgl. § 34 StGB) in Anschlag bringen zu können, die auf die Gefahren der Klimakrise verweist. Dadurch wird die Klimakrise in das Zentrum des politischen Diskurses gerückt.[68] Wäre ziviler Ungehorsam begrifflich rechtswidrig, könnte diese kommunikative Strategie nicht erklärt werden. Auch kann von der Rechtswidrigkeit die Wirksamkeit nicht abhängen, ist doch gerade die Diskussion darüber, ob eine Aktion des zivilen Ungehorsams gerechtfertigt ist, ein maßgeblicher strategischer Faktor für ihre Wirksamkeit.[69]

3 Schluss

Es hat sich gezeigt, dass eine rechtliche Rechtfertigung von zivilem Ungehorsam nicht „logisch widersprüchlich" ist. Die Rechtswidrigkeit des zivilen Ungehorsams ist keine analytische Wahrheit. Zwar kann man dieses Merkmal stipulieren und durch begriffliche Ausweichmanöver eine argumentative Abkürzung nehmen; die demokratietheoretischen Aspekte werden dabei jedoch aus dem Begriff des zivilen Ungehorsams herausgekürzt. Eine Aktion des zivilen Ungehorsams lässt sich als Verhaltensnormverstoß beschreiben, der einer Rechtfertigung zugänglich ist. Auch nimmt die Rechtfertigung dem zivilen Ungehorsam nicht seine Wirksamkeit. Er lässt sich mithin als rechtsimmanente Praxis konzeptualisieren.

Zur Person: Sebastian Tober ist wissenschaftlicher Mitarbeiter am Lehrstuhl für deutsches und internationales Strafrecht und Strafprozessrecht, Strafrechtsvergleichung sowie Strafrechtsgeschichte von Prof. Dr. Carl-Friedrich Stuckenberg an der Universität Bonn. Er promoviert als Stipendiat der Heinrich-Böll-Stiftung zu zivilem Ungehorsam bei Prof. Dr. Michael Kahlo an der Universität Leipzig.

Sebastian Tober
stober@uni-bonn.de.

68 Näher dazu Tober, Sebastian (2024), „Ziviler Ungehorsam – Eine undemokratische und instrumentalisierende Praxis?". In: Stiftung der Hessischen Rechtsanwaltschaft (Hg.): Ziviler Ungehorsam im 21. Jahrhundert, Coburg: Sieversmedien, 73–113, 78–82.

69 P lässt sich sinnvollerweise schwächer formulieren; so sind verschiedene rechtspolitische Einwände erhoben worden, sowohl von mit zivilem Ungehorsam sympathisierenden Autoren als auch von solchen, die ihn ablehnen; s. dazu nur Dreier, (1985a), 309–316 und Brockhaus (2023), 534–537; es sei hier angedeutet, dass sich die Frage, unter welchen Umständen mit einer rechtlichen Rechtfertigung ein Wirksamkeitsverlust einhergeht, kaum pauschal beantworten lässt; so zielt Bönte (2021), 169 mit guten Gründen gerade unter dem Gesichtspunkt der Wirksamkeit auf eine umfassende Rechtfertigung der Aktivist*innen der Letzten Generation.

Was heißt, das Recht immanent zu kritisieren?
Ein methodologischer Beitrag zur Kritischen Theorie des Rechts

RODRIGO MARUY VAN DEN BROEK

What does it mean to criticize the law immanently?
A methodological contribution to the Critical Theory of Law

Abstract: This article delineates a methodological program for an immanent critique of modern law. To this purpose, I reconstruct four approaches to the critique of law within the tradition of Frankfurt School Critical Theory. First, I claim that Jürgen Habermas and Axel Honneth offer a model of internal legal critique which falls prey to both a normative reformism and institutional conservatism, thus concealing the possibility of a radical disruption of the modern legal form. Secondly, I argue that Christoph Menke and Daniel Loick propose a model of genealogical critique which, by condemning the formation of legal subjects as a pathological process in itself, ends up relying on external normative criteria that lack both normative and explanatory power to account for an overcoming of the modern legal form. Finally, following Rahel Jaeggi, I programmatically outline a set of tasks for an immanent critique of modern law on the basis of concepts such as contradiction and legitimation crisis.
Keywords: Immanent critique of law, Habermas, Menke, contradiction, legitimation crisis

1 Einleitung

Rechtskritik ist ein Leitmotiv, das von Anfang an mit dem interdisziplinären Projekt der Frankfurter Schule einherging.[1] Weil die praktische, ja institutionelle Verwirklichung emanzipatorischen Wandels umfangreich auf das Recht angewiesen ist, haben die in den letzten Jahrzehnten erschienen Beiträge zu diesem Topos zwar ein nicht

1 Zum Überblick s. Scheuerman, William (2019): „Critical Theory and the Law". In: Gordon, Peter / Hammer, Espen / Honneth, Axel (Hg.): The Routledge Companion to the Frankfurt School. New York/London: Routledge, 486–499; sowie Loick, Daniel (2019): „Aufgaben einer kritischen Theorie des Rechts". In: Bohmann, Ulf / Sörensen, Paul (Hg.): Kritische Theorie der Politik. Berlin: Suhrkamp, 330–347.

zu unterschätzendes Gewicht.[2] In der Debatte bleibt dennoch unklar, wie eine Kritik des modernen Rechts *der Sache nach* herangehen soll. Obgleich mehrere Stimmen für eine „immanente Rechtskritik" plädieren, werden sowohl die Beschaffenheit der Immanenz als auch deren Verhältnis zur Transzendenz dabei unterthematisiert.[3] Entsprechend zielt dieser Aufsatz darauf, methodologische Überlegungen zur *Form* einer immanenten Rechtskritik darzustellen.

Für mein Argument bedarf ich dreier Schritte. *Erstens* rekonstruiere ich Jürgen Habermas' und Axel Honneths rechtsphilosophischen Beiträge. In ihnen lässt sich ein Modell *interner Kritik* erkennen, dessen Zweck hauptsächlich darin besteht, die moderne Idee der Autonomie auf eine bessere Art und Weise zu verwirklichen. Der Rekurs auf diesen normativen Maßstab, welcher letztendlich in den Institutionen westlicher liberaler Demokratien gründet, birgt leider ein strukturelles Manko. Denn interne Rechtskritik erweist sich darin als ein reformistisches Projekt. Aus diesem Grund tendieren beide Ansätze dazu, die konstitutive Widersprüchlichkeit, die der modernen Rechtsform innewohnt, zu verschleiern.

Weil Christoph Menke und Daniel Loick sich vornehmen, anhand einer radikalen Kritik des modernen Rechtssubjekts ebendieser Widersprüchlichkeit gerecht zu werden, rekonstruiere ich *zweitens* deren Ansätze. Dabei kristallisiert sich ein Modell *genealogischer Kritik* heraus, dessen Ziel nichts anderes als eine Überwindung, ja Revolution der bestehenden Rechtsform ausmacht. Allein indem die Rechtsform selbst für einen pathologischen Fallstrick gehalten wird, schlagen beide Ansätze Alternativen vor, die sich normativ auf andere, der Rechtsform *externe* Kriterien stützen (müssen). So verfehlen sie das transformative Potential, das sich nicht zuletzt aus der Widersprüchlichkeit des modernen Rechts ergibt.

Notabene: Meine kritische Rekonstruktion jener vier Autoren behauptet nicht, dass ihre Beiträge sich *ausschließlich* auf ein entweder intern-reformistisches oder genealogisch-externes Modell reduzieren lassen. Habermas' Entgegensetzung von Geltung und Faktizität des modernen Rechts, um nur ein Beispiel zu nennen, weist in der Tat Züge dessen auf, was ich unter dem Begriff immanenter Kritik erfassen werde. Meine Rekonstruktion beansprucht nur zu zeigen, inwiefern den entweder intern-reformistischen oder genealogisch-externen *Strukturmomenten* der Kritik bei jenen Autoren ein problematisches Übergewicht zukommt.

---

2 Gemeint sind vor allem Habermas, Jürgen (1998): Faktizität und Geltung. Beiträge zur Diskurstheorie des Rechts und des demokratischen Rechtsstaats. Frankfurt a. M.: Suhrkamp; Honneth, Axel (2011): Das Recht der Freiheit. Grundriß einer demokratischen Sittlichkeit. Berlin: Suhrkamp; Brunkhorst, Hauke (2014): Critical Theory of Legal Revolutions. Evolutionary Perspectives. London: Bloomsbury; Menke, Christoph (2015): Kritik der Rechte. Berlin: Suhrkamp; und Loick, Daniel (2017): Juridismus. Konturen einer kritischen Theorie des Rechts. Berlin: Suhrkamp. Im Folgenden beschränke ich mich auf diese Beiträge.

3 Zur immanenten Kritik im Allgemeinen s. Stahl, Titus (2013): Immanente Kritik. Elemente einer Theorie sozialer Praktiken. Frankfurt a. M.: Suhrkamp; sowie Jaeggi, Rahel (2014): Kritik von Lebensformen. Berlin: Suhrkamp, 255–309.

In Abgrenzung zu diesen Modellen werde ich *drittens* programmatische Überlegungen zur Form einer *immanenten Rechtskritik* entwerfen, die vornehmlich auf Rahel Jaeggis Ansatz aufbauen. Deutet man die Gegenüberstellung beider vorheriger Kritikformen als einen Gegensatz zwischen Reform oder Revolution des Rechts, dann wäre dies für eine immanente Rechtskritik kein Dilemma. Denn immanente Kritik, so die These, geht in jenem anscheinenden Gegensatz nicht auf. Ihr Vorhaben zielt vielmehr auf eine aus dessen eigenen Widersprüchen getriebene Transformation des modernen Rechts, die erst im Nachhinein reformistische oder revolutionäre Züge aufweisen kann. Dies soll im Folgenden geklärt werden.

Vorab lohnt sich, den Unterscheid zwischen interner und externer Kritik zu thematisieren.[4] Aufschlussreich ist hier die folgende Einsicht: Formen der Gesellschaftskritik lassen sich zunächst dadurch voneinander unterscheiden, wie sie die Frage nach dem *Ursprung* ihrer normativen Maßstäbe behandeln. Führen die Maßstäbe auf ein *Jenseits* oder *Außerhalb der Gesellschaft* zurück, so liegt ein Modell externer Kritik vor. Illustrative Beispiele dafür sind Platons Idealstaat, Kants kategorischer Imperativ oder Rawls' Gerechtigkeitstheorie.[5] Ist es hingegen der Fall, dass die normativen Maßstäbe *aus der Sache selbst* hervorgehen, dann handelt es sich vorerst um ein Modell interner Kritik. Eine Gesellschaft, die sich laut ihrer eigenen Verfassung als eine demokratische Republik versteht, darf man z. B. intern kritisieren, wenn Verletzungen von Grund- und Mitbestimmungsrechten stattfinden. Denn in solchem Fall gäbe es eine Inkonsistenz zwischen sozialen Normen und denjenigen Praktiken, die im Prinzip ebendiese Normen zu verwirklichen hätten, ihnen aber faktisch widersprechen.

Zwischen beiden Modellen herrscht eine Spannung. Vis-à-vis ihrem externen Pendant hat interne Kritik freilich den „praktisch-pragmatischen Vorteil", dass ihre Ansprüche kein bloßes Sollen darstellen.[6] Das heißt, diese Form der Kritik ist deshalb an normativer Kraft überlegen, weil sie einen internen Zusammenhang zwischen sozial anerkannten Normen und deren entsprechenden Praktiken in Anspruch nimmt. Es geht also darum, eine „Wiedergewinnung oder Reetablierung der durch abweichende Praktiken teilweise außer Kraft gesetzten Normen" zu erringen.[7] Allein solch eine Gebundenheit interner Kritik an ihre normativen Maßstäbe impliziert zugleich, dass sie nicht die Geltung dieser Maßstäbe zu hinterfragen vermag. Daher ist interne Kritik sowohl für einen „normativen Konventionalismus" als auch für einen „strukturellen

---

4 Den Weg für diese methodologische Gegenüberstellung hat Honneth, Axel (2007): „Rekonstruktive Gesellschaftskritik unter genealogischem Vorbehalt. Zur Idee der ‚Kritik' in der Frankfurter Schule", in: ders.: Pathologien der Vernunft. Geschichte und Gegenwart der Kritischen Theorie. Frankfurt a. M.: Suhrkamp, 57–69, bereitet.

5 Ob die Einordnung dieser tradierten Beispiele zutreffend ist, mag hier dahingestellt bleiben. Zu Platon s. beispielhaft Maruy van den Broek, Rodrigo (2020): „Dialéctica de la justicia. Una apología de Platón como crítico social". In: Estudios de Filosofía 18, 112–136.

6 Jaeggi (2014), 268 f.

7 Ebd., 265.

Konservatismus" anfällig.[8] Im Gegenteil dazu weist externe Kritik wohl radikalere Züge auf, indem ihre Maßstäbe einen größeren Abstand zur sozialen Wirklichkeit halten. So betrachtet hat externe Kritik zwar ein utopisches, ja die bestehende Gesellschaft transzendierendes Moment. Der Preis, den sie für diese Radikalität zu bezahlen hat, ist allerdings ein Mangel an normativer Kraft. Das bloße Sollen externer Maßstäbe befindet sich zudem kaum in der Lage, auf die schwierige Frage nach dem Übergang vom bestehenden zum idealen Zustand eine überzeugende Antwort zu geben. Wie ist dieses Spannungsverhältnis nun für die Kritik des Rechts relevant?

2 Intern-reformistische Kritik: Die rechtliche Aufspaltung der Autonomie und ihre institutionelle Versöhnung

Das moderne Recht, so Habermas' späte Grundthese, zeichnet sich dadurch aus, in welcher Form es die positive, zwingende Faktizität seiner Normen *einerseits* und deren freiheitsverbürgenden Geltungsanspruch *andererseits* miteinander verzahnt:

> [D]er Umstand, daß die mit staatlichen Sanktionsdrohungen bewehrten Normen auf die änderbaren Beschlüsse eines politischen Gesetzgebers zurückgehen, wird mit der Erwartung verknüpft, daß sie die Autonomie aller Rechtspersonen gleichermaßen gewährleisten. Diese Legitimitätserwartung verschränkt sich mit der Faktizität von Rechtsetzung und -durchsetzung.[9]

Das Argument darf man in drei Thesen rekonstruieren: Die Legitimität des Rechts hängt *erstens* von dessen Fähigkeit ab, zur Integration moderner Gesellschaften beizutragen. Dafür braucht das Rechtsmedium *zweitens* eine gewisse funktionale Durchsetzbarkeit. Aber um diese Zwangsbefugnis und somit sich selbst zu legitimieren, sind Rechtsordnungen *drittens* auf das moderne Ideal der Autonomie angewiesen. Daraus ergibt sich eine notwendige Verschränkung zwischen Faktizität und Geltung, die sich entsprechend „im ambivalenten Geltungsmodus des Rechts" spiegelt:

> Das moderne Recht wendet sich nämlich seinen Adressaten mit einem Janusgesicht zu: es stellt ihnen frei, ob sie die Rechtsnormen nur als Befehle im Sinne faktischer Einschränkungen des eigenen Handlungsspielraums betrachten und mit den kalkulierbaren Folgen möglicher Regelverletzungen *strategisch* umgehen wollen oder ob sie dieselben in *performativer* Einstellung als gültige Gebote ansehen und „aus Achtung vor dem Gesetz" befolgen wollen.[10]

---

8 Ebd., 272 ff.
9 Habermas (1998), 661.
10 Ebd., 661 f.

Die Autonomie moderner Rechtssubjekte gilt insofern doppelt: *zum einen* als private Autonomie bzw. als „Willkürfreiheit des rational entscheidenden Aktors“, *zum anderen* als öffentliche Autonomie bzw. als kommunikative „Freiheit der ethisch entscheidenden Person“.[11] Eine eigentümliche „Aufspaltung der Autonomie“ drückt sich also darin aus, dass Rechtssubjekte sich entweder als Adressat:innen oder als Autor:innen des geltenden Rechts betrachten dürfen.[12] Diese Ambivalenz manifestiert sich schließlich in der Form von subjektiven Rechten. Folgt man einer wohlbekannten Einordnung, so stehen negative Freiheitsrechte und soziale Teilhaberechte wohl aufseiten der privaten Autonomie, während dem Wesen politischer Teilnahmerechte ein öffentliches Moment innewohnt.[13]

Aus der Janusköpfigkeit des Rechts leitet Habermas zwei entgegengesetzte Prinzipien ab, denen zwei Traditionen des neuzeitlichen politischen Denkens zugesprochen werden: die liberal geprägte „Herrschaft des Gesetzes“, welche Habermas mit dem Schutz der Grundrechte identifiziert, und das vom Republikanismus befürwortete Prinzip der „Volkssouveränität“.[14] Die institutionelle Form des Rechtsstaats soll demgemäß die private Autonomie von Rechtssubjekten sichern; die der Demokratie hat eher ihre öffentliche Autonomie zu verwirklichen. Dass zwischen beiden autonomieverbürgenden Institutionen kein einseitiger Primat, sondern vielmehr ein interner Zusammenhang der Gleichursprünglichkeit besteht, ist der Kern von Habermas „prozeduralistischer Rechtsauffassung“. Deren Begründung lautet: Das Rechtsmedium, an deren öffentlicher Gestaltung die Rechtssubjekte als Staatsbürger:innen aktiv teilnehmen dürfen, setzt in transzendentaler Hinsicht die private Autonomie von Rechtspersonen voraus. Ohne Grundrechte kann diese private Autonomie jedoch nicht gewährleistet werden. Hieraus folgt, dass die demokratische Volkssouveränität den rechtsstaatlichen Schutz von Grundrechten braucht. Das ist die eine Seite. Dass Grundrechte hingegen imstande sind, die private Autonomie von Individuen angemessen zu berücksichtigen, setzt eine kollektive Teilnahme an der politischen Öffentlichkeit voraus. Denn ohne die Ausübung von kommunikativen Freiheiten wäre es unmöglich, den Bedürfnissen und Forderungen des Volkes bzw. dessen Minderheiten gerecht zu werden. Im Umkehrschluss heißt das, dass der Rechtsstaat ebenso die Demokratie braucht. Dieser Zusammenhang der Gleichursprünglichkeit legt nahe, dass private und öffentliche Autonomie nur im Gleichschritt verwirklicht werden können.[15]

Dass es sich um ein Modell interner Kritik handelt, kommt zum Vorschein, sobald man die abschließenden Sätze von *Faktizität und Geltung* ernst nimmt. Da charakterisiert Habermas das von ihm befürwortete Modell wie folgt:

---

11 Ebd., 665.
12 Ebd., 164.
13 Ebd., 104 f.
14 Ebd., 669 f.
15 Ebd., 671.

> Dieses [prozedurale Rechtsparadigma, R. M. B.] behält gewiß, wie der Rechtsstaat selber, einen dogmatischen Kern: die Idee der Autonomie, wonach Menschen nur in dem Maße als freie Subjekte handeln, wie sie genau den Gesetzen gehorchen, die sie sich gemäß ihren intersubjektiv gewonnenen Einsichten selber geben. „Dogmatisch" ist diese Idee freilich nur in einem unverfänglichen Sinne. Denn in dieser Idee spricht sich eine Spannung von Faktizität und Geltung aus, die mit dem Faktum der sprachlichen Verfassung soziokultureller Lebensformen „gegeben", d. h. *für uns*, die wir einer solchen Lebensform unsere Identität ausgebildet haben, unhintergehbar ist.[16]

Wohlgemerkt, Habermas' Auffassung kommunikativer Freiheit schließt nicht aus, dass die Rechtssubjekte in öffentlichen Diskursen ihre unterschiedlichen Verständnisse von Autonomie hinterfragen. Zwischen der sozialen Praxis und der Norm besteht vielmehr die Möglichkeit einer reflexiven, durchaus pluralistischen Rückkopplung. Eine Diskurstheorie des demokratischen Rechtsstaats müsste also nicht unbedingt auf einem normativen Konventionalismus beruhen. In der Art und Weise, wie mit dem Spannungsverhältnis zwischen privater und öffentlicher Autonomie umgegangen wird, stößt dieses Modell jedoch an seine unhintergehbaren Grenzen. Es läuft, so meine These, auf einen *normativen Reformismus* und *institutionellen Konservatismus* hinaus. Denn Habermas' Systematik zielt nicht darauf, kraft jener Aufspaltung der Autonomie eine Transformation des bestehenden Rechts erahnen zu lassen. In Wahrheit bemüht sich er darum zu zeigen, inwiefern die institutionelle Form des demokratischen Rechtsstaats jene Aufspaltung des Subjekts überwinden kann. Im Rahmen einer prozeduralen Rechtsauffassung, welche der Gleichursprünglichkeit von Rechtsstaat und Demokratie Rechnung trägt, wird demgemäß eine rationale Versöhnung von privater und öffentlicher Autonomie nachvollziehbar.[17] Nicht umsonst gilt das Recht als „Kategorie der gesellschaftlichen Vermittlung zwischen Faktizität und Geltung".

Dabei zieht Habermas z. B. die pathologischen Wirkungen des modernen Rechts auf den Subjektivierungsprozess so gut wie nicht in Betracht. Von der frühen Kritik einer Kolonisierung oder Verrechtlichung der Lebenswelt sind allenfalls in *Faktizität und Geltung* nur nachhallende Überreste zu finden.[18] Der Frage danach, inwiefern das moderne Recht eine juridifizierte Subjektivitätsform oktroyiert, spricht der späte Habermas, wenn überhaupt, ein marginales Gewicht zu. Vor diesem Hintergrund stellt es sich als eine Errungenschaft Honneths heraus, dieses Leitmotiv der Kritischen Theorie prägnant aufgegriffen zu haben, als er die sogenannten „Pathologien rechtlicher

---

16 Ebd., 537.

17 Dass man aber aus der Einhaltung formalpragmatischer Verfahrensbedingungen nicht ohne Weiteres auf rationale Ergebnisse schließen darf, zeigt Peters, Bernhard (1991): Rationalität, Recht und Gesellschaft. Frankfurt a. M.: Suhrkamp, 260.

18 Zur Entschärfung seiner eigenen Kritik der sozialstaatlichen Materialisierung des Rechts s. Habermas (1998), 502; sowie Loick (2017), 242.

Freiheit" untersuchte. Unter „Pathologien" versteht Honneth die reflexionsfeindliche „Verabsolutierung" eines einseitigen Freiheitsverständnisses, nämlich des negativen, durch Eigentums- und Vertragsrechte definierten Freiheitsverständnisses von Rechtspersonen und deren strategischen, ja nutzenmaximierenden Einstellungen.[19] Interagieren Subjekte miteinander so, als ob sie hauptsächlich eigeninteressengeleitete Personen wären, dann liegt etwas Pathologisches vor. Denn daraus erfolgt eine Verzerrung von sittlichen Anerkennungsbeziehungen, die entsprechend in bloße Rechtsverhältnisse umschlagen.[20] Doch wie ist das genauer zu begründen?

Die allgemeine, wohl liberale Prämisse des Arguments lautet: So wie die Moral oder die Ökonomie vermag das Recht eine freiheitsverbürgende Sphäre von modern ausdifferenzierten Gesellschaften darzustellen, nur insofern als seine eigenen „Mauern" nicht überschritten werden.[21] Habermas' frühe Verrechtlichungsdiagnose hatte dieses Phänomen als eine pathologische „Ausdehnung" des Rechtsmediums in vorher nicht juridifizierte Bereiche der Lebenswelt thematisiert.[22] Nun besteht Honneths besondere Einsicht darin, jene Pathologien mit einem systematisch verzerrten Selbstverständnis des Subjekts zu identifizieren. Das bedeutet, dass die Aufspaltung der Autonomie nicht nur die anscheinend dilemmatische Art und Weise betrifft, wie das Subjekt sich gegenüber dem Recht betrachten kann, nämlich entweder als dessen Adressat oder Autor: „Die Spannung zwischen privater und öffentlicher Autonomie (…) verläuft mitten durch die Rechtspersonen hindurch".[23] Die rechtsförmige Aufspaltung des Subjekts ist also immer zugleich eine Aufspaltung *im* Subjekt und *zwischen* Subjekten. In diesem Sinne bringt jene pathologische „Überstrapazierung der rechtlichen Freiheit" einen Zustand hervor, wo Menschen von sich selbst und von deren sittlicher Welt entfremdet werden.[24] Der Gebrauch von subjektiven Rechten, deren primäre Funktion eine Sicherung der privaten Autonomie war, tendiert schließlich zu dieser pathologischen Verkehrung, sobald man vergisst, dass der eigentliche „Daseinsgrund der Privatheit" nichts anderes als die Ermöglichung einer ethisch reflektierten Beteiligung an der politischen Öffentlichkeit ist.[25]

---

19 Den Ausdruck „Verabsolutierung" hat Loick (2017), 243 ff., geprägt. Zum Begriff sozialer Pathologien bei Honneth s. nur Zurn, Christopher (2001): „Social pathologies as second-order disorders". In: Petherbridge, Danielle (Hg.): Axel Honneth. Critical Essays. Leiden: Brill Academic, 345–370.

20 Zur Kritik s. Möllers, Christoph (2015): Freiheitsgrade. Elemente einer liberalen politischen Mechanik. Berlin: Suhrkamp, 212 f.

21 Zu dieser Charakterisierung s. Walzer, Michael (1984): „Liberalism and the Art of Separation". In: *Political Theory* 12 (3), 315–330.

22 Habermas, Jürgen (1981): Theorie des kommunikativen Handels. Band 2. Zur Kritik der funktionalistischen Vernunft. Frankfurt a. M.: Suhrkamp, 522 ff.

23 Honneth (2011), 144.

24 Ebd., 160.

25 Ebd., 136 ff., 160 f. Der Ausdruck „Daseinsgrund der Privatheit" kommt von Loick (2017), 244.

Dass auch Honneth ein Modell interner Kritik vertritt, ist bereits am Anfang von *Das Recht der Freiheit* nahegelegt. Da beginnt er seine normative Rekonstruktion mit dem folgenden Satz:

> Unter all den ethischen Werten, die in der modernen Gesellschaft zur Herrschaft gelangt sind und seither um Vormachstellung konkurrieren, war nur ein einziger dazu angetan, deren institutionelle Ordnung auch tatsächlich nachhaltig zu prägen: Die Freiheit im Sinne der Autonomie des einzelnen.[26]

Die „ungeheure Sogwirkung" der Autonomie erklärt Honneth daraus, dass diese Idee wie keine andere imstande war, einen Legitimationszusammenhang zwischen dem individuellen Selbst und der gesellschaftlichen Ordnung geltend zu machen. Der Clou vom Autonomiegedanken liegt daher in dessen Fähigkeit, soziale Gerechtigkeit und die Selbstbestimmung des Individuums begrifflich so zu verknüpfen, dass beide nur im Gleichschritt verwirklicht werden können.[27] Eine angemessene Vermittlung dieser Januskopfigkeit der Autonomie, deren legales Pendant „die eigentümliche Doppelnatur der subjektiven Rechte" ausmacht, bedarf allerdings einer Verwirklichung sozialer bzw. kommunikativer Freiheit.[28] Der institutionelle Rahmen dafür ist das, was Honneth in Anlehnung an Hegel und Dewey als „demokratische Sittlichkeit" begreift. Deren höchste Sphäre ist das sogenannte „Wir" der demokratischen Willensbildung. Dazu nur zwei Anmerkungen.

Zum einen betont Honneth in seiner Rekonstruktion der demokratischen Öffentlichkeit, dass die staatliche Gewährung von individuellen Rechten der freien Meinungsäußerung und der politischen Teilnahme zwar eine notwendige, nicht aber eine hinreichende Bedingung für die Verwirklichung kommunikativer Freiheit darstellt.[29] Denn eine gleichberechtigte Ausübung dieser Freiheit verlangt, dass solche Rechte in ein breiteres Gefüge von Praktiken und Institutionen eingebettet werden. Entscheidend sind z. B. ein schichtübergreifender, mit Massenmedien ausgestatteter Kommunikationsraum, die diskursive Teilnahmebereitschaft der Staatsbürger:innen sowie die Existenz einer politischen Kultur und eines demokratischen Rechtsstaats.[30] *Zum anderen* konstatiert Honneth in den letzten Jahrzehnten eine vom Kapitalismus getriebene Krise des demokratischen Rechtsstaats. Diesem Phänomen mag nur „die Bündelung der öffentlichen Macht von Verbänden, sozialen Bewegungen und zivilen Assoziationen" entgegenwirken.[31] Solch ein staatsjenseitiger Vorschlag artikuliert sich in der folgenden, das Buch fast abschließenden These: „Der Motor und das Medium von

26 Honneth (2011), 35.
27 Ebd., 36.
28 Ebd., 132 f.
29 Ebd., 539.
30 Ebd., 540 ff.
31 Ebd., 608.

geschichtlichen Prozessen der Realisierung institutionalisierter Freiheitsprinzipien ist nicht in erster Linie das Recht, sondern sind soziale Kämpfe um deren angemessenes Verständnis und die sich daraus ergebenden Verhaltensänderungen".[32] So spannenden wie insgesamt seltenen Äußerungen zum Trotz verrät Honneths Systematik, dass sein Hauptanliegen darin besteht, die bereits erreichten normativen Verständnisse sozialer Freiheit entweder im Rahmen einer demokratischen Sittlichkeit besser zu verwirklichen oder, wenn sich ein institutioneller Verfall ergibt, mit extra-institutionellen Mitteln wiederzugewinnen.[33]

Alles zusammengerechnet handelt es sich um ein Modell der Kritik, das sowohl für einen normativen Reformismus als auch für einen institutionellen Konservatismus anfällig ist. Denn abermals kommt hier die Möglichkeit eines radikalen Bruches mit der bestehenden Form subjektiver Rechte und deren pathologischen Wirkungen so gut wie nicht in Betracht. Dafür bräuchte man ersichtlich ein Modell, das in der Lage wäre, die strukturellen Beschränkungen interner Rechtskritik zu transzendieren, indem es die Rechtsform selbst in Frage stellte – ein Modell, das nicht mehr bloße Alternativen im Recht, sondern nun eine Alternative zum Recht erahnen ließe.

3 Genealogisch-externe Kritik: Die rechtliche Verzerrung des Subjekts und ihre menschliche Überwindung

Das moderne Recht, so Menke, zeichnet sich durch den funktionalen Primat subjektiver bzw. bürgerlicher Rechte aus. Im Unterschied zu traditionellen Rechtsauffassungen, denen zufolge Rechte eher eine schiere Ableitung vom objektiven Recht darstellten, drehen sich moderne Rechtsordnungen um die Gewährleistung subjektiver Rechte überhaupt. Aus diesem Grund bezeichnet Menke das moderne Recht als „das Recht der Rechte", denn „das Recht ist jetzt *dazu da,* Rechte zu sichern".[34] Der neuzeitliche Stellenwert von subjektiven Rechten geht aber nicht ohne eine Transformation von deren *Form* einher. Hatten Rechte im Rahmen traditioneller Auffassungen die Form von Anteilen, die jeder gemäß der objektiven Ordnung des Rechts als das Seinige beanspruchen dürfte, so strukturiert sich die moderne Rechtsform eher als eine eigentümliche Art Verfügungsmacht, die völlig imstande ist, sittliche Überzeugungen auszuschließen. Insofern kann der Inhalt von diesen sittlich entbundenen Rechten nichts anderes als die vermeintlich „natürlichen" Ansprüche des Individuums sein. Allein daraus, dass subjektive Rechte private Ansprüche legalisieren, ergeben sich patholo-

32 Ebd., 613 f.
33 Eine ähnliche Kritik in Celikates, Robin (2019): „Critical Theory and the Unfinished Project of Mediating Theory and Practice". In: Gordon, Peter / Hammer, Espen / Honneth, Axel (Hg.): The Routledge Companion to the Frankfurt School. New York/London: Routledge, 206–220, hier 213–216.
34 Menke (2015), 31.

gische Phänomene sozialer Atomisierung, Naturalisierung und Entpolitisierung. Das Argument dürfte man wie folgt rekonstruieren: Moderne Subjekte, indem sie sich als Rechtsträger verstehen, betrachten sich *zum einen* als grundsätzlich vereinzelte Individuen bzw. als voneinander abgespaltene, ja eigenwillige Bürger. *Zum anderen* kommt die rechtsförmige Legalisierung von individuellen Ansprüchen weiterhin einer ideologischen Verleihung von Natürlichkeit bzw. einer Immunisierung solcher Ansprüche gegen die Möglichkeit politischer Infragestellung gleich. Nicht also erst die faktische Implementierung, sondern bereits die normative Verfasstheit der bürgerlichen Rechtsform bringt ein systematisch verzerrtes Selbstverständnis des Subjekts hervor.

Dabei vollzieht die Rechtsform eine Doppelbewegung. *Einerseits* etabliert sie innerhalb des Subjekts eine Trennung zwischen Rechten und natürlichen Ansprüchen, also eine Trennung zwischen dem Recht und dem Nichtrecht. Im Anschluss daran werden diese Ansprüche *andererseits* verrechtlicht. Das heißt, die Rechtsform erlegt sich selbst dem Nichtrecht auf. An dieser Stelle geht Menkes Kritik allerdings so weit, dass er die Legalisierung des Natürlichen auch als eine „ontologische Gewalt" beschreibt, die jedem Recht innewohnen muss.[35] Der Grund für dieses schicksalhafte Moment der rechtlichen Gewalt liegt nämlich darin, dass ein gewalt- und somit kraftloses Recht nicht dessen herrschaftsregulierende Funktion zu erfüllen vermöchte. Obwohl Loicks Ansatz sich von Menkes gerade dadurch unterscheidet, dass ersterer die Möglichkeit eines gewaltlosen Rechts nicht nur nicht ausschließt, sondern ebenfalls anvisiert, sind beide Autoren doch in ihrer Diagnose einstimmig. „Das Recht", so lautet Loicks Juridismuskritik in Anlehnung an Hegel, „fabriziert Subjekte, die ideologisch verblendet, affektiv verarmt, kommunikativ ausgedörrt und politisch passiviert sind."[36] Mit anderen Worten, ein rechtsförmiges Selbstverständnis verursacht *erstens* eine ideologische Verschleierung unserer konstitutiven Sozialität und gegenseitigen Abhängigkeiten, *zweitens* eine emotionale Abkapselung des Individuums zugunsten instrumenteller, ja verdinglichender Einstellungen zueinander und zu sich selbst, *drittens* eine Entlastung von diskursiven Rechtfertigungspflichten bezüglich unserer privaten Ansprüche, weshalb eine Zirkulation schlechter Gründe systematisch ausgelöst wird, und *viertens* eine Neutralisierung, Domestizierung oder Pazifizierung von potenziell revolutionären Forderungen, sobald diese sich der normativen Zwangsjacke von subjektiven Rechten bedienen, die ihrer Form nach mit einer normalisierenden Staatsgebundenheit behaftet sind.

Die These, dass beiden Ansätzen ein Modell genealogischer und somit externer Kritik zugrunde liegt, möchte ich in zwei Schritten untermauern. Versteht man *einerseits* Genealogie als eine im etymologischen Sinne radikale Kritik, die sich mit der schwierigen Frage nach der Subjektivierung bzw. nach der Herausbildung eines „Selbst" überhaupt befasst, dann ist es leicht zu sehen, inwiefern Menke und Loick

---

35 Menke, Christoph (2018): Law and Violence. Christoph Menke in Dialogue. Manchester: Manchester University Press, 213 f.
36 Loick (2017), 54.

eine genealogische Kritik des Rechtssubjekts unternehmen.[37] Indem sie sowohl die fragwürdigen Entstehungsbedingungen als auch die pathologischen Wirkungen der Rechtssubjektivität bloßstellen, tragen beide Autoren im Umkehrschluss zu einer „Verflüssigung" des Bestehenden bei. Dadurch kristallisiert sich die moderne Rechtsform in ihrer historischen Kontingenz sowie in ihrer prinzipiellen Überwindbarkeit heraus. An dieser Stelle kommt dennoch die normative Beschränktheit genealogischer Kritik zum Vorschein. Denn diese Form der Kritik nimmt sich eine radikale Vernehmung der geltenden Maßstäbe vor, kraft derer unser rechtsförmiges Selbstverständnis strukturiert wird. Dabei ist sie allerdings kaum in der Lage, *eigene* normative Kriterien zu begründen, anhand derer sich dieses Selbstverständnis als pathologisch, defizitär oder gar problematisch identifizieren ließe.[38] Nicht zuletzt deshalb hat man Genealogie als ein gewissermaßen „parasitäres Kritikverfahren" bezeichnet.[39] Parasitär heißt in diesem Zusammenhang, dass die genealogische Unfähigkeit, eigene Kriterien konsequent zu rechtfertigen, sich in eine normative Angewiesenheit auf *andere* Kritikformen übersetzt. Gerade solche Angewiesenheit ist m. E. das Einfallstor für normative Maßstäbe, die nicht aus der Sache selbst, sondern von außen kommen (müssen). Das genealogische Modell schlägt auf diese Weise in ein externes um.

Diese Verkehrung wird umso deutlicher, wenn man *andererseits* die von Menke und Loick entworfenen Alternativen zum Recht in Betracht zieht. Am Ende seiner *Kritik der Rechte* plädiert Menke für ein „neues Recht", dessen Form natürlich nicht in bürgerlichen Rechten, sondern vielmehr in dem gründet, was er als „Gegenrechte" kennzeichnet.[40] Obwohl der Begriff „zu vage und – bewusst – unbestimmt" bleibt,[41] lässt sich Folgendes sagen: Gegenrechte sollen zur „Emanzipation des Menschen" führen, indem sie der wesentlichen „Spaltung des Subjekts" als aktiver Teilnehmer und passiver Nichtteilnehmer des Sozialen gerecht werden.[42] Im Gegensatz zur modernen Dynamik der gesetzförmigen Positivierung, Naturalisierung und Entpolitisierung von privaten Ansprüchen haben Gegenrechte demnach einer „Affirmation der Passivität"

37 Zum Begriff genealogischer Kritik s. Saar, Martin (2007): Genealogie als Kritik. Geschichte und Theorie des Subjekts nach Nietzsche und Foucault. Frankfurt a. M.: Campus.

38 Vgl. bereits Peters (1991), 154.

39 Honneth (2007), 63.

40 Inwiefern der moderne Begriff der Rechte nicht nur die subjektiv-bürgerlichen, sondern auch die Gegenrechte umfasst, weil Letztere ebenfalls die „Grundoperation" der modernen Rechtsform, nämlich die „Selbstreflexion des Rechts" vollziehen, ist eine interessante Frage, die ich leider hier nicht behandeln kann. S. Menke (2015), 101. Aber selbst wenn das so wäre, das heißt wenn Menke mit den Gegenrechten vorhätte, eher eine „rettende Kritik" des modernen Rechts zu betreiben, würde dies nicht ohne Weiteres die These widerlegen, dass den genealogisch-externen Strukturmomenten bei ihm ein theoretisches Übergewicht zukommt. Den Hinweis auf diese Herausforderung verdanke ich Simon Kneip.

41 Forst, Rainer (2018): „Das Recht der Negativität". In: Khurana, Thomas / Quadflieg, Dirk / Raimondi, Francesca / Rebentisch, Juliane / Setton, Dirk (Hg.): Negativität. Kunst, Recht, Politik. Berlin: Suhrkamp, 196–206, hier 199.

42 Menke (2015), 367, 397.

Rechnung zu tragen, sodass die negative Kraft von passiven, etymologisch betrachtet von ästhetischen Empfindungen eine transformative Rolle in der Urteilsbildung des Subjekts spielen kann.[43] Auf diese Weise soll die schicksalhafte Gewalt des Rechts, ja die von der Rechtsform selbst getriebene Verrechtlichung der Normativität innerhalb des Subjekts eine „Entsetzung“ erfahren. Solch eine Depotenzierung der rechtlichen Normativität wird im Folgenden, für das Subjekt der Gegenrechte gemeinten Satz prägnant ausgedrückt: „[N]ichts ist Grund, alles wird zum Moment“.[44] Wie ist aber das konkret zu verstehen? Nicht unprovokativ hat Christoph Möllers Stichwörter wie „Verflüssigungsromantik“ oder „schlichten Gattungshumanismus“ geprägt, um den Tenor von diesem Ansatz zu kritisieren.[45] In der Tat erweckt die Rede von einem „neuen Menschen“, der sich Menke am Ende seiner existentiell grundlegenderen *Theorie der Befreiung* bedient, den Eindruck, dass seine Argumentation einen gewichtigen anthropologischen oder mindestens ontologischen Ballast mit sich trägt.[46]

Ähnliches mag wohl für Loick gelten, aber jedenfalls nicht ohne theoretische Vorbehalte. Am Ende von *Juridismus* wird beispielhaft der Ausblick für ein „postjuridisches Recht“ erarbeitet. Es ist zwar auffällig, dass Loick ebenfalls anthropologische Redewendungen wie „das menschliche Dasein des Gesetzes“ oder „menschliches Recht“ benutzt, um seinen Vorschlag einer *„radikalen Transformation von Recht“* auszubuchstabieren.[47] Die Idee eines ethisch gehaltvollen Rechts bzw. einer „Eu-Nomie“ wird dennoch mithilfe von sozialphilosophischen Thesen zur konstitutiven Sozialität des Menschen substantiiert. In Anlehnung an Hegel und Marx schildert Loick ein Bild der menschlichen Natur, und die Kritik weist entsprechend darauf hin, inwiefern das Recht diesem Bild nicht passt: „Anstatt den Menschen auf die Befolgung staatlicher Imperative zu fixieren, soll das Gesetz also umgekehrt die realen Bedürfnisse des Menschen in seiner Menschlichkeit zum Maß haben.“[48] Dieser Begriff des Menschlichen ist jedoch deshalb plausibel, weil es nicht essentialistisch, sondern vielmehr formal begründet wird: „Was der Mensch ist, kann nicht im Vorhinein festgelegt werden, sondern ist Ergebnis menschlicher Selbstbestimmung.“[49] Nicht zuletzt anhand der jüdischen Tradition konturiert Loick schließlich drei emanzipatorische Eigenschaften von

43 Ebd., 365, 399 ff.
44 Ebd., 380.
45 So etwa Möllers, Christoph (2018): „Herr, Knecht und Maschine in der künftigen Rechtsphilosophie“. In: Khurana, Thomas / Quadflieg, Dirk / Raimondi, Francesca / Rebentisch, Juliane / Setton, Dirk (Hg.): Negativität. Kunst, Recht, Politik. Berlin: Suhrkamp, 184–195, hier 195.
46 Ester, Marvin / Maruy van den Broek, Rodrigo (2023): „Christoph Menke: Theorie der Befreiung“. In: Zeitschrift für philosophische Literatur 11 (1), 24–35, insb. 32 ff.
47 Loick (2017), 295, 330, 18.
48 Ebd., 297.
49 Ebd., 301. Trotzdem stellt sich die Frage, ob der von Honneth bereits identifizierte Verdacht eines „allzufreundlichen, harmonischen Menschenbildes“ hinter Loicks Zurückweisung jeglicher souveränen Staatsgewalt ebenso auf *Juridismus* zutrifft. Siehe Loick, Daniel (2012): Kritik der Souveränität. Frankfurt a. M.: Campus, 17.

einer menschlichen Rechtlichkeit, nämlich die diskursive Offenheit eines interpretativen Pluralismus, die rationale und somit zwangslose Einsehbarkeit des Gesetzes, und die universelle Möglichkeit der Mitgliedschaft in politischen Gemeinschaften ohne nationalstaatliche Grenzregimes.[50] Dadurch wäre die entsetzliche, ja pathologische Verzerrung des Rechtssubjekt auf eine menschliche Art und Weise zu überwinden.

Dass es sich hier auch um ein Modell externer Kritik handelt, könnte man aus mehreren Gründen anfechten. Die normativen Maßstäbe für ein menschliches Recht, so dürfte man in positivistischer Hinsicht gegenargumentieren, ließen sich dadurch intern rechtfertigen, dass es gerade Menschen waren, die das realexistierende Recht geschafft haben. Dieses sollte also nichts anderes als ein Recht der Menschen, durch und für die Menschen sein. Die anthropozentrischen Resonanzen hierbei mögen irritierend wirken, aber sie verraten tatsächlich ein internes Moment. Ausschlaggebender für den Verdacht einer externen Kritik ist allerdings Loicks normativ motivierte Zurückweisung und somit Vernachlässigung der weitgehenden Funktionen, die das Recht innerhalb moderner Gesellschaften ausüben muss, um minimale Bedingungen eines reproduktionsfähigen Zusammenlebens zu gewährleisten. Es ist bemerkenswert, dass der erste Absatz von *Juridismus* sich mit der Idee befasst, modernes Recht konstituiere das gesellschaftliche Integrations- und Interaktionsmedium schlechthin, dessen Rolle als politisches Steuerungsinstrument sowohl für die friedliche Vermittlung von sozialen Konflikten als auch für den Schutz der Gesellschaftsmitglieder:innen durchaus unerlässlich ist.[51] Bereits ab dem zweiten Absatz widmet sich Loick hingegen einer schonungslosen Widerlegung dieser These. Aber dabei – und das ist der springende Punkt – wird die Frage nach der Funktionalität des modernen Rechts größtenteils ausgeblendet.[52] Inwiefern bestehende Rechtsordnungen eine integrative Funktion im Rahmen ausdifferenzierter Gesellschaften erfüllen müssen, um den legitimationsbedürftigen Zwangscharakter von Rechtsnormen zu rechtfertigen, ist zum Beispiel eine ergiebige Frage, die Loick wohl aus prinzipiellen Gründen nicht behandelt. Mindestens in diesem Sinne bleibt die Kritik *der Sache gegenüber* eine äußerliche, weshalb der daraus resultierende Mangel an normativer Kraft sowie die theoretische Lücke hinsichtlich eines nachvollziehbaren Übergangs zum menschlichen Recht kaum überraschend sind.

---

50 Loick (2017), 331 f.
51 Ebd., 9.
52 Zum Vergleich s. etwa Preuß, Ulrich K. (1979): Die Internalisierung des Subjekts. Zur Funktionsweise des subjektiven Rechts. Frankfurt a. M.: Suhrkamp.

4 Zur immanenten Kritik: Die legitimationstheoretische Widersprüchlichkeit des modernen Rechts und ihre krisengetriebene Transformation

Das moderne Recht, so meine Grundthese, wird durch ein Spannungsverhältnis zwischen dessen normativen und funktionalen Legitimationsforderungen bestimmt. Bevor ich dies erläutern kann, sind zwei Anmerkungen zur Form immanenter Kritik einzuführen. *Zum einen* ähnelt immanente Kritik ihrem internen Pendant eben darin, dass beide Modi ihre Maßstäbe aus der Sache selbst herausarbeiten. Deswegen liegt ihnen eine nicht zu unterschätzende normative Kraft zugrunde. Mit ihrem externen Pendant hat immanente Kritik hingegen gemein, dass sie sich weder auf einen institutionellen Konservatismus noch auf einen normativen Reformismus beschränken muss. Das heißt, sie vermag wohl auf eine Überwindung der bestehenden Rechtsform zu zielen. *Zum anderen* dürfte solch einen Anspruch auf Transzendenz beim Modell immanenter Kritik gleichwohl nicht von außen kommen. Andernfalls würde sie ersichtlich ihrer normativen Kraft entsagen. Immanente Kritik anvisiert insofern eine Art „Transzendenz von innen" bzw. eine aus dessen eigener Widersprüchlichkeit getriebene Transformation des modernen Rechts.[53] Dabei gilt zu beachten, dass diese Widersprüchlichkeit weder etwas bloß Gegebenes noch beliebig Erfundenes sein kann. Denn immanente Kritik zielt in Wahrheit darauf, in der Sache selbst widersprüchliche Zusammenhänge *hervorzubringen*.[54] Mit „Widerspruch" ist allerdings nicht eine zu versöhnende Inkonsistenz zwischen Normen und Praktiken gemeint. Dies ist wohl ein verbreitetes Missverständnis dessen, was immanente Kritik von einer bloß internen zu unterscheiden hat.[55] Vielmehr heißt Widerspruch ein systematisch erzeugtes, ja konstitutives *„Spannungsverhältnis innerhalb einer Formation, das diese über sich selbst hinaustreiben wird."*[56] Prägnant ausgedrückt: „Immanente Kritik setzt an der *Krisenhaftigkeit* eines bestimmten sozialen Arrangements an."[57] Wie genau ist solch eine dialektische Krisenhaftigkeit des modernen Rechts nun zu begreifen?

Obschon eine ausführliche Begründung meines Arguments hier nicht geleistet werden kann, dürfte man dessen Grundlinien *programmatisch* so skizzieren: Versteht man die Rechtsform als eine Problemlösungsinstanz vis-à-vis der Rechtfertigungsbedürftigkeit von Herrschaftsverhältnissen innerhalb moderner Gesellschaften, dann

---

53 Zum Begriff Transzendenz von innen s. Habermas, Jürgen (1992): „Exkurs: Transzendenz von innen, Transzendenz ins Diesseits". In: ders.: Texte und Kontexte. Frankfurt a. M.: Suhrkamp, 127–156, hier 142, 155; sowie Habermas (1998), 30–31. Zur rechtsphilosophischen Aneignung s. Brunkhorst (2014), 316.

54 Jaeggi (2014), 286, 291 f., 300.

55 Ausdrücklich befindet sich solch eine Gleichsetzung in Loick (2017), 12, 336. Den Hinweis auf dieses Missverständnis verdanke ich Robert Ziegelmann.

56 Jaeggi (2014), 287.

57 Ebd., 292.

steht das Recht unter einem ambivalenten Legitimationsdruck.[58] *Normativ* betrachtet hat sich das moderne Recht *einerseits* dadurch zu legitimieren, dass es eine formale Möglichkeit reflexiven Wandels zulassen muss, welche sich immanent aus der demokratischen Rechtsdynamik zwischen subjektiven Rechten und der positiven Rechtsordnung zu ergeben hat.[59] Das *moderne* Recht ist insofern wandelbares, kritikfähiges Recht. *Funktional* betrachtet hat sich *andererseits* das moderne *Recht* dadurch zu legitimieren, dass es Rechtssicherheit und sittliche Kohäsion in komplex differenzierten, ja kapitalistischen Gesellschaften bewerkstelligen muss. Dies erfordert ein komplementäres Austarieren zwischen mechanischen und organischen Solidaritätsformen, die idealtypisch vom Straf- und Kooperationsrecht jeweils sanktioniert werden. Die koordinationsfähige Sanktionierung von Solidaritätsformen setzt aber voraus, dass das Recht, indem es sittliche Praktiken in einer positiven Form zum Ausdruck bringt, von diesen normativ bekräftigt wird. Das heißt, die normative Kraft der Rechtsordnung geht bis zu einem gewissen Grad auf deren Verhältnis zur Sittlichkeit zurück.[60] Dies hat dennoch die ambivalente Kehrseite, dass die Rechtsform dabei zu einer ideologischen Naturalisierung ihrer eigenen Autorität zu führen vermag. Kraft der funktionalen Positivierung von Rechtsnormen schlägt deren normative Legitimationsbedürftigkeit in einen Legitimitätsanspruch um, der sich seiner Form nach als kaum kritikfähig darstellt.[61] Das *moderne* Recht gerät also mit dem modernen *Recht* in Konflikt.[62]

Immanente Kritik versucht jedoch nicht, diese Spannung zugunsten von sozialer Integration auszutragen. Es kommt vielmehr darauf an, sie so zu begreifen und zuzuspitzen, dass sich daraus transformative Konflikte qua *Legitimationskrisen* ergeben können.[63] In der Tat scheint es der Fall zu sein, dass emanzipatorischer Wandel aufseiten der Rechtsordnung oft als eine normative Reaktion auf gesellschaftliche Legitimationskrisen erfolgt. Weil legale Emanzipationsakte aber einen gewissen Kompromiss-

---

58 Zum Legitimitätsproblem politischer Herrschaft s. etwa Hofmann, Hasso (1977): Legitimität und Rechtsgeltung: Verfassungstheoretische Bemerkungen zu einem Problem der Staatslehre und der Rechtsphilosophie. Berlin: Duncker & Humblot, 11–24.

59 Diese formal-dynamische Auffassung der rechtlichen Normativität gründet in Kelsen, Hans (2017): Reine Rechtslehre. Mit einem Anhang: Das Problem der Gerechtigkeit (Studienausgabe der 2. Auflage 1960). Hg. Jestaedt, Matthias. Tübingen: Mohr Siebeck, S. 346 ff.

60 Klassisch dazu: Durkheim, Émile (2013): De la division du travail social, Paris: Presses Universitaires de France, 117 f. Ein konziser Versuch, diesen Zusammenhang zu reaktualisieren, befindet sich in Honneth, Axel (2021): „Recht und Sittlichkeit: Aspekte eines komplexen Wechselverhältnisses". In: Forst, Rainer / Günther, Klaus (Hg.): Normative Ordnungen. Berlin: Suhrkamp, 42–73.

61 Zur Ambivalenz schriftlicher Verselbständigung von Verfassungsnormen s. Möllers, Christoph (2015): Die Möglichkeit der Normen. Über eine Praxis jenseits von Moralität und Kausalität. Berlin: Suhrkamp, 288–297.

62 Obwohl dies im Rahmen einer sehr voraussetzungsreichen Theorie sozialer Evolution eingerahmt wird, befindet sich die Idee einer „dialektischen Spannung" im Recht zwischen dem Normativen und dem Funktionalen bereits in Brunkhorst (2014), 38.

63 Zur Begriffsbestimmung s. Brunkhorst, Hauke (2012). Legitimationskrisen: Verfassungsprobleme der Weltgesellschaft. Baden-Baden: Nomos, 21–46.

charakter zwischen den normativen und funktionalen Legitimationsforderungen des modernen Rechts haben, verwundert es kaum, dass erstere mit sozialen Rückschlägen einhergehen.[64] Aus dem Versuch, gesellschaftliches Unrecht durch Recht zu überwinden, ergeben sich im Rechtsmedium neue Formen des Unrechts. Dieser moderne Widerspruch lässt sich allerdings im Recht weder versöhnen noch auflösen. Es macht vielmehr den immanenten Zusammenhang aus, innerhalb dessen die reale Möglichkeit einer „Transzendenz von innen" artikuliert werden muss.

Dies erfordert *schließlich* eine Auseinandersetzung mit sozialen Praktiken, Bewegungen und Kämpfen, die sich aktiv darum bemühen, das geltende Recht radikal zu verändern. Eine Schlüsselkategorie hier wäre z. B. die vom zivilen Ungehorsam, dessen Begriff sich gerade als eine emanzipatorische Reaktion auf rechtliche Legitimationsdefizite deuten lässt.[65] Weil ziviler Ungehorsam ein Rechtsbruch bzw. eine Form von „Unrecht" ist, die aber den eigenen Legitimitätsanspruch des modernen Rechts einzulösen hat, stellt es eine Alternative dar, um widersprüchliche Zusammenhänge hervorzubringen. Aus der Perspektive einer immanenten Kritik wäre also ziviler Ungehorsam, wenn nicht der, dann doch wenigstens ein dialektisch aufschlussreicher Weg dazu, im Recht Alternativen zum Recht zu schaffen. Wie das konkret aussehen wird und ob daraus eher reformistische oder revolutionäre Transformationen entspringen werden, sind umkämpfte Fragen, welche in der Praxis selbst ausgehandelt werden müssen. Immanente Rechtskritik hat sich insofern an der Schnittstelle zwischen Theorie und Praxis zu verwirklichen.

Zur Person: Rodrigo Maruy van den Broek ist wissenschaftlicher Mitarbeiter am Lehrstuhl für Praktische Philosophie und Sozialphilosophie der Humboldt-Universität zu Berlin. Er promoviert im Rahmen des Graduiertenkollegs 2638 „Normativität – Kritik – Wandel". Seine Dissertation untersucht das Verhältnis von Recht und Emanzipation in modernen Gesellschaften aus der Perspektive der Kritischen Theorie.

Rodrigo Maruy van den Broek
rodrigo.maruy@hu-berlin.de.

---

64 Man denke nur an die Abschaffung der Sklaverei als eine Vorbedingung kapitalistischer Ausbeutung. Weitere historische Beispiele in Koselleck, Reinhart (2006): „Grenzverschiebungen der Emanzipation. Eine begriffsgeschichtliche Skizze", in: ders.: Begriffsgeschichten. Berlin: Suhrkamp, 182–202.

65 So etwa Celikates, Robin (2016): „Democratizing civil disobedience". In: Philosophy & Social Criticism 42/10, 982–994.

Kommunistisches Recht – ein Oxymoron?*

D. E. H. JACOBS

Communist Law – an Oxymoron?

Abstract: Form the viewpoint of orthodox Marxism the notion of "Communist Law" can be rejected as an oxymoron. Since law is equated with violent enforcement, it must wither away in a communist society. This standard position shall be challenged, arguing that law itself implies a utopian aspect which might mediate the establishment of a classless society. My core claim is, that if law is defined as the negation of violence and if Marx critique of capitalism implies a broader notion of violence, then "Communist Law" can be perceived as establishing the necessary conditions of a society free from all domination.
Keywords: Communism, Oxymoron, Utopia, Freedom, Natural Law, Marxism.

1 Einleitung

Hat selbst ein Verein freier Menschen noch eine Verfassung? Kann Marx Ausspruch – „Jeder nach seinen Fähigkeiten, jedem nach seinen Bedürfnissen!"[1] – als Rechtsprinzip gelten? Gibt es ein Recht, welches das Absterben des Staates garantiert? Fragen wie diese müssen im Rahmen marxistischer Orthodoxie als Affront gelten. Am prominentesten durch Friedrich Engels[2], Vladimir Ilitsch Lenin[3] und Eugen Paschukanis[4] vertreten dominiert bis heute die These vom Absterben des Rechts die innermarxistische Diskussion. Recht wird einerseits als Instrument der Klassenherrschaft (Engels, Le-

* Der folgende Text basiert teilweiße auf meiner an der University of Chicago verfassten Masterarbeit „On the Paradox oft he Law".

1 Marx, Karl (1973), MEW 19: 21.

2 Engels, Friedrich / Kautsky, Karl, MEW 21: 491–509.

3 Lenin, Wladimir Iljitsch (1972): „Staat und Revolution" (Erstdruck 1918). In: Ders.: Lenin Werke. Berlin: Karl Dietz Verlag, Band 25: 393–507.

4 Paschukanis, Eugen (2003): Allgemeine Rechtslehre und Marxismus. Versuch einer Kritik der juristischen Grundbegriffe. Freiburg: Ça Ira.

nin), und anderseits als Strukturanalog zur Warenform (Paschukanis) begriffen, weshalb die Überwindung des Kapitalismus zugunsten einer klassenfreien Gesellschaft zugleich die Abschaffung eines jeden Rechts impliziert. Die Möglichkeit eines „Kommunistischen Rechts" kann entsprechend als Oxymoron abgetan werden.

Postkapitalistisches Recht dennoch zu thematisieren, riskiert einen Tabubruch. Entscheidender als die Infragestellung marxistischer Klassiker ist, dass Kommunistisches Recht die Utopie eines „Vereins freier Menschen"[5] selbst zu unterminieren droht. Im Zentrum orthodox-marxistischer Rechtskritik steht die These, dass Recht immer an seine gewaltsame Durchsetzung gebunden bleibt. Somit würde selbst Kommunistisches Recht eine soziale Hierarchie implizieren, die unweigerlich in eine neue Form der Herrschaft umschlagen muss. Die Annahme eines Kommunistischen Rechts erscheint entsprechend nicht bloß als eine contradictio in adiecto, sondern als Frontalangriff auf die kommunistische Utopie schlechthin. Das scheinbar pragmatische Zugeständnis, dass es auch in einer postkapitalistischen Gesellschaft noch irgendeiner Form des Rechts bedarf, verleugnet den radikalen Anspruch auf Befreiung. Die These vom Absterben des Rechts bleibt hingegen dem Imperativ treu, jeder Herrschaft von Menschen über Menschen ein Ende zu setzten.

Der unbedingte Wille auf dem Anspruch der Herrschaftsfreiheit zu beharren, läuft allerdings Gefahr die Frage nach der praktischen Umsetzbarkeit herrschaftsfreier Sozietät zu übergehen. Dem entspricht eine Tendenz an Utopie nur um den Preis ihrer Entrückung in eine unerreichbare Ferne festzuhalten. Utopismus verkommt selbst zur Stütze falscher Verhältnisse, fällt der projizierte Begriff der Befreiung so „radikal" aus, dass dessen Verwirklichung zugleich als Ding der Unmöglichkeit erscheint. Die These vom Absterben des Rechts droht das Schicksal eines solchen „Vulgärradikalismus" zu erleiden, insofern mindestens zwei Aspekte ausgemacht werden können, die Recht im Zuge des Übergangs zu einer befreiten Gesellschaft als praktische Notwendigkeit erscheinen lassen.

Ernstgenommen werden muss zunächst, dass ein Leben ohne Recht und Staat nur noch den wenigsten als realistische oder auch nur erstrebenswerte Perspektive erscheint. Das „Rechtssubjekt" hat sich unter dem Druck der bestehenden Verhältnisse als Grundzug jeglicher Subjektivität festgesetzt.[6] Ermächtigt die Form subjektiver Rechte den Einzelnen als Subjekt, so bleibt dieser zugleich an das Recht als seine zweite Natur gekettet. Freie Subjektivität jenseits von Recht und Staat entzieht sich somit zunehmend der politischen Vorstellungskraft. Diesem Vorbehalt kann einerseits die Kraft der Sozialisation entgegengesetzt werden: Der radikalen Neugestaltung gesellschaftlicher Verhältnisse entspricht zugleich die Möglichkeit eines „neuen Menschen".

---

5 Marx, Karl (1962), MEW 23, 92.

6 Zur subjektivierenden Kraft des Rechts siehe: Menke, Christoph (2018): Kritik der Rechte. Berlin: Suhrkamp Verlag. Sowie: Loick, Daniel (2020): Juridismus. Konturen einer kritischen Theorie des Rechts. Berlin: Suhrkamp Verlag.

Ausschlaggebend ist jedoch, dass der Übergang zum Neuen immer noch durch den „alten Menschen“ vollzogen werden muss. Zählt Recht zu dessen zweiter Natur, so kann zumindest während einer Übergangsphase nicht auf Recht verzichtet werden. Einer „Übergangsphase“ scheint die praktische Notwendigkeit eines „Übergangsrecht“ zu entsprechen.

Zweitens verweist der Gedanke eines „Übergangsrechts“ auf ein tieferliegendes revolutionstheoretisches Paradox: Soll der revolutionäre Bruch ein für alle Mal Gewaltverhältnissen ein Ende setzen, so erscheint es als grundlegend problematisch, dass gerade die Revolution nicht auf Gewalt verzichten kann.[7] Kann gewährleistet werden, dass revolutionäre Gewalt tatsächlich jeder Gewalt ein Ende setzt? Ohne entsprechende Konzepte droht der revolutionäre Bruch lediglich einen Gewaltexzess zu initiieren, dessen Resultat nur eine neue Form der Herrschaft sein kann. Recht erscheint als mögliche Antwort für diese Problemstellung: Kodifiziert Recht tatsächlich die Bedingungen der Möglichkeit gewaltfreier Sozietät, so müsste der revolutionären Durchsetzung des Rechts, die Etablierung gesellschaftlicher Verhältnisse entsprechen, die auf kurz oder lang jeglicher Gewalt entsagen können. Zweifelsohne kann diese These hier noch nicht als erwiesen gelten. Angemerkt werden muss allerdings, dass der marxistische Rechtsnihilismus von vornherein die Möglichkeit verstellt den Rechtsgedanken revolutionstheoretisch zu wenden. Impliziert Recht immer Herrschaft, so kann auch der Übergang in einen herrschaftsfreien Zustand nicht rechtsförmig vermittelt werden. Es folgt, dass der Staat – welcher gemäß der marxschen Tradition während einer Übergangsphase erhalten bleibt – kein Rechtsstaat sein kann.[8] Die Identifikation von Recht mit nackter Gewalt rächt sich in der Form sozialistischer Willkürherrschaft.[9]

Diese Konsequenz zu vermeiden rechtfertig über die Möglichkeit eines kommunistischen Rechts nachzudenken. Der These vom Absterben des Rechts als Voraussetzung für eine herrschaftsfreie Gesellschaft steht die Einschätzung entgegen, dass auf Recht zur praktischen Verwirklichung eben jenes Zieles nicht verzichtet werden kann. Das Oxymoron „Kommunistisches Recht“ ist somit nicht als reine Begriffsverwirrung abzutun, sondern Ausdruck einer konkreten historischen Problemstellung: Wie kann

---

7 Die Notwendigkeit revolutionärer Gewalt ergibt sich aus der Bestimmung von Herrschaft als Gewaltverhältnis. Wird Herrschaft immer schon durch Gewalt aufrechterhalten, so ist dies erst recht der Fall, wenn sie ernsthaft herausgefordert wird.

8 Gunnar Hindrichs macht darauf aufmerksam, dass der revolutionäre Staat, obgleich kein Rechtsstaat, dennoch kein Unrechtsstaat sein muss. Stattdessen gilt es diesen als „Rechtsaufhebungsstaat“ zu erfassen. Dem Anspruch nach ist dies zutreffend: Ein Staat ist nur dann revolutionär, wenn er die Notwendigkeit zur Durchsetzung des Rechts (und somit sich selbst) aufhebt. Problematisch ist hingegen, wenn keinerlei Konzepte vorhanden sind, welche eine solche Selbstaufhebung des Staates garantieren. Im Folgenden soll gezeigt werden, dass eine rechtsphilosophische Wendung der Idee des Kommunismus diesen Missstand behebt. Hindrichs, Gunnar (2017): Philosophie der Revolution. Berlin: Suhrkamp Verlag, 134.

9 Christine Sypnowich Darstellung der stalinistische Rechtspraxis erlaubt diese als konsequenten Ausdruck der marxschen Reduktion von Recht auf ein Herrschaftsinstrument zu begreifen. Sypnowich, Christine (1990): The Concept of Socialist Law. Oxford: Oxford University Press, 46–58.

Herrschaft überwunden werden, ohne diese zu reproduzieren? Gelingt die Konzeption eines „Kommunistischen Rechts", so ist ein Lösungsansatz für diese Frage vorhanden. Dem entspricht die Aufgabe ein Recht zu denken, welches die notwendigen Bedingungen von Herrschaftsfreiheit kodifiziert und gerade so den Übergang zu einer klassenfreien Gesellschaft vermittelt. Recht muss als Vermittlungsinstanz radikaler Befreiung begriffen werden.

Im Folgenden soll, der im Anspruch und Umfang limitierte Versuch unternommen werden, dieser Herausforderung gerecht zu werden. Intendiert ist die Möglichkeit einer rechtsphilosophischen Wendung der kommunistischen Idee aufzuweisen, ohne diese zugleich zu entfalten. Gleichsam kann keine systematische Rekonstruktion marxistischer Rechtskritik geleistet werden.[10] Ob Marx Rechtskritik tatsächlich jeder Form des Rechts eine Absage erteilt oder selbst – ex-negativo – auf eine neue Form des Rechts verweist muss unbeantwortet bleiben. Stattdessen gilt es den positiven Ausgangspunkt einer genuin marxistischen Theorie postkapitalistischen Rechts auszumachen. Erschlossen werden soll eine neue Möglichkeit kreativ an Marx Werk anzuknüpfen, welche weder durch Marx selbst noch durch die marxistische Tradition wahrgenommen wurde. Eine solche Denkbewegung mit Marx gegen Marx und über Marx hinaus, erscheint gerechtfertigt, gelingt es Lösungsansätze für jene praktischen Problemstellungen zu finden, die sich im Zuge vergangener Befreiungsversuche als fatal erwiesen haben.

2 Recht als Negation von Gewalt

Meine erste These lautet, dass bereits der frühneuzeitliche Anspruch auf eine rationale Rechtfertigung des Rechts ein utopisches Moment birgt, dessen Radikalisierung die Möglichkeit eines kommunistischen Rechts eröffnet.[11] Kurz umrissen kann dieser Gedanke wie folgt erfasst werden: Nicht mehr die Gewalt des Souveräns, sondern freie Zustimmung basierend auf rationaler Einsicht legitimiert das Recht. Die Heteronomie der Herrschaft soll durch die Autonomie der vereinten Bürgerschaft ersetzt werden. Dieser legitimationstheoretische Ansatz rückt den Willen ins Zentrum der Aufmerksamkeit: Recht ist dann legitim, wenn es durch einen auf seine eigenen Voraussetzungen reflektierenden Willen gewollt werden kann. Ex-negativo wird so das bestimmende Prinzip des Rechts als Negation von Gewalt definiert.[12] Da der Wille nicht seine

---

10 Für eine systematisierenden Überblick siehe: Buckel, Sonja (2015): Subjektivierung und Kohäsion: Zur Rekonstruktion einer materialistischen Theorie des Rechts. Weilerswist: Velbrück Wissenschaft.

11 Die Möglichkeit einer genuin marxistischen Rechtsphilosophie als Radikalisierung klassischen Naturrechts hat bereits Hans Kelsen angedeutet. Kelsen, Hans (1955): The Communist Theory of Law. London: Stevens & Sons Limited, 105.

12 Die Bestimmung des Recht als Negation von Gewalt hervorzuheben ist ein wesentliches Verdienst von Christoph Menke: „Law begins with the experience of violence. Law exists because there is violence, and

eigene Unterwerfung wollen kann, ist nur jenes Recht legitim, dass Gewalt radikal negiert. Die Zustimmung zum Recht kann somit auch als Affirmation der Konstitutionsbedingungen des eigenen Willens erfasst werden. Im Rechtsbruch unterminiert der Wille hingegen seine eigenen Voraussetzungen.

Gleichwohl die Entgegensetzung von Recht und Gewalt als ein Grundzug frühneuzeitlicher Rechtsphilosophie ausgemacht werden kann, soll im Folgenden Hegels *Grundlinien der Philosophie des Rechts* als Beispiel dienen. Hegel affirmiert Recht als Negation von Gewalt, indem er das Rechtssystem als „Reich der verwirklichten Freiheit"[13] bestimmt, dessen „Ausgangspunkt der Wille"[14] ist:

> Weil der Wille, nur insofern er Dasein hat, Idee oder wirklich frei und das Dasein, in welches er sich gelegt hat, Sein der Freiheit ist, so zerstört Gewalt oder Zwang in ihrem Begriff sich unmittelbar selbst, als Äußerung eines Willens, welche die Äußerung oder Dasein eines Willens aufhebt. Gewalt oder Zwang ist daher, abstract genommen unrechtlich.[15]

Gewalt wird als Willensakt bestimmt, welcher das Dasein eines anderen Willens negiert. Hegel begreift diese willentliche Negation eines Willens als begrifflichen Selbstwiderspruch: Da der Wille des Einzelnen nur durch die harmonische Übereinstimmung mit dem Willen aller Mitbürger dauerhaft Bestand haben kann, negiert der Wille zur Gewalt in letzter Konsequenz sich selbst.[16] Hegel zieht hieraus den Schluss, dass die gewaltsame Durchsetzung des Rechts legitim ist, um die allgemeinen Ermöglichungsbedingung des freien Willens zu gewährleisten:

> Der Zwang hat davon, daß er sich in seinem Begriffe zerstört, die reelle Darstellung darin, daß Zwang durch Zwang aufgehoben wird; er ist daher nicht nur bedingt rechtlich, sondern notwendig – nämlich als zweiter Zwang, der eine Aufhebung eines ersten Zwangs ist.[17]

Die Gewalt des Staates negiert die Gewalt des Rechtsbruchs. Entsprechend besteht die Rechtfertigung der Staatsgewalt darin die notwendigen Bedingungen von Gewaltfreiheit abzusichern. Ungeklärt bleibt allerdings, warum es überhaupt zum Rechts-

---

because recognizing the existence of violence appears to be tantamount to saying that violence should not exist. ‚Pain says: ‚Refrain! Away, you pain!'' This is the underlying drive behind law. Its raison d'être is to fight against the violence which one inflicts upon another." Menke, Christoph (2018): A Reply to my Critics. In: Ders.: Law and Violence: Christoph Menke in Dialogue. Manchester: Manchester University Press, 207.

13 Hegel, Georg Wilhelm Friedrich (2009): „Grundlinien der Philosophie des Rechts. Naturrecht und Staatswissenschaft im Grundrisse" (1820/21). In: Ders.: Gesammelte Werke. Hg. Grotsch, Klaus / Weisser-Lohmann, Elisabeth. Hamburg: Felix Meiner Verlag, Band: 14,1: 14.

14 Hegel (2009), 14.

15 Ebd., 92.

16 Diese These eingehender zu entfalten, bedürfte eine Auseinandersetzung mit dem Verhältnis Hegels zur kontraktualistischen Tradition. Siehe hierzu: Neuhouser, Frederick (2000): Foundations of Hegel's Social Theory: Actualizing Freedom. Cambridge Massachusetts: Harvard University Press.

17 Hegel (2009), 92.

bruch kommen muss. Die von Hegel proklamierte Notwendigkeit rechtlichen Zwangs scheint die Unvermeidbarkeit des Rechtsbruchs stillschweigend vorauszusetzen. Diese Annahme steht jedoch in einem eklatanten Gegensatz zur legitimationstheoretischen Begründung des Rechts: Harmoniert die Rechtsordnung tatsächlich mit dem rational reflektierten Willen eines jeden Einzelnen, so müssten Bürger_innen von sich aus und ohne der Androhung eines äußeren Zwanges im Einklang mit dem Gesetz leben. Rationale Einsicht und nicht Zwang entspräche dem Fundament der Rechtsordnung.

Nimmt man diesen Gedanken ernst, so entspricht der Verwirklichung des Rechts nicht der Rechtfertigung des Staates, sondern dessen Überwindung. Zumindest die repressive Funktion des Staates erscheint als überflüssig, sobald davon ausgegangen werden kann, dass Recht seinem eigenen rationalen Anspruch gerecht wird. Im Kern des Rechts findet sich somit ein anarchistisches Moment, dessen utopische Kraft weit über den Horizont der bestehenden Verhältnisse hinausweist. Das überraschende Resultat einer „Rechtsutopie", wirft allerdings die Frage auf warum die Vision eines Rechts ohne Staat ganz und gar nicht unserer Lebensrealität entspricht. Drei mögliche Antworten müssen hier in Betracht gezogen werden:

1. Der Mensch ist schlecht: Sowohl im Rahm der politischen Philosophie sowie für den Alltagsverstand kann die verkommene Natur des Menschen als populärster Ansatz gelten, um zu klären, warum es dem Menschen nicht gelingt aus freien Stücken im Einklang mit dem Recht zu leben. Auch wenn nicht geleugnet werden kann, dass der Mensch vernunftbegabt ist, so erweist sich dessen Vernunft dennoch niemals als hinreichend, um ein wahrhaft vernünftiges Recht zu affirmieren.
2. Das Recht ist Paradox: Erfordert die Form des Rechts seine eigene gewaltsame Durchsetzung, so unterminiert Recht seinen Zweck Gewalt zu unterbinden. Die Gewalt des Rechts gilt entsprechend nicht als „zweiter Zwang", welcher die Bedingungen gewaltfreier Sozietät garantiert und entsprechend auch ausbleiben könnte, sobald das Recht aus freien Stücken affirmiert werden würde. Stattdessen ist Recht selbst Quelle und Ursprung der Gewalt, insofern Recht soziale Verhältnisse konstituiert, welche die gewaltsame Durchsetzung des Rechts erfordern.
3. Das bestehende Recht ist illegitim: Das Scheitern des Rechts kann als Ausdruck einer konkreten historischen Gesellschaftsformation begriffen werden. Statt auf zeitlose Bestimmungen des „Menschen" oder des „Rechts" zu verweisen, ist das Ausbleiben gewaltfreier Sozietät durch die unzureichende historische Verwirklichung des Rechtsbegriffs zu erklären. Die Verwirklichung eines Rechts, welches seinem eigenen Anspruch entspricht, bleibt somit weiterhin ausständig und kann als konkrete politische Herausforderung begriffen werden.

Unter den drei Antwortmöglichkeiten erlaubt lediglich letztere am Anspruch des Rechts festzuhalten. Diese Intention teilend, werde ich im Folgenden argumentieren, dass das Scheitern des Rechts weder der Natur des Menschen noch der Rechtsform selbst, sondern deren Konstitution unter kapitalistischen Bedingungen anzulasten ist. Kann die Diskrepanz zwischen der Realität und dem Begriff des Rechts als Pathologie der kapitalistischen Gesellschaftsformation ausgewiesen werden, so muss in Betracht gezogen werden, dass die Utopie des Rechts durch postkapitalistisches Recht eingelöst werden kann.

3 Hegels Pöbel

Meine zweite These lautet, dass bereits die Diskussion des Pöbels in Hegels *Grundlinien der Philosophie des Rechts* – publiziert 1820 – den Selbstwiderspruch des Rechts unter kapitalistischen Bedingungen zum Ausdruck bringt. Erfasst wird das Phänomen, dass die bürgerlich-kapitalistische Eigentumsordnung seine eigenen „Kriminellen" produziert und somit selbst zur gewaltsamen Durchsetzung des Rechts nötigt. Von einem „Paradox des Rechts" kann also insofern die Rede sein, als die sich im Rechtsbruch offenbarende Verkommenheit des Menschen selbst Produkt der Rechtsordnung ist. Erklärungsansätze, welche das Scheitern des Rechts auf die menschliche Natur oder die Rechtsform ansich zurückführen, können unter Verweis auf Hegels Pöbels als Naturalisierungen einer konkreten historischen Gesellschaftsformation zurückgewiesen werden.

Die Problematik des Pöbels kann ausgehend von Hegels Konzeption der Sittlichkeit rekonstruiert werden. Bestimmt als „das lebendige Gute"[18] gilt Sittlichkeit als die soziale Verwirklichung einer ausgeglichenen „Einheit des Begriffs des Willens und des besonderen Willens."[19] Die Subjektivität des Einzelnen kann entsprechend nicht der gesellschaftlichen Allgemeinheit untergeordnet, sondern muss durch diese vermittelt und erhalten werden. Hegel geht jedoch noch einen Schritt weiter: Die sittliche Einheit des allgemeinen und des einzelnen Willens erfordert die Allgemeinheit selbst temporär zu suspendieren, um dem Einzelnen zu ermöglichen ungehemmt seinen egoistischen Interessen nachzugehen.[20] Dem entspricht die Sphäre der „bürgerlichen Gesellschaft" – ein Art Prototyp der kapitalistischen Gesellschaft – in welcher lediglich die bürgerlichen Eigentumsordnung die Willkür des Einzelnen begrenzt. Individuelle Selbstverwirklichung durch Arbeit ist somit als wesentliches Moment hegelscher Sittlichkeit anerkannt.

---

18 Hegel (2009), 156.
19 Ebd., 125.
20 Ebd., 188.

Die Schattenseite der hegelschen Affirmation individueller Willkür ist, dass die Ökonomie der bürgerlichen Gesellschaft insgesamt unter dem Vorzeichen der Zufälligkeit steht. Gleichwohl als „System allseitiger Abhängigkeit"[21] eine neue Form der gesellschaftlichen Allgemeinheit entsteht, bleibt weitgehend kontingent, wie und ob der Einzelne an dieser Allgemeinheit partizipiert. Ein Zusammenspiel aus unglücklichen Zufällen, natürlichen Unterschieden und der ökonomischen Eigendynamik der bürgerlichen Gesellschaft, führt schließlich zur Spaltung der Gesellschaft in Arm und Reich und zur Erzeugung des Pöbels:

> Das Herabsinken einer großen Masse unter das Maaß einer gewissen Subsistenzweise […] und damit zum Verlust des Gefühls des Rechts, der Rechtfertigung und der Ehre, durch eigene Tätigkeit und Arbeit zu bestehen – bringt die Erzeugung des Pöbels hervor […][22]

Ausschlaggebend ist nicht allein die Armut des Pöbels, sondern der mit einem gewissen Grad materieller Verelendung einhergehende Verlust des sittlichen Anspruchs auf individuelle Selbstverwirklichung durch Arbeit. Zugleich produziert gerade die ungehemmte Realisation desselben sittlichen Prinzips – der Selbstverwirklichung durch Arbeit – jene Armut, welche einem Teil der Gesellschaft vom sittlichen Versprechen der bürgerlichen Gesellschaft ausschließt. Im Pöbel offenbart sich somit tatsächlich der Selbstwiderspruch des bürgerlich-kapitalistischen Rechts: Der für den Pöbel charakteristische „Verlust des Gefühls des Rechts" ist keinesfalls Ausdruck einer in der menschlichen Natur angelegten Verkommenheit, sondern Effekt des Scheiterns des Rechts an seinem eigenen sittlichen Anspruch. Negiert der Pöbel das Recht, so lediglich aufgrund der Negation des Pöbels durch das Recht.

Nichtsdestotrotz erlaubt Hegels Pöbel am rationalen Kern des modernen Rechtsgedankens festzuhalten. Dies erfordert jedoch dessen Radikalisierung. Die „Utopie des Rechts" harrt der Einlösung durch postkapitalistisches Recht.

4 Marx' Begriff der Gewalt

Meine dritte These lautet, dass Marx Kritik des Kapitalismus als Herrschaftsverhältnis einen umfassenderen Begriff der Gewalt impliziert, dessen Negation eine rechtsphilosophische Wendung der kommunistischen Idee ermöglicht. Dieser Gedanke kann in Absetzung zur hegelschen Rechtsphilosophie entfaltet werden. Bleibt es umstritten, ob für Hegel das Phänomen des Pöbels eine strenge Notwendigkeit darstellt, so steht

---

21 Ebd., 187.
22 Ebd., 232.

dies für Marx außer Frage.[23] Die Möglichkeit von Mehrwertproduktion und somit der Kapitalakkumulation erfordert, dass ein erheblicher Teil der Gesellschaft keine andere Wahl hat, als die eigene Arbeitskraft zu verkaufen. Diese Voraussetzungen reproduzierend, entspricht die Entlohnung der Arbeit lediglich den zur alltäglichen Reproduktion notwendigen Lebensmitteln, ohne jedoch jemals vom Zwang zur Lohnarbeit zu entbinden. Relative Armut ist somit keine Anomalie der bürgerlichen Gesellschaft, sondern Voraussetzung sowie Resultat der kapitalistischen Ökonomie.

Diese Verschiebung von Hegel zu Marx markiert einen Unterschied ums Ganze: Die Notwendigkeit des Ausschlusses eines Teils der Gesellschaft von dessen sittlichen Versprechen stellt die Legitimität der kapitalistischen Rechtsordnung grundsätzlich in Frage. Die ausbleibende Vermittlung des einzelnen Willens mit dessen allgemeinen Konstitutionsbedingungen ist kein unglücklicher Zufall, sondern systematischer Kern der kapitalistischen Ökonomie. Die Durchsetzung des Rechts garantiert somit nicht die Bedingungen der Möglichkeit gewaltfreier Sozietät, sondern zementiert selbst ein Gewaltverhältnis. Recht ist Klassenherrschaft mit anderen Mitteln:

> Den bürgerlichen Ökonomen schwebt nur vor, dass sich mit der modernen Polizei besser produzieren lasse als z. B. im Faustrecht. Sie vergessen nur, dass auch das Faustrecht ein Recht ist, und dass das Recht des Stärkeren unter andrer Form auch in ihrem „Rechtsstaat" fortlebt.[24]

Die begriffliche Gleichsetzung von Recht mit nackter Gewalt erscheint hier tatsächlich als naheliegend. Fällt die Wirklichkeit des Rechts hinter seinen eigenen Anspruch zurück, so kann Recht als reines Trugbild zurückgewiesen werden. Verkompliziert wird die Sachlage jedoch durch Marx Bemerkung, dass Gewalt im bürgerlichen Rechtsstaat eine neue Form annimmt. Rechtsstaatlichkeit impliziert durchaus einen qualitativen Unterschied zum Faustrecht, wenn auch dem bürgerlichen Rechtsstaat keine vollständige Negation von Gewalt entspricht.

Folglich bedarf es einer „Formanalyse" der Gewalt des bürgerlichen Rechtsstaates. Hierbei kann als Grundzug marxscher Kapitalismuskritik festgehalten werden, dass die Gewalt der bürgerlich-kapitalistischen Gesellschaft nicht auf direkte physische Gewalt reduziert werden kann. Bekommt man physische Gewalt lediglich als ultima ratio der herrschenden Ordnung zu fühlen, so strukturiert ökonomisch vermittelte Gewalt die alltägliche Reproduktion der kapitalistischen Ökonomie. Was Lohnabhängige in ihrer misslichen Lage festhält, ist primär die Abhängigkeit individueller Reproduktion vom gesamtgesellschaftlichen Stoffwechsel mit der Natur. Noch vor Polizei und Militär sind es Hunger, Kälte, Krankheit, Schutzlosigkeit, Langeweile, usw. welche zur

---

23 Frank Ruda diskutiert sieben Lösungsansätze für die Pöbel-Problematik und gelangt zum Ergebnis von dessen Unvermeidbarkeit. Ruda, Frank (2011): Hegels Pöbel. Eine Untersuchung der Grundlinien der Philosophie des Rechts. Konstanz: Konstanz University Press, 37–59.

24 Marx, Karl (1971), MEW 13: 620.

Akzeptanz von Ausbeutung und Fremdbestimmung zwingen. Dem entspricht die Erfahrung, dass der Bedarf alltäglicher Güter keine andere Wahl lässt als seine Arbeitskraft zu verkaufen. Die Abhängigkeit des Lebens von sogenannten „Lebensmitteln" verkommt im Kapitalismus zum Mittel der Unterwerfung.

Die Tatsache, dass Marx den Kapitalismus als Herrschafts- und somit als Gewaltverhältnis kritisiert, ohne dieses zugleich auf direkte physische Gewalt zu reduzieren, verweist auf einen umfassenderen Gewaltbegriff. Gleichermaßen werden physische und ökonomisch vermittelte Gewalt nicht einfach gleichgesetzt, sondern der Form nach unterschieden. Der wesentliche Unterschied besteht im Ausgangspunkt der Überwältigung: Physische Gewalt setzt direkt am menschlichen Körper an, insofern dieser mechanischen Kräften unterworfen werden kann. Ökonomische Gewalt instrumentalisiert hingegen den „anorganischen Leib des Menschen"[25] d.h. die Tatsache, dass die Reproduktion des menschlichen Körpers auf natürliche Ressourcen angewiesen ist. Beiden Formen der Gewalt ist gemeinsam, dass die Natürlichkeit des Menschen gegen dessen Willen gewendet wird. Eine Übereinstimmung, welche sich nicht zuletzt darin abzeichnet, dass die praktischen Konsequenzen beider Formen der Gewalt gleichermaßen vom körperlichen Unbehagen bis hin zum Tod reichen.

Erhärtet sich die These, dass Marx Kapitalismuskritik ein umfassenderer Begriff der Gewalt entspricht, so ergeben sich weitreichende rechtsphilosophische Implikationen. Bürgerlich-kapitalistisches Recht kann als „halbiertes Recht" begriffen werden, dessen Scheitern sich auf eine unvollständige Negation der Gewalt zurückführen lässt. Negiert wird lediglich direkte physische Gewalt, während die ökonomisch vermittelte „Gewalt am anorganischem Leibe" nicht nur legal bleibt, sondern selbst durch rechtliche Sanktionen abgesichert wird. Der Doppelcharakter des bürgerlichen Rechts, einen realen Fortschritt zu manifestieren und dennoch keine vollständige Befreiung zu gewährleisten, kann so auf den Begriff gebracht werden. Gleichermaßen fällt neues Licht auf Marx Kritik des Rechts als Form der Klassenherrschaft. Statt Recht pauschal als Instrument von Herrschaft zu begreifen, kann der Fortbestand von Herrschaft auf die unvollständige Verwirklichung des Rechts zurückgeführt werden. Marx Kapitalismuskritik eröffnet somit gleichsam die Möglichkeit einer Radikalisierung des Rechts: Kodifiziert Recht die Bedingung der Möglichkeit gewaltfreier Sozietät, so impliziert ein über dessen bürgerliche Bestimmung hinausgehende Begriff der Gewalt zugleich die Notwendigkeit eines neuen Rechts. Die Negation ökonomischer Gewalt kann analog zur Negation physischer Gewalt als systematischer Ausgangspunkt einer postkapitalistischer Rechtstheorie begriffen werden.

Im Raum steht somit die Möglichkeit einer rechtsphilosophischen Wendung der kommunistischen Idee. Unter Voraussetzung der marxschen Kapitalismuskritik erfordert die Bestimmung des Rechts als Negation von Gewalt selbst die grundlegende

---

25 Marx, Karl (1932), MEW Ergänzungsband, Teil 1: 516.

Neuordnung der Ökonomie. Kommunismus als rechtsförmig vermittelt zu begreifen erscheint somit als naheliegende Option. Die notorisch schwierige Frage, was genau unter Kommunismus zu verstehen ist, könnte entsprechend durch die Entfaltung postkapitalistischen Rechts beantwortet werden.

Offen bleibt allerdings, ob der von Marx und Engels skizzierte Begriff des Kommunismus selbst zugunsten eines „marxist legal turn" fruchtbar gemacht werden kann. Obgleich eine entsprechende Intention Marx und Engels keinesfalls ex-post zugeschrieben werden kann, gibt es durchaus Passagen, welche eine rechtsphilosophische Wendung nahelegen. Beispielsweise wird im Rahmen der *Deutschen Ideologie*, Kommunismus als die Negation des in jeder arbeitsteiligen Gesellschaft latent vorhandenen Gewaltpotentials begriffen. Hintergrund dieser Bestimmung ist die im Rahmen geschichtstheoretischer Überlegungen vorgebrachte These, dass die materielle Reproduktion des Einzelnen immer schon im sozialen Zusammenhang, d. h. als „gesellschaftliches Naturverhältnis" erfolgt. Selbstbestimmung im Verhältnis zur Natur, kann somit nie durch das vereinzelte Individuum, sondern immer nur durch den gesellschaftlichen Gesamtzusammenhang gewährleistet werden. Die im gesellschaftlichen Naturverhältnis angelegte menschliche Interdependenz birgt jedoch zugleich die Gefahr in ein Mittel der Unterwerfung verkehrt zu werden. Eine Problematik die sich im Phänomen der Arbeitsteilung konzentriert:

> Und endlich bietet uns die Teilung der Arbeit das erste Beispiel davon dar, dass solange die Menschen sich in der naturwüchsigen Gesellschaft befinden, solange also die Spaltung zwischen den besonderen und dem gemeinsamen Interesse existiert, solange die Tätigkeit also nicht freiwillig, sondern naturwüchsig geteilt ist, die eigne Tat des Menschen ihm zu einer fremden, gegenüberstehenden Macht wird, die ihn unterjocht, statt dass er sie beherrscht.[26]

Marx und Engels Lösungsansatz – Kommunismus – ist entsprechend nichts anderes als die Negation des in der gesellschaftlichen Arbeitsteilung latent vorhandenen Gewaltpotentials:

> Die allseitige Abhängigkeit [...] wird durch die kommunistische Revolution verwandelt in die Kontrolle und bewusste Beherrschung dieser Mächte, die, aus dem Aufeinander-Wirken der Menschen erzeugt, ihnen bisher als durchaus fremde Mächte imponierte und sie beherrscht haben.[27]

Der Begriff des Kommunismus sowie die oben skizzierte Bestimmung eines postkapitalistischen Rechts stimmen also in der Negation ökonomisch vermittelter Gewalt überein. Kommunismus als Rechtsphilosophie zu rekonzeptualisieren, kann somit

---

26 Marx, Karl / Engels, Friedrich (1932), MEW 3: 33.
27 Ebd., 37.

auch im Bezug auf dessen Bestimmung durch Marx und Engels ein Stück weit gerechtfertigt werden. Diesen Eindruck verstärken zahlreichen Reminiszenzen zur klassischen Rechtsphilosophie. Augenfällig ist, dass die kritisierte „Spaltung zwischen den besonderen und dem gemeinsamen Interesse" der hegelschen Bestimmung von Sittlichkeit die Treu hält. Gleichermaßen spricht die Forderung „freiwilliger" statt „naturwüchsiger" Arbeitsteilung für eine materialistische Radikalisierung der Idee vom Gesellschaftsvertrag. An der Vision freier Übereinstimmung wird festgehalten, allerdings unter dem Gesichtspunkt der materiellen Voraussetzungen des freien Willens. Kurz gesagt: Kein Gesellschaftsvertrag ohne „kommunistischen Arbeitsvertrag".

Ausschlaggebend sind allerdings nicht einzelne Textstellen, welche dem marxschen Rechtsnihilismus zu widersprechen scheinen, sondern der systematische Gesichtspunkt, dass jeder arbeitsteiligen Gesellschaft ein latentes Gewaltpotential innewohnt. Die Abhängigkeit des Einzelnen von fremden Arbeitsprodukten birgt stehts das Potential in eine Mittel der Unterwerfung verkehrt zu werden. Bleibt Arbeitsteilung selbst in einer kommunistischen Gesellschaft erhalten, so besteht auch in dieser die Möglichkeit eines Rückfalls in Herrschaftsverhältnisse. Entsprechend muss eine kollektive Wirtschaft eine spezifische Form annehmen, um eine solche Regression zu vermeiden. Solche Minimalbedingungen der Herrschaftsfreiheit werden durch Kommunistisches Recht expliziert und gerade so in eine politisch wirksame Form gebracht. Oder in anderen Worten: Kann selbst eine kommunistische Gesellschaft, die in Arbeitsteilung selbst angelegte Möglichkeit von Herrschaft nicht aus der Welt schaffen, so bedarf es rechtlich garantierter Standards, welche es erlauben die Aktualisierung von Herrschaft im Ernstfall zu unterbinden. Kommunistisches Recht kann entsprechend als ultima ratio der Herrschaftsfreiheit gelten.

5 Konklusion

Zwei Bedingungen müssen erfüllt werden, um Kommunistisches Recht als Alternative zur These vom Absterben des Rechts zu etablieren: Erstens darf Kommunistisches Recht nicht hinter den Anspruch zurückfallen jeder Herrschaft von Menschen über Menschen ein Ende zu setzen. Zweitens muss erwiesen werden, dass Kommunistisches Recht den praktischen Anforderungen einer radikaler Gesellschaftstransformation besser gewachsen ist als am Absterben des Rechts orientierter Gegenmodelle. Ob der skizzierte Begriff postkapitalistischen Rechts diesen Ansprüchen gerecht wird, soll abschließend kurz umrissen werden.

Das Verhältnis von Recht und Befreiung zu bestimmen, erfordert zunächst auf die These vom Absterben des Rechts zurückzukommen. Deren zentrale Prämisse lautet, dass Recht immer auf seine gewaltsame Durchsetzung und somit in letzter Konsequenz auf Herrschaftsverhältnisse verwiesen ist. Trifft dies zu, so blamiert sich „Kommunistisches Recht" in dem Moment, wo selbst dieses sich der Gewaltmittel bedienen muss. Herrschaftsfreiheit entspricht somit tatsächlich dem Absterben eines jeden Rechts, während „Kommunistisches Recht" als Oxymoron abgetan werden muss.

Kommunistisches Recht kann also nur dann als Vermittlungsinstanz radikaler Befreiung begriffen werden, wenn es gelingt Recht von der Notwendigkeit seiner gewaltsamen Durchsetzung zu trennen. Argumentiert wurde, dass ein solcher Rechtsbegriff unter Rückgriff auf die klassische Rechtsphilosophie der Frühen Neuzeit entfaltet werden kann. Wird Recht auf freier Übereinkunft, d. h. als Bedingung der Möglichkeit kollektiver Selbstbestimmung begründet, so ergibt sich ein entgegengesetztes Verhältnis von Recht und Gewalt. Als Konstitutionsbedingung des Einzelnen im Einklang mit dem allgemeinen Willen, entspricht Recht dem rational reflektierten Eigeninteresse und kann somit auch ohne der Androhung äußerlichen Zwangs affirmiert werden. Fluchtpunkt des Rechts ist nicht die Rechtfertigung seiner gewaltsamen Durchsetzung, sondern deren Überwindung. Rational gerechtfertigtes Recht schlägt um in „Rechtsutopie": Nicht die Abschaffung, sondern die Verwirklichung des Rechts etabliert herrschaftsfreie Verhältnisse.

Freilich spottet unsere Lebensrealität der im Rechtsbegriff inbegriffenen Utopie. Dieser Umstand kann allerdings auf die mangelhafte Verwirklichung des Rechts zurückgeführt werden. Die Unterwerfung des einzelnen Willens ist weiterhin ein Grundzug unserer Gesellschaft, wenn auch vermittelt durch ökonomische und nicht durch direkte physische Gewalt. Als „halbiertes Recht" bleibt die bürgerlich-kapitalistische Rechtsordnung hinter ihrem eigenen Anspruch zurück. Die Utopie des Rechts – als Bedingung der Möglichkeit kollektiver Selbstbestimmung darauf verzichten zu können sich als Zwangsordnung zu konstituieren – harrt somit seiner Einlösung durch die Rechtsordnung einer postkapitalistischen Gesellschaft. Das Versprechen klassischer Rechtsphilosophie muss aufgegriffen, radikalisiert und so seiner Vollendung zugetrieben werden.

Die vollständige Verwirklichung des Rechts als Befreiung zu begreifen, impliziert zugleich die Frage nach der Wirklichkeit des Rechts in einer befreiten Gesellschaft. Woran kann Kommunistisches Recht als Recht ausgemacht werden, wenn nicht an seiner gewaltsamen Durchsetzung? Entscheidend ist zunächst, dass ein Leben in Freiheit zugleich die Bedingungen der Möglichkeit von Freiheit affirmiert. Der Wirklichkeit des Rechts entspricht eine Lebensrealität welche – bewusst oder unbewusst – in jenen Bahnen verläuft die allein ein gewaltfreies Zusammenleben ermöglichen. Gerade weil Recht nicht mehr erzwungen werden muss, ist es in der objektiv vorhandenen Form gesellschaftlicher Verhältnisse inbegriffen.

Die Wirklichkeit postkapitalistischen Rechts zu bestimmen, erfordert zudem die Notwendigkeit zur gewaltsamen Durchsetzung des Rechts von deren Möglichkeit zu unterscheiden. Kommunistisches Recht erhebt den Anspruch ersteres zu überwinden. Wird Recht seinem eigenen Begriff gerecht, so besteht keinerlei im Recht selbst angelegte Notwendigkeit Recht durch Gewaltmittel abzusichern. Markiert ist somit ein entscheidender Unterschied zum bürgerlichen Recht, welches – wie bereits anhand von Hegels Pöbel veranschaulicht wurde – selbst Verhältnisse konstituiert, die nur durch Gewalt aufrechterhalten werden können. Dem widersprich jedoch nicht, dass auch Kommunistisches Recht gegen kontingente, d. h. auf keinerlei systematische Ursache zurückführbare Umstände, durchgesetzt werden kann.[28] Die Existenz von Recht in einer postkapitalistischen Gesellschaft kann also auch an den der Möglichkeit seiner Durchsetzung entsprechenden Institutionen festgemacht werden. Der Grad der Verwirklichung des Rechts bemisst sich allerdings gerade daran, auf die Möglichkeit der Durchsetzung des Rechts möglichst vollständig verzichten zu können. Die Institutionen kommunistischen Rechts können mit einem Sicherheitsnetz verglichen werden, von welchem die geübte Trapezkünstler_in im Idealfall niemals Gebrauch macht, dessen Vorhandensein jedoch nicht geleugnet werden kann.

Recht von der Notwendigkeit seiner gewaltsamen Durchsetzung zu trennen, entspricht der Vereinbarkeit von Recht mit dem Anspruch auf eine herrschaftsfreie Gesellschaft. Die Möglichkeit auch Kommunistisches Recht durch Gewaltmittel zu stützen, erlaubt hingegen den Übergang in einen Zustand der Freiheit als realistische Perspektive zu begreifen. Oder in anderen Worten: Nicht allein die Idee des Kommunismus, sondern auch die Konzepte zu dessen Durchsetzung können rechtsphilosophisch gewendet werden. In der Tat kann Revolution als die Einführung eines neuen Rechts begriffen werden. Revolutionäre Gewalt entspricht dem hegelschen „zweiten Zwang", welcher gegenüber den vorherrschenden Gewaltverhältnissen die Bedingungen der Möglichkeit gewaltfreier Sozietät herstellt. Als Übergangsphase kann gelten, wenn die aus dem revolutionäre Bruch hervorgehenden Wirrungen keine andere Wahl lassen als von der Möglichkeit der Durchsetzung des Rechts Gebrauch zu machen. Zu einem erfolgreichen Abschluss gelangt die Revolution hingegen, sobald Verhältnisse etabliert sind, die vollständig oder zumindest weitgehend auf Gewaltmittel verzichten können.

Vermittelt Kommunistisches Recht den Übergang zwischen beiden Phasen, so kann es als „Recht des Einschlafen des Staates"[29] begriffen werden. Vorhanden ist somit ein Ansatz, welcher gewehrleistet – obgleich dies möglicherweise nie vollständig möglich ist – dass der revolutionäre Bruch zum gewünschten Ergebnis führt. Revolution muss nicht mehr als Zustand völliger Rechtlosigkeit begriffen werden, in welcher allein die Gewalt entscheidet. Stattdessen wird die Gewalt der Revolution selbst dem Zweck unterworfen ein neues Recht zu etablieren. Als Mittel zu diesem Zweck unterliegt selbst revolutionäre Gewalt noch rechtlichen Limitationen. Selbiges gilt für die

---

28 Die Rede von „kontingenten Umständen" kann als Achillesferse der vorgestellten Konzeption gelten, scheint sie doch Tür und Tor zu öffnen um „Kommunistisches Recht" in eine neue Form der Herrschaftslegitimation zu verkehren. Dies wäre dann der Fall, wenn eine neue Form der Herrschaft unter dem Vorwand der Durchsetzung „Kommunistischen Rechts" gegen „kontingente Umstände" etabliert werden würde.

29 Diese Formulierung ist exakter als die Rede vom „Absterben des Staates", da die Möglichkeit Recht durchzusetzen auch dann erhalten bleibt, wenn diese kaum jemals aktualisiert wird.

Gefahr einer Verselbständigung revolutionärer Kräfte zugunsten der Etablierung neuer Formen der Herrschaft. Ein „kommunistischer Rechtsstaat" erscheint als die erfolgversprechendere Perspektive als eine „Diktatur des Proletariats".

Die zivilisierende Kraft des Rechts soll also in der revolutionären Situation selbst zur Geltung gebracht werden. Mehr noch als in der Limitation revolutionärer Gewalt besteht die befreiende Kraft des Rechts allerdings darin überhaut auf Gewalt Verzicht zu leisten. Konstituiert den Kern Kommunistischen Rechts die Frage nach den Bedingungen der Möglichkeit freier Übereinstimmung, so muss die öffentliche Auseinandersetzung mit derselben Frage zum Leitmotiv politischer Praxis gemacht werden. Recht zur Diskussion zu stellen, erlaubt die Herstellung eines breiten Konsenses, gerade weil sich lediglich über die Minimalbedingungen friedlicher Koexistenz verständigt werden muss. Umso breiter dieser Konsens ausfällt, umso friedlicher der Übergang ins Reich der Freiheit.

Folglich wäre nichts verfehlter als eine kleine Avantgarde, welche sich auf den Standpunkt kommunistischen Rechts stellt und zu dessen Durchsetzung übergeht, ohne hierbei den expliziten Willen einer überwiegenden Mehrheit umzusetzen. Geltungsgrund Kommunistischen Rechts ist kein philosophisches Argument in abstracto, sondern der Einzelnen welcher dieses übernehmend zum anderen spricht: „Überzeugt durch diese Gründe bin ich bereit mit dir und allen anderen nach diesen Prinzipien zu leben, solange ihr es mir gleichtut." Der Prüfstein, an welchem sich der Wahrheitsgehalt Kommunistischen Rechts letztlich erweisen muss, ist also der freie Wille eines jeden Einzelnen. Zur Auseinandersetzung mit der philosophischen Rechtfertigung kommunistischer Rechtstheorie gesellt sich die Frage: Wäre ich selbst bereit mein Leben im Einklang mit kommunistischen Rechtsprinzipien auszurichten?

Gleichsam gilt es die Idee des Gesellschaftsvertrages nicht auf ein Gedankenexperiment zu reduzieren, sondern als reales geschichtliches Ereignis zu realisieren. Diese Perspektive wird dem Umstand rechtsförmiger Subjektivierung gerecht. Kann vorausgesetzt werden, dass sich Recht als zweite Natur festgesetzt hat, so ist der Übergang zu einer neuen Ordnung durch die Einführung eines neuen Rechts zu erreichen. Statt sich der Illusion hinzugeben einen „neuen Menschen" im Hier und Jetzt vorwegnehmen zu können, gilt es die, durch die Radikalisierung des „Rechtssubjekts" ein neues „revolutionäres Subjekt" zu konstituieren. Der Furcht vor dem Umbruch und dem entsprechenden Festhalten an der halbierten Freiheit des bürgerlichen Rechts, kann entgegnet werden, dass lediglich der Anspruch auf eine rationale Rechtsordnung eingelöst werden soll, welcher auch unter kapitalistischen Bedingungen vorhanden ist und doch stehts prekär bleiben muss. Die Antizipation einer neuen Ordnung kann als Vollendung der bereits im bestehenden rudimentär vorhanden progressiven Elemente begriffen werden. Die Kontinuität zur alten Ordnung ermöglicht den revolutionären Bruch.

Konkret bedeutet dies, dass die grundlegenden Prinzipien des Rechtsstaates in den Rahmen kommunistischen Rechts übersetzt werden müssen. Eine kollektive Wirtschaft ohne Kollektivismus ist möglich, wenn die Partizipation des Einzelnen an derselben durch ein System klar definierter Rechte und Pflichten geregelt und zugleich demokratischen Aushandlungsprozessen sowie juridischer „Checks and Balances" unterworfen ist. Totalitären Tendenz steht gleichsam entgegen, dass Kommunistisches Recht einer rein negativen Bestimmung von Freiheit als Abwesenheit von Gewalt treu bleibt. Der Grundsatz, dass die Freiheit des Einzelnen dort beginnt, wo die Freiheit des Anderen aufhört, wird lediglich dahingehend neubestimmt als die Möglichkeit individueller Freiheit eine Form kollektiver Ökonomie voraussetzt. Die rechtliche Verpflichtung zur Partizipation an derselben beschränkt sich gleichsam auf ein nötiges Minimum. Es folgt, dass ein Kommunismus, der sich allein auf die Beachtung des rechtlich Gebotenen beschränkt, lediglich dessen rudimentärste Form darstellt. Fluchtpunkt Kommunistischen Rechts ist jedoch gerade jene Bedingungen zu gewährleisten, die es erlauben weit über das bloß rechtlich Gebotene hinaus zu gehen. Individuelle Selbstverwirklichung sowie die volle Entfaltung des menschlichen Potentials werden ermöglicht, ohne selbst rechtlich geboten zu sein. Die negative Freiheit des Rechts eröffnet das Reich positiver Freiheit.

Zur Person: David Jacobs, studierte Geschichte und Philosophie in Wien, Berlin, Jerusalem und Chicago. Er promoviert an der Universität Potsdam und ist in der politischen Bildungsarbeit tätig.

David Jacobs
david.haunschmid@uni-potsdam.de.

Benjamin's *Trauerspiel*
Model for Another Legality of Language

William Ross

Benjamins Trauerspiel
Modell für eine andere Gesetzlichkeit der Sprache

Abstract: This article argues that Walter Benjamin's *Origin of German Trauerspiel* gives an account for an alternative form of presentation in language of the habit breaking experience without such a presentation being a performance of determination itself. This becomes clear only through the distinction made by Benjamin between the forms of tragedy and *Trauerspiel*. This paper will argue that both forms are mode of presentation of the habit breaking experience, but while tragedy presents this experience in an ambiguous manner in which a new law will emerge, the *Trauerspiel* by recourse to allegorical presentation will hold on to this ambiguity challenging the law of identity.
Keywords: Philosophy, Walter Benjamin, Determination, Presentation, Tragedy, Baroque Drama

1 Introduction

Thought I saw an eagle
But it might have been a vulture
I never could decide
– Leonard Cohen, *Story of Isaac* –

In *Theorie der Befreiung*, Christoph Menke argues that liberation is an act of determination that does not reproduce habitual determination. By this is meant that liberation lies in the capacity to break through the 'given' meaning carried by the totality of habit, by a 'given' second nature. Simultaneously, liberation is not a mere breaking through the wall of determination, but it is also to determinate anew. Experience of liberation as determination takes place in a legal framework: "If to determine habitually is to subsume something to a given general according to the law of identity, then to determine something freely is to determine it as if for the first time, because solely from itself."[1] This means, however, that the liberation that is the negation of a given law is simultaneously the positing of a new law, a new determination that states under which new identity something ought to be subsumed. Or, to use Walter Benjamin's terminology, the alternative in determination is either lawmaking or law preserving.[2]

Within the frame of the topic of *Utopie einer neuen normativen Ordnung* and the alternative that it posits, namely the alternative between an alternative *to* right and an alternative *in* right; the liberation that seems like an alternative to right is *simultaneously* an alternative in right. This is one way of understanding the intricate relation between freedom and bondage diagnosed by Menke throughout the history of philosophy and that is challenged in *Theorie der Befreiung* by proposing a "radical" theory of liberation.

To think and to enact radical liberation, one has to go beyond the liberation that performs a determinate negation in the Hegelian sense by which the determination of the negative is always the negation of a given determination that generates a new, better, more precise, determination. In order to think of a more radical form of liberation, one has to do a determinate negation of the (Hegelian) determinate negation and move towards the negation of the form of determination. This implies that we need to find an alternative to the alternative between the alternative to right and the alternative in right as they are dialectically identical.[3] This, I suggest, demands an alternative form of presentation in language of the habit breaking experience without such a presentation being a performance of determination itself. A form in which language succeeds in negating without being itself immediately affirmative of a new determination.

In what follows, I will interpret Walter Benjamin's theory of the allegory in the *Origin of the German Trauerspiel* as contributing to the formulation of a theory of presentation in language of the habit breaking experience without such a presentation being a performance of determination itself. Benjamin's account for the *Trauerspiel*'s form of presentation, however, becomes clear only through the distinction made by him between the forms of tragedy and *Trauerspiel.* This paper argues that both forms are mode of presentation of the habit breaking experience, but while tragedy presents this experience in an ambiguous manner through which a new law will emerge, the *Trauerspiel* by recourse to allegorical presentation will hold on to this ambiguity and challenge the law of identity that structures the habitual experience. In order to do

1 Menke, Christoph (2022): Theorie der Befreiung. Berlin: Suhrkamp, 194 f. (my translation).

2 Benjamin, Walter (1996a): "Critique of Violence". (trans. Edmund Jephcott) In: Ders.: Selected Writings I (1913–1926). Cambridge: The Belknap Press of Harvard University Press, 243; Benjamin, Walter (1972–1989): Gesammelte Schriften. Frankfurt am Main: Suhrkamp, Bd. II, 190.

In the following citations, the reference to Benjamin's *Gesammelte Schriften* will be in parentheses following the English pagination.

3 The alternative to the alternative is not to be conceptualized as the positing of a transcendental from without that would dissolve the tension in the alternative between an alternative to right and an alternative in right. If we are to go beyond this alternative, it is only by working through its tensions as constituents of it.

so, I will first establish the base for a theory of presentation (*Darstellung*) that will set the stage for what is being performed in both tragedy and *Trauerspiel.* Second, I will engage with the question of the presentation of liberation in tragedy: While tragedy portrays the liberation from the "mythical" world, it is also the presentation that leads to the threshold of the "historical" world. This threshold which is the ambiguous negotiation between the inside and the outside of a legal order is presented in the tragic conclusion but lifted out of its ambiguity in its subjection to a judgement that actualizes a new legal order. However, this actualization of a new legal order is simultaneously the erasure of the content of the habit breaking experience. Finally, it will be argued that the allegorical presentation at work in the *Trauerspiel* presents the dissolution of a legal order without exposing the resolution of a legal order as its consequence: the *Trauerspiel* is able to do so only because it internalizes the outside of the legal order as an effect of its own totality.

2 *Darstellung*

The *Origin of German Trauerspiel* opens with the following sentence: "It is proper to philosophical writing to stand, with every turn, before the question of presentation anew."[4] In short presentation is an act of determination that does not reproduce habitual determination.[5] While the act of presentation is traditionally conceived as an objective formation of a determination, it also testifies that a habit breaking experience has taken place: the need to present something stems from the experience of something that has not yet been determined. To present, therefore, is "to determine it as if for the first time, because solely from itself."[6] Philosophy stands before the question of presentation because every turn it takes is an expression of its capacity to enact liberation from previous determination. Or, to say it differently, it is the habit of philosophy to not reproduce habitual determination and to challenge any positing or grounding of habits that might result from philosophy itself. This does not mean that philosophy *in* its habit was successfully able to break *out* of the lawmaking / law preserving alternative: philosophical presentation has until now been the presentation of the new

---

4 Benjamin, Walter (2019): Origin of the German Trauerspiel. (trans. Howard Eiland) Cambridge: Harvard University Press, 1. (Trans. mod.) (Bd. I, 207). The translation used is from Kristina Mendicino: Mendicino, Kristina (2017): "Before the Truth". In: Qui Parle 26, no. 1, 19. DOI: 10.1215/10418385-3822439.
5 The term "*Darstellung*" was introduced in philosophy by Kant who used it to "designate (the act of) the effective realization of a concept." (Gasché, Rodolphe (2003): The Idea of Form: Rethinking Kant's Aesthetics. Stanford: Stanford University Press, 92.) From this initial use in Kant, the concept of presentation was developed in German Romanticism as well as in the philosophy of Hegel. In all cases, "to present" is to give reality to something which before it being presented was not present. In this sense, it plays an essential role in the question of giving actuality to something that does not pertain to the totality of habit.
6 Menke (2022), 195.

determination replacing the old one. The question of presentation in a radical sense becomes the question of presenting the interruption of habit without reconducting it.

As previously said, the experience of liberation takes place in the act of breaking through the given legal framework of determination of second nature. This implies that the experience of liberation testifies of a relation *in* experience with something that appears to lie *outside* of the given lawfulness. To say it differently, experience in its full meaning is the experience of the non-identity between the content of experience and the legal form in which it is supposed to be subsumed. This relation between the inside and the outside of social totality is central to Benjamin's argument about both tragedy and *Trauerspiel*.

As theatrical forms, tragedy and *Trauerspiel* are both practices through which something is being presented (*dargestellt*) through scenic portrayal and theatrical performance which in German is also *Darstellung*. Beyond the presentation of the narrative of the play, tragedy and *Trauerspiel* have in common to present a semantic space through which a community presents itself to its own members. They also share the characteristic that their presentation depicts the community at the moment of their demise.

On the one side, Attic tragedy portrays the mythical world at the breaking point of the unity between the gods and the humans; it exposes the contradiction or the ironic doubling between the liberating intent of the hero's deed and its performance. Tragedy, for Benjamin is characterized by the ultimate repetition of a habit within the mythical world in order to present the liberation from that same mythical world.

On the other side, German *Trauerspiele* portray a community living in the violent limbo of a world witnessing "the collapse of all eschatology"[7] and for which the only possible answer lies in "the attempt to find consolation in the renunciation of a state of grace in reversion to the bare creaturely condition."[8]

As they are portraying downfall and collapse of a totality, both tragedy and *Trauerspiel* are animated by an immanent need to *present* what transcends the given totality; to present the form of experience that allows to break through the totality. What Simon Sparks says here about tragedy is equally valid for *Trauerspiel*:

> [For Benjamin both forms are] *presentation* in the strictest sense of the term – it is the saying of something, it exposes something or gives something to be seen – he is nevertheless still careful to insist that what is decisive is to be found less in what it is tragedy presents *(das Dargestellte)*, than in the presentation itself *(der Darstellung selbst)*.[9]

By giving something to be seen, tragedy and *Trauerspiel* present something new, that is something that before being presented remained absent and unseen. However, what

---

7 Benjamin (2019), 67. (Bd. I, 259)
8 *Ibid.* (Bd. I, 260)
9 Sparks, Simon (2005): "Fatalities: freedom and the question of language in Walter Benjamin's reading of tragedy". In: de Beistegui, Miguel / Sparks, Simon (Hg.): Philosophy and Tragedy. London: Routledge, 187.

is also novel about them is how their performance of presentation enables them to present something which without their form of presentation (*Darstellungsform*) could not have been presented. To understand the performance of presentation in tragedy and *Trauerspiel* signifies to focus, not in what is being presented, but on the form of presentation itself. This task is a reflexive performance: to present the presentation.[10]

Through this reflexive performance tragedy and *Trauerspiel* can therefore be understood as a type of 'transcendental' presentation as defined by Menke in an essay on "The possibility of the revolution" in which he argues that "the revolution neither stands within history nor is external to it, but is rather the act which places us in a different relation *to* history."[11] Hence, the revolution is understood as the performance of an "operation of transcendental self-reflection"[12] which implies "a specific form of presentation (*or Darstellung*)."[13]

If presentation in general is the presentation of something – the presented – it is at the same time the act of presenting the presented. "In a 'transcendental' […] presentation, the 'producing' as such (*das Produzierende*) is presented together with the product; that which produces the presentation becomes part of the presented subject matter, and hence of the product that it brings about."[14] In what follows, I will argue that tragedy and *Trauerspiel* perform such a 'transcendental' presentation as they perform the reflexivity of presenting the presentation or, as Menke says: "The revolution is the (transcendental or critical) act of inscribing the activity and power of producing *into* the product that it brings about – of *co*-presenting the act of presenting in the presentation."[15]

However, what distinguishes the form of presentation in the *Trauerspiel* from the one at play in tragedy lies in the way that it accomplishes its own going beyond of the existing order under the constrain of going back to its own ground – the "reversion to the bare creaturely condition."[16] This return to one's own ground is another character-

---

10 As a reflexive performance, it is also a *critique* as Benjamin understands it following Schlegel's definition of critique: "This poetic criticism … presents the presentation of the new (*von Neuem*), it will once again form what is already formed … It will supplement, rejuvenate, shape anew the work." In: Schlegel, Friedrich (1882): Seine prosaischen Jugendschriften. Wien: Karl Konegen Verlag, Bd. II, 177; quoted by Benjamin, Walter (1996c): "The Concept of Criticism in German Romanticism". (trans. David Lachterman, Howard Eiland, and Ian Balfour) In: Ders.: Selected Writings I (1913–1926). Cambridge: The Belknap Press of Harvard University Press, 154. (Trans. mod.) (Bd. I, 69)

11 Menke will explicitly refer to Schlegel as well, this time in regard to his understanding of "revolution" as rejuvenation. Menke, Christoph (2020): "The Possibility of the Revolution". In: Telios, Thomas / Thomä, Dieter / Schmid, Ulrich: The Russian Revolution as Ideal and Practices. Cham: Palgrave Macmillan, 249.

12 *Ibid.*, 250.

13 *Ibid.* (Menke uses in his text the term "representation" as a translation of *Darstellung*. In order to not create confusion, I have decided to translate *Darstellung* as "presentation" and *darstellen* as "present.").

14 *Ibid.*, 250 f.

15 *Ibid.*, 251.

16 Benjamin (2019), 67. (Bd. I, 260)

istic of the revolution as a form of presentation. Menke, once again, summarizes this movement succinctly:

> As an act of transcendentalization, the revolution goes only beyond the existing order by going *back* to that which produced it in the first place […]. The revolution transforms, even transgresses the given order precisely by returning to its ground […]; the revolution becomes a new beginning only by remembering and repeating the forgotten, hidden origin of the given order. The origin is the goal.[17]

In order, however, to understand the performance of presentation in the *Trauerspiel,* one has to be able to understand where the performance of tragedy fails. Its failure does not lie in the fact that it does not remember its origin, but that the presentation of this remembering is itself forgetful of the origin. This paradox which is fateful for the tragic form of presentation will be presented anew in the *Trauerspiel* with a form of presentation that internalizes reflexively the ambiguous relation to the origin. In other words, if tragedy is the presentation of a determinate negation of an existing configuration of second nature, then, the *Trauerspiel* is the reflexive determinate negation of that form of determinate negation.

3 Tragedy

Benjamin opens his reflections on "The Role of Language in *Trauerspiel* and Tragedy" with the following statement: "The tragic rests on a lawfulness governing the spoken word between human beings."[18] The legality of language, discussed earlier, is here clearly indicated as the ground of the tragic. The emphasis on "the spoken word between human beings" indicates that Benjamin understood human language in tragedy as forming a totality closed on itself,[19] meaning that language does not communicate an extra-linguistic reality but rather only communicate human reality to itself separately from what lies outside of it.[20] This totality is contingent and historical but presents itself as necessary and natural. Tragic is the moment in which the legality governing

---

17 Menke (2020), 251.

18 Benjamin, Walter (2019b): "The Role of Language in Trauerspiel and Tragedy". (trans. Howard Eiland) In: Ders.: Origin of the German Trauerspiel. Cambridge: Harvard University Press, 267. (Bd. II, 137)

19 One can remember here Aristotle's definition of tragedy as the "imitation of an action that is complete and whole" (τραγῳδίαν τελείας καὶ ὅλης πράξεως εἶναι μίμησιν) (1450b, 25) which focuses on the quality for the tragic work to be a successful synthesis of events that form a unity.

20 In another text, Benjamin will qualify human language of this type as "prattle" (*Geschwätz*) in the Kierkegaardian sense. See: Benjamin, Walter (1996b): "On Language as Such and on the Language of Man". (trans. Edmund Jephcott) In: Ders.: Selected Writings I (1913–1926). Cambridge: The Belknap Press of Harvard University Press, 71. (Bd. II, 153)

actual language is failing to comprehend the situation at play and, at the same time, is not able to open itself to its other, to what lies beyond it.

Benjamin's idea of tragedy as form rests, however, on its portrayal of liberation. The theologian Florens Christian Rang, who was instrumental in the development of Benjamin's theory of tragedy, describes the content of this liberation in a letter from January 1924 addressed to Benjamin: "*Tragedy is the breaching of astrology* and consequently the escape from the destiny determined by the course of the stars [...] humanity's consciousness of victory over hieratic petrifaction."[21] Tragedy is liberation from myth, from the category of fate, from the legally bounded sacred tradition. It is liberation from the immutable, from what one – according to the 'given' categories – should not be able to free oneself.

The tragic frame is therefore paradoxical. It is, on the one hand, "a tendentious recasting of tradition."[22] However, on the other hand, "invention is incompatible with the tragic."[23] Tragedy is a confrontation with the mythical world, it is the portrayal of the attempt to recast the tradition passed down generations through the performing of legends (*Sage*). Nevertheless, the mythical world of the ever sameness does not tolerate to be transformed and Attic tragedy is therefore also a portrayal of this impossibility. Hence, Simon Sparks is right in saying that tragedy is "a matter of the transformation *not* of *muthos* [...] but of *die Sage* as the primordial saying of mythic existence."[24] This means that legend and tragedy are both mode of presentation of the mythical world: while legends are a retelling of the myth, its repetition within difference[25]; tragedies are the attempt of articulating the difference beyond repetition; the presentation of the (im)possibility to give a presentation of what conjures the mythical order. Attic tragedy is here a transformation of the portrayal of mythical existence. As a form of presentation, Attic tragedy *is* an invention. It is an invention that allows a transformation in the performative presentation of the myth, a transformation that portrays the impossibility of transformation inside the mythical world that still governs existence inside Attic tragedies. It is only as such that tragedy can present liberation. To play on a formula of Werner Hamacher, tragedy performs the farewell to myth in myth,[26]

---

21 Benjamin, Walter (1994): The correspondence of Walter Benjamin 1910–1940. (trans. Manfred R. Jacobson and Evelyn M. Jacobson) Chicago: University of Chicago Press, 234; Benjamin, Walter (1978): Briefe. Frankfurt am Main: Suhrkamp, 336 f.

22 Benjamin (2019), 106. (Bd. I, 285)

23 *Ibid.* (Bd. I, 285)

24 Sparks (2005), 205.

25 Legends are multiple and different but their unity as form is to repeat the mythical order, to ground it anew at every utterance of the legend.

26 Werner Hamarcher describes the effect of *kátharsis* (κάθαρσις; purification) as "the farewell *to* drama *in* drama (*der Abschied* vom *Drama* im *Drama*)" by which is meant that *kátharsis* as a result of the dramatic process is not to be conceived merely as an act of purification that would create as its own effect the process of integration of the tragedy and therefore confirm its unity. *Kátharsis* also denotes a process of differentiation, of separation, of critique which leaves the drama behind at the moment of its unification.

because the presentation of the impossibility of presenting what lies beyond the myth conjures its spell simultaneously: "*Kátharsis* is a stratagem for liberation from the cult of *kátharsis*."[27]

The structure of the form of presentation in tragedy lies in the necessity of an ultimate repetition of the myth in order to actualize the liberation. As Peter Szondi explains:

> In Benjamin's interpretation, all the following situations must be called tragic: The emancipation of an "ancient right" can occur only by revering it once again; the removal of "fatal obligation" demands, in turn, death as its price; "the new aspect of the life of the nation" require for their realization the individual as hero, but must also destroy him, for they are "inadequate for the single will."[28]

This reading is to be distinguished from the Hegelian reading of the tragedy. While both Benjamin and Hegel are attached to the dissolution of the second nature portrayed in tragedy, Hegel focuses on how the contradictory tension between given norms, values, moral obligation that are held to be equally important but cannot coexist forces the "ruins of the ethical Substance[29] *and its passage in another*."[30] The accent here is to be put on the fact that the ruins of a form of legality implies immediately[31] the passage in another, the negation of a determination *is* the positing of a new determination. Benjamin, on the other hand, will try to present how the demise of second nature in tragedy testifies to a radical liberation that is not presented as such within

---

As we will see this is exactly what happens within Benjamin's portrayal of the tragic sacrifice which enacts liberation from myth in myth. Hamacher, Werner (2018): "Das eine Kriterium für das, was geschieht". In: Ebert, Olivia et al. (Hg.): Theater als Kritik. Bielefeld: Transcript, 22 f.

27 *Ibid.*, 24.

28 Szondi, Peter (2002): An Essay on the Tragic. (trans. Paul Fleming) Stanford: Stanford University Press, 51.

29 "Ethical Substance" translates "*sittlichen Substanz*" which signifies the substance in which habits, norms, and mores obtain their concrete existence. It is synonymous to *second nature*.

30 Hegel, Georg Wilhelm Friedrich (1977): Phenomenology of Spirit. (trans. A. V. Miller) Oxford: Oxford University Press, 289; Hegel, Georg Wilhelm Friedrich (1970): Werke. Frankfurt am Main: Suhrkamp, Bd. 3, 354. (Added emphasis.)

31 Of course, there are mediations involved in the passage from the Greek ethical Substance to the Stoic one which is the following figure of Spirit considered in the *Phenomenology of Spirit*. However, it is important to see that Hegel's own *Darstellung* is here erasing this mediation. In fact, the text of the *Phenomenology* repeats this passage as a conjunction twice in a row: "The ethical shape of Spirit has vanished and another takes its place. This ruin of the ethical Substance and its passage into another form is thus determined by the fact that the ethical consciousness is directed on to the law in a way that is essentially immediate." Hegel (1977), 289; Hegel (1970), Bd. 3, 354. Benjamin's focus on repetition *in* tragedy can here be read as applicable to Hegel: the progress of spirit can only make place to the new determination through the repetition of the ancient. Hegel's own prose does not sublate this principle and its attachment to mythical repetition. Like Szondi notes, it is telling in this case that Hegel "posits the tragic as identical with the genesis of the dialectic" (Szondi (2002), 51.) because it means, from a Benjaminian perspective, that dialectical *Darstellung* is to be understood as sharing the same form as tragic *Darstellung*.

the tragic form. Also, as we will see, Benjamin portrays the passage to another form of second nature as something happening outside of the tragic text, i. e. in the reception of tragedy by the public.

The riddle of tragedy lies therefore in its capacity to be a presentation of liberation while presenting the impossibility of liberation. To interpret this riddle, the performance of liberation in the sacrifice of the tragic hero must be analysed. What commands this liberation takes place in the experience of a boundary which is also simultaneously the experience of the transgression of the limit indicated by the boundary. This experience of the limit and its transgression is the entry point in 'tragic time': "The time of history passes over in tragic time at a determinate and outstanding points of its course: namely, in the action of great individuals."[32] Here, both the historical time of tragedy and its relation to the actions of individuals must be explained.

3.1 Tragic time

'Tragic time' names the confrontation between a given actuality and an experience whose content is not compatible with what is actual. The actuality of the mythical order presented in tragedy is at a tipping point: the façade of unity between humankind and the gods is receding and what appears is a non-united world characterized by a gap: the overcoming of fate can only be actualized through the fateful category of sacrifice and the experience of the forging of a new unity is only delivered in the death of the hero. This death, however, is not a revelation of an ultimate truth. Tragic presentation is a portrayal of the ideological content of the myth of unity. Like all other ideologies, the myth that governs Attic tragedy is not simply an abstract and false belief, the portrayal of the limits of myth by tragedy is not the portrayal of the true essence that lies behind the veil of appearance. As Sparks aptly puts it: "For in saying this confrontation [between humankind and the gods], what tragedy exposes or gives to be seen is not so much the 'essence' of it in the sense of what it is, than the confrontation itself in its historical happening."[33]

Hence, tragic time has to be understood as a modality of historical time for history is the breaching of the new inside mythical ever sameness.[34] Tragic time is a modality

---

32 Benjamin, Walter (2019c): "Trauerspiel and Tragedy". (trans. Howard Eiland) In: Benjamin, Walter: Origin of the German Trauerspiel. Cambridge: Harvard University Press, 261. (Trans. mod.) (Bd. II, 133 f.)
33 Sparks (2005), 187.
34 History and myth form a conceptual coupling in the dialectical unity of unicity and repetition. Benjamin's treatment of these categories is to be understood as a critique of Wilhelm Windelband's strict separation between nomothetic sciences and ideographic sciences, that is between the natural sciences whose truth involves establishing laws (*nomoi*) for the phenomena they explain and the historical sciences whose activity is the descriptive procedure that specify particular phenomena and emphasizes their singularity, gives shape to what pertains to one's own (*idio*). In this regard, Benjamin's concept of natural history

in which the new – that which becomes manifest – not only modifies the content of the totality of meaning or second nature, but also and more precisely interrupts meaning and the way we relate to it. Accordingly, Benjamin says that "historical time is infinite in every direction and unfulfilled at every moment."[35] By this he means that historical time is the negation of the finite, it corresponds to the experience of going beyond the boundary of given signification, of going beyond the limit ascribed to meaning by tradition. If it is infinite in every direction, it is because as a negation of the limits imposed by tradition it is simultaneously the negation of the finite understanding of the directionality of time. Tragic, for instance, is the moment in which the past cease to have an actuality in the present, opening the possibility for a new future – now.

In other words, tragic time is, in the course of time, an interruption of meaning. The manifestation of this interruption is an opportunity: on the one hand, it negates the totalizing effect of habitual meaning and negates its form *qua* totality. On the other hand, then, this interruption gives rise to the reconfiguration of our relation *to* meaning.[36]

The manifestation of the interruption of meaning is the manifestation of an effect; an effect for which the cause is unknown. This unknown disturbs meaning: it is meaningless and, at the same time, challenges the structure of meaning. But if the tragic is not merely the irruption of an unknown new content but a content whose indeterminateness shatters the structure of meaning then this means that tragic events should not be considered as the immediate fulfilment – by the means of positing a new meaning – of this unknown. For, as Benjamin pursues: "Time is for the empirical event only a form, but, what is more important, as a form it is unfulfilled. The event does not fulfil the formal nature of the time in which it lies."[37] The event of the tragic time takes place in time, but its relation to time is not its essential determination; rather its essential relation lies in the opening of the web of signification; the event is essentially a semiotic relationship. The event is a semiotic opening, the event is not the fulfilling of time, nor the fulfilling of signification, it is the experience of this opening as such. The properties of the form of experience implied by the event can be described through Menke's portrayal of the 'true experience':

> Experience, every true experience, is the experience of an indeterminate – of something that cannot be habitually determined. Because what is experienced cannot be habitually determined, experience is the cessation of subjective (determining) activity. Experience

(*Naturgeschichte*) emphasizes the presence of repetition within the realm of history and of unicity within the realm of nature. The mythical world is one example of the realm of history taking the form of naturally given law, of the forced repetition. Mythical time is therefore also a modality of historical time. A modality that is blind to its own historical becoming and produces an erasure of history from within. See: Hanssen, Beatrice (1998): Walter Benjamin's Other History: *Of Stones, Animals, Human Beings, and Angels*. Berkeley: University of California Press, 43 f.

35 Benjamin (2019c), 261. (Bd. II, 134)

36 Just as the revolution "places us in a different relation *to* history". Menke (2020), 249.

37 Benjamin (2019c), 261. (Bd. II, 134)

> goes beyond determining; it is nothing other than this going out. The moment in which this happens is the moment of fascination. In fascination, a self suffers (*erleidet*) the cessation of its activity of determination and affirms this suffering (*Erleiden*).[38]

'Tragic time' is therefore an event, to which corresponds a form of experience whose content manifests as the interruption of meaning. This interruption is therefore the cessation of the determining activity of the subject which reproduces – consciously or not – the totality of meaning. This interruption or this cessation is not linked to an entering a new realm of meaning. The emphasis of this interruption is to be located in the movement of going beyond what was previously given; it is 'nothing other than this going out.' In the tragic form, the experience of the opening as a suspension of meaning is the structure of the experience of the tragic hero. Or to say it differently, the tragic hero is the subject suffering the interruption.

3.2 Individual Experience

The cessation of subjective activity and the emphasis on passivity through *Erleiden* is symbolically presented in tragedy through the fact that the actions of great individuals are determined in their moment of passivity. Which means that tragedy does not portray them on stage as such:

> Not infrequently it is in moments of complete calm – during the hero's sleep, as it were – that the fatality of his time fulfils itself, and likewise the meaning of fulfilled time in the tragic fate emerges in the great moments of passivity: in the tragic decision, in the retarding moment, in the catastrophe[39].

For Benjamin, "Truth is the death of intention."[40] Intentionality, which is the correlate of the subject, is at its most relaxed in passive moments. Akin to the totalizing limits of habits, the totalizing form of intentionality preserves the subject to experience what is not compatible with its own categories. Therefore, it is what lies beyond intentionality, in the subject's suspension of its activity, that matters for truth: to have the capacity to have an experience of what is non-identical. However, such an experience results in a paradoxical situation: the actual concepts and categories available to the subject fail to adequately translate what is being expressed in the object of experience. Hence, the experience of what matters most for truth results in muteness. This is why Benjamin, following here Franz Rosenzweig, claims that the individual experience of tragic time is expressed by the silence of the hero:

---

38 Menke (2022), 485 f.
39 Benjamin (2019c), 263. (Bd. II, 135)
40 Benjamin (2019), 12. (Bd. I, 216)

> The tragic hero has only one language which completely corresponds to him: precisely keeping silent. [...] Tragedy casts itself in the artistic form of drama just in order to be able to *present* speechlessness. [...] By keeping silent, the hero breaks down the bridges which connect him with God and the world, and elevates himself out of the fields of personality, delimiting itself and individualizing itself from others in speech, into the icy solitude of self.[41]

The experience of the tragic hero is nothing else than the experience of the suspension of meaning for which the appropriate language can only be silence. Silence here is not the negation of language: silence "is neither impossibility, namely the impossibility of speaking, nor possibility, namely the negative possibility of not speaking. Rather, it belongs essentially to language as a positive possibility of it. It is, even, language in its most originary and proper sense."[42] This idea that silence belongs to language as a positive possibility can be fleshed out by recourse (again) of Menke's conceptualization of the experience of going beyond determination:

> The experience [...] is the experience that something [...] cannot be determined: the existence of the indeterminate; the existence of negativity, as a thing or an event; this here not as something determinate, but as indeterminate. Because the indeterminate, which eludes all determination, yet appears to us in experience, the real, indeterminate, which we experience, is at the same time the determinable. In the fascinating experience, the pure possibility of determination appears to us. By experiencing this, we are freed from the law of identity. We ourselves become determinable – free of determination.[43]

The cessation of determination which pushes the subject outside of the given totality of meaning has to be understood in a radical sense as the experience of something that cannot be determined. Paradoxically, this indeterminate appears to the subject *in* experience. It is the experience of our determinability: every given form of determination relies on this capacity to produce a determination. Determinability is the *origin* of determination. More precisely, determination is an effect of determinability, and, in its activity, determination translates an aspect of determinability; as a translation, determination betrays determinability as it gives a specific content to the capacity of determination as such.[44] This, in turn, helps us to understand the experience of the tragic hero: against the mythical experience which reifies determination, the tragic hero experience determinability. He experiences that every determination is the result

---

41 Rosenzweig, Franz (1970): The Star of Redemption. (trans. William W. Hallo) New York: Holt, Rinehart and Winston, 77.
42 Sparks (2005), 197.
43 Menke (2022), 486.
44 The form of this experience has been also described in relation to Benjamin's critique of the Kantian form of experience by Caygill, Howard (1998): Walter Benjamin: The Colour of Experience. New York: Routledge, 1–7.

of a historical production relying on the capacity of determinability. The tragic hero wants to communicate this capacity, but every act of communicating determinability will transform it in a specific determination. This paradox forces the tragic hero to silence. Silence is the negative indication of the performance of the transcendental presentation in tragedy. If transcendental presentation is characterized by the fact that in it the "'producing' as such is presented together with the product,"[45] the silence of the tragic hero is here the mark that what needs to be presented – the experience of determinability – can only appear as a product under a specific determination and hence erasing the producing within the product. Silence echoes this impossibility and manifest that it can achieve transcendental presentation only negatively. This is how one can understand Sparks' conclusion that "in order to keep silent, the hero must have something to say, something to communicate."[46] But what is to be communicated here is nothing determinate, but the "pure possibility of determination." The structure of determination inside the Attic tragedy does not allow for such a *Darstellung* from the mouth of the hero: "The heroic defiance contains closed up in itself, this unknown word; that distinguishes it from the hubris of a man in whom the fully developed consciousness of the community acknowledges no hidden content anymore."[47] The tension between the "unknown word" and the Parousia which manifests "no hidden content anymore" cannot be explained from within the individual experience of the hero but understood as a result of the sacrificial ambiguity.

3.3 Sacrificial ambiguity

The incapacity of the community to acknowledge the content of the Hero's experience is what leads to the heroic sacrifice and, to its duality and ambiguity for the community:

> Tragic poetry rests on the idea of sacrifice. But the tragic sacrifice differs in its object – the hero – from every other form of sacrifice, and it is at the same time a first and a last measure. Last, in the sense of the expiatory sacrifice that falls to the gods, who uphold an ancient right; first, in the sense of the representative action in which new circumstances in the life of the people are announced.[48]

Tragic sacrifice is a *last* sacrifice to the mythical order, one last acknowledgment that all deviation to its legal totality will be punished. It is a *first* sacrifice because it is not itself the positing of a new law, but the offer to a coming community of the possibility

45 Menke (2020), 250.
46 Sparks (2005), 197.
47 Benjamin (2019), 111. (Bd. I, 294)
48 *Ibid.*, 100. (Bd. I, 285)

of inaugurating a new era. It is the farewell to myth in myth. However, one must stress that the "new circumstances of the life of the people" do not find their moment of presentation *in* the language of tragedy.

These circumstances announce themselves, express themselves, because the people in question – i. e. the audience – only receive from tragedy the saturation and mythical overdetermination that refers to death. But sacrificial death is itself an ambiguous limit: in it the divine law is not strengthened, on the contrary it represents the "first fruits of a new human harvest."[49] The hero's silence at the moment of their death is not simply the sign of natural domination, silence is the expression that the limit has been crossed, but that language fails precisely to gather the event within itself. The audience receives this silence as the negative sign that the ethical order of the mythical world is no longer actual without being replaced. To actualize a new determination, one must posit a judgement on the meaning of the sacrifice. It is here that the known parallel between Attic tragedy and the Ancient Greek trial process is articulated by Benjamin:

> The ancient legal process – the criminal trial, in particular – is dialogue, because it is based on the double role of accuser and accused, without official intervention. […] For Athenian law, the important and characteristic element is the Dionysian irruption – namely, the fact that the intoxicated, ecstatic word can break through the regular encirclement of the agon, that a higher justice could spring from the force of conviction in living speech than from the trial of factions opposing each other with weapons or prescribed verbal forms. By means of the logos, in freedom, the ordeal is broken through. This is at bottom the kinship (*Verwandtschaft*) of juridical process and tragedy in Athens.[50]

This affinity between tragedy and right is this capacity in the act of judgement for a new determination to come to the fore. This is the victory of logos over myth. However, the resolution presented by tragedy implies, also, in a way, a regression of logos back to mythos. If the tragic hero is witness to a "higher justice," this higher realm is not presented in language.

> The content of the hero's works belongs to the community, just as language does. Since the community denies this content, it remains speechless in the hero. And so the latter must formally enclose within the boundaries of his physical self every deed and every piece of knowledge – and must do so the more violently the greater and more effective those matters turn out to be.[51]

That doesn't stop, however, the whole tragic setting to move forward from the presentation of the case to the moment of judgement:

---

49 *Ibid.* (Bd. I, 285)
50 *Ibid.*, 111 f. (Trans. mod.) (Bd. I, 295)
51 *Ibid.*, 102. (Bd. I, 287)

> But if the myth, in the understanding of the poet, is the legal procedure, then his poetry is at once a reproduction and a revision of the proceedings. And this entire process has unfolded according to the dimensions of the amphitheatre. The community takes part in this resumption of the process as a controlling, indeed judging authority. For its part, it seeks to arrive at some verdict concerning the confrontation, in the interpretation of which the poet renews the memory of heroic deeds.[52]

The judgement of the public in regard to tragedy then becomes the determining act by which the hero becomes the ground of a new way of determination. As Simon Sparks notes: "Language, then, begins in the response of the community – its learning thanks or gratitude – to what is given to it by the death of the hero, a death which is now to be thought ecstatically and not metaphysically. From out of this sacrifice, language happens."[53] This turns a negative into a positive: while the speechlessness of the hero testifies to our own determinability, to our "being free of determination," the judgement of the community upon the sacrifice of the hero, on the contrary, makes the hero and not the experience made by the hero the grounding event of language. This results in a πρῶτον ψεῦδος: through the judgement of the public, the origin of the community is now symbolically tied to the hero and not to the experience of breaching through the limits of determination that characterized his sacrifice. While the sacrifice, under this aspect, is understood as an expression of his own heroic intentionality; the essential content of his experience, on the other hand, testified to the suspension of intentionality. The hero now serves as the starting point of a new law of subsumption and determination: the hero is the particular that is identical to the universal, the individual through which a totality of determination emerges. In this judgement, the tragic results in leaving *outside* the outside of language that manifested itself *inside* the experience of the hero. In the positing that accompanies the judgement, the negativity at work in the experience of the hero is erased. This is what Benjamin underlines with the concept of the *non liquet*: a fundamental ambiguity, an original unclarity that proceeds from the tragic form. "But there always sounds in the conclusion of the tragedy a *non liquet*. To be sure, the resolution is always also salvation – but only a temporary, problematic, limited one."[54]

Thrown as a riddle to the audience, tragic silence is the tipping point at the uncertain outcome of the ἀγών between the mythical and the historical world. The hero's silence points towards a historical supplement that cannot be incorporated into the mythical world: the fact that human language can make law and history. Benjamin treats this supplement as the *non liquet* of tragedy, its surplus whose assimilation by the community is not guaranteed. Florens Christian Rang summarizes this idea: "The tragic

52 *Ibid.*, 112. (Bd. I, 295 f.)
53 Sparks (2005), 199.
54 Benjamin (2019), 112 f. (Bd. I, 296)

resolution (*Lösung*) discovered each time is, of course, redemption (*Erlösung*), but a problematical one, postulated in prayer, but not realized in such a way as to preclude it from again producing conditions that would require a new resolution = redemption."[55]

Joel White has rightfully argued that the Idea of tragedy, its truth, lies in "the emergence of the new as *Einmaligkeit*"[56] (singularity). As previously shown, this singularity is the result of repetition, it is the singular experience of the Hero which confirms and denies the mythical realm. In its singularity, it is the experience of something that lies beyond the realm of what can be habitually subsumed; the experience of something new – that is the crux of the tragic frame. This singular experience, however, is described, on the one hand, as the dismantling of the subjectivity of the Hero and, on the other hand, presents the Hero as the 'origin' of the new determination. The subjective experience of the hero is the experience that goes beyond determination; it is the experience of experience, the experience of determinability. However, subsumed under the judgement that grounds the community, the experience of the hero becomes the grounding event of a new determination: the coming community is not the mythic community in unity with the gods, it is the human community, the descendants of the hero – "humanity's consciousness of victory over hieratic petrifaction."[57] The experience of the hero becomes the new law; it is law making and it is reproducing the cycle of determination as identity. The objective perspective that is expressed in the judgement of the audience is the erasure of the subjective experience; it is the creation of a new totality that creates its own outside from its own blind spots.

In this sense, the singularity in tragedy is bound with its fateful repetition: every time a community experiences the saturation of determination or a contradiction inside its totality of meaning, it will have to go through this tragic event that would redefine the identification between *Lösung* and *Erlösung*. In order to escape this fateful repetition, one has to portray it: one has to be able to present on a stage the subjective perspective of the experience of the hero.[58] Accordingly, the presentation of the community to itself through the form of theatrical presentation should also not take the so-called identity between the individual and the community as the origin of the community. This origin is to be found less in any determination that might arise in the course of history, but in the fundamental ambiguity that any foundation is but a result of negotiating the determinability of the content of experience. This is what is at stake in the baroque theory of the allegory which is at work in the *Trauerspiel*.

---

55 Benjamin (1994), 233; Benjamin (1978), 335.
56 White, Joel (2014), "The Betrayal and Rescue of the New: Walter Benjamin's and Carl Schmitt's Interpretations of Hamlet". (Master's Thesis Kingston University London), 17.
57 Benjamin (1994), 234; Benjamin (1978), 336 f.
58 Something that will only become available much later with the establishment of the dispositive of 'consciousness' which will open up the possibility for language to talk about the interior life of characters. For Benjamin, Socrates is an intermediary figure between the tragic hero and the proto-modern baroque character. Benjamin (2019), 108 f. (Bd. I, 292 f.)

4 *Trauerspiel* and Allegory

The tragic ends in the establishment of the symbolic unity between the hero and the community under the grounding of a new legality of determination. The *Trauerspiel* begins with the sovereign as a symbol: "The sovereign represents history."[59] In this regard, the sovereign is the object of the *Trauerspiel* because "historical life, as that epoch represented it to itself, is [the] content [of *Trauerspiele*], its true object."[60] Benjamin pursues: "The sovereign, as chief exponent of history, might almost be considered its incarnation."[61]

The sovereign is the symbol of history. A symbol which is depicted, however, at the threshold of the failure of symbolic representation. In the *Trauerspiel*, symbols fail to represent the unity they ought to create because the artificial forging between image and meaning appears for what it is: a forced reconciliation. However, the *Trauerspiel* goes beyond the mere negation of the symbol, it deconstructs it and with it the pretension of language of creating a definitive, legally binding, identity. By recourse to allegorical presentation, the *Trauerspiel* presents the interruption of determination in language by the means of language. This interruption has its locus in the sovereign itself as a fundamental ambiguity runs through him: "The king is both man (an end of nature) and also king (bearer and symbol of meaning)."[62] In his human condition, the sovereign is both a piece of nature and history in the flesh. Through him the negotiation of the threshold between history and nature is being interwoven. The *Trauerspiel* reveals history not as the movement that leaves behind nature, but that the movement of separation with nature was a possibility of nature itself. As a symbol of history, the sovereign is only severed from nature through forgetfulness. Nature in the sovereign survives but as a fragment: "the nature of the *Trauerspiel* remains a torso in this sublime symbol; sorrow fills the sensuous world in which nature and language meet."[63]

It has been said that the presentation of the symbolic unity in tragedy was the result of the outward portrayal of the hero's experience. Tragedy depicts the hero going beyond determination and entering in dumbness. It does not portray the perspective of the hero as they plunge beyond determination in a deconstruction of their subjectivity. This is the lacuna of the form of presentation in tragedy that the *Trauerspiel* takes on by recourse to allegorical presentation.

The formal distinction between symbol and allegory on which Benjamin draws upon has been formulated by Friedrich Creuzer. However, while Creuzer holds the symbol to be superior then allegory; Benjamin will invert this hierarchy:

---

59 *Ibid.*, 48. (Bd. I, 245)
60 *Ibid.*, 46. (Bd. I, 242 f.)
61 *Ibid.* (Bd. I, 243)
62 Benjamin (2019b), 269. (Bd. II, 139)
63 *Ibid.* (Bd. II, 139)

> The "difference between symbolic and allegorical presentation": "The latter merely signifies a general concept or idea that is distinct from it; the former is the idea itself bodied forth and rendered sensible. On one hand, a substitution takes place; [...] on the other hand, this concept itself has descended into the bodily world, and it itself is what we see immediately in the image." But with this Creuzer returns to his original conception. "The difference between the two modes is therefore to be found in the quality of the momentary, which allegory lacks".[64]

It is precisely the momentary aspect of the symbol its instantaneity – that Creuzer defines as "a suddenly appearing spectre, or like a lightning flash that suddenly lights up the dark night"[65]–that characterizes the erasure of the historical mediation that takes part in the construction of meaning. The symbol as form is erasure and reification of the historical labour at work in meaning. The allegory, on the other hand, shows that a substitution is taking place, it shows the non-identity between meaning and its presentation – allegory signifies an "idea that is distinct from it." Allegory as a form of presentation shows the construction of meaning through the mediations as they take place into language. It is immanent to allegory to be a transcendental presentation as previously defined, for by laying bare the mediations that produce meaning – instead of hiding them behind the unity of the symbol – allegory posits its producing along with the product of presentation. Benjamin also underlines that the mediations presented by allegory are the ones that obtain between nature and history: "Allegorical expression itself enters the world with a strange interlacing of nature and history."[66] Its most vivid expression is the historical dissolution of the natural appearance of signification: "In the field of allegorical intuition, the image is fragment, rune. Its symbolic beauty evaporates once the light of divine learning falls upon it. The false semblance of totality is extinguished. For the *eidos* is effaced, the simile perishes, the cosmos within it is desiccated."[67] This capacity to portray dissolution of meaning enables allegory to be the translation of experience into language. Hence it is appropriate to portray the inner experience of a subject who experiences the transient character of meaning, the passing away of a habitual determination. As Bainard Cowan demonstrated, the role of allegory, for Benjamin, was to articulate the outward portrayal with the inner experience:

> In Benjamin's analysis, allegory is pre-eminently a kind of experience. A paraphrase of his exposition might begin by stating that allegory arises from an apprehension of the world as no longer permanent, [...] or a conviction [...] that "this world is not conclusion."

---

64 Creuzer, Friedrich (1819): Symbolik und Mythologie der alten Völker, besonders der Griechen. Leipzig-Darmstad, 70 f; Quoted in: Benjamin (2019), 172. (Bd. I, 341)
65 Creuzer (1819), 59 f; Quoted in: Benjamin (2019), 170 f. (Bd. I, 340)
66 Benjamin (2019), 175. (Bd. I, 344)
67 *Ibid.*, 186. (Bd. I, 352)

> Allegory would then be the expression of this sudden intuition. But allegory is more than an outward form of expression; it is also the intuition, the inner experience itself. The form such an experience of the world takes is fragmentary and enigmatic.[68]

Allegorical presentation in the *Trauerspiel* is, therefore, both the presentation of the insufficiency of the 'symbolic' legality in language determined by the law of identity and the presentation of the experience that replaces the symbolic determination with a language whose own legality goes beyond identity. It does so by exposing the diremption between nature and history in the body of the sovereign. This diremption involves, in *Trauerspiele,* two relevant aspects: first, the experience of mourning and, second, the return to the creaturely condition.

The *Trauerspiele,* whose historical frame are the Counter-Reformation, present the disappearance of any given realm outside of the everlasting actuality:

> Where the Middle Ages exhibits the precariousness of worldly events and the transitoriness of the creature as stations on the path to salvation, the German *Trauerspiel* wholly buries itself in the desolation of the earthly estate. Such redemption as it knows will lie more in the depths of these vicissitudes themselves than in the fulfilment of a divine plan of salvation. The repudiation of eschatology in religious plays is characteristic of the new drama throughout Europe; nevertheless, the headlong flight into a nature without grace is specifically German.[69]

In the *Trauerspiele,* says Howard Caygill: "time is open-ended; God is remote, and the completion of time in the advent of the absolute has both already happened in the birth of Christ and is eternally deferred in the Last Judgement. In the mourning play, the organizing principle is not completion in and of time, but repetition; not praise but mourning."[70]

The passage from repetition to mourning takes the following path: "The two metaphysical principles of repetition interpenetrate in the *Trauerspiel* and establish its metaphysical order: cycle and repetition, circle and two."[71] The word in the tragic is two, it is either law preserving or law making. This duality forms a circle of determination in which the experience that matters, the experience that goes beyond the determination of the word cannot be presented. This is the principle of the *mourning* play – the *trauer*-Spiel: by giving a conscious account of the overdetermination created by the tragic frame, the *Trauerspiel* presents the feeling of sadness, the sadness that human language will never be able to present what lies outside of itself, to do justice of what lies outside

---

68 Cowan, Bainard (1981): "Walter Benjamin's Theory of Allegory". In: New German Critique, no. 22, 110. DOI: 10.2307/487866.
69 Benjamin (2019), 67 f. (Bd. I, 260)
70 Caygill (1998), 52.
71 Benjamin (2019b), 269. (Bd. II, 139)

of its totality by the means of determination. For determination is the tragic *in* the word: "Thus, with the double-dealing of the word, with its meaning nature comes to a standstill."[72] This fixation of nature in language is the erasure of the content of the experience that breached the wall of determination, for it is precisely the historical determination that fixes the becoming of nature. *Trauerspiel* opposes the tragic precisely on this aspect: "For mourning is not, like the tragic, a ruling force, the indissoluble and inescapable law of orders that attain closure in the tragedy; rather, it is a feeling. What metaphysical relation does this feeling have to language, to the spoken word? That is the riddle of the Trauerspiel."[73]

The riddle of the *Trauerspiel* is to present the content of the experience that goes beyond determination which lies outside of spoken language in language itself. This is the meaning of the mourning *play* – trauer-*Spiel*. In this play, the speaker of language experiences and surpasses the limits of language's legal form by giving voice to its other – ἄλλος ἀγορεύω. This play is ambiguous: it creates a semantic space for the event disrupting the order of language by assigning it a place in language. What seems to be unfaithful to the content of experience – not respecting the fact that its content lies outside of the limits of language by forcing it inside the presentation of language – is actually and paradoxically its salvation. It is the transgression of the limit of what transgresses the limit of habit. For the so-called faithfulness to the unnameable in the experience reifies the outside of language and contributes to the reproduction of the cycle of lawmaking and law preserving determination. The outside is as much outside of the totality of language as it is an effect of this totality. To give it an ontological priority would establish it on a transcendental realm and claim that one cannot speak about it. This would be a reification of both the totality of language and its own exteriority. This is why betrayal is a necessary category in presentation: one can choose between the faithfulness to the outside of language and therefore provoke an erasure of nature inside language, which is the historical betrayal of nature; or, one can choose to betray the externality of the outside, consider it seriously as also an effect of the inside and therefore be able to give a voice to nature inside history. As Benjamin says contemplating the second option: "midway through this passage [into language], nature sees itself betrayed by language."[74] This betrayal of nature by language is, of course, the effect of determination which puts nature at a standstill. But this determination is the act of the subject negotiating its own subjectivity and, as such, the emphasis put by the *Trauerspiel* on the creaturely condition of humankind's springs forth: the betrayal has its locus in the human subject as she is both a piece of nature and a subject of language. This is the revolutionary movement of the *Trauerspiel* as it is the presentation of the experience that goes "beyond the existing order by going *back* to that which produced

---

72 *Ibid.* (Bd. II, 138)
73 *Ibid.*, 267 f. (Bd. II, 137 f.)
74 *Ibid.*, 268. (Bd. II, 138)

it in the first place."[75] The betrayal is therefore duplicated; it betrays the existing order as it betrays nature. It is experienced as mourning, because it is the act by which the human subject frees herself from the realm of nature and the realm of meaning without severing ties with neither of them. The *Trauerspiel* allegorical presentation plays on this mourning as negative sign: the passing away of both nature and determination in the subject is itself the expression of the need of history understood as the event in which the possibility of a new determination that would also restore nature lies but remains uncertain.

Accordingly, the spectator of the *Trauerspiel* does not experience the play as a common shared experience, rather the allegorical presentation as a portrayal of the inner experience is experienced by the audience as *reading*:

> Fundamentally, then, the *Trauerspiel* too, having arisen in the realm of the allegorical, is – by virtue of its form – a drama to be read. [...] Such recognition does make it clear that the select viewer of such *Trauerspiele* immersed himself in them as though brooding on a problem, and in this respect at least was like a reader; that the situations on stage did not change very often, but when they did it was in a flash, like the aspect of the printed page when it is turned.[76]

With this experience, the spectators are kept separated, individualized in their inner experience of reading the inner experience of the *Trauerspiel* whose result is neither their subjectivation as members of a community, nor their desubjectivation as *disjecta membra* of a coming community. The allegorical presentation in the *Trauerspiel* does not deliver a new determination. As Benjamin says, in the allegory,

> any person, any object, any relation can signify any other whatever. With this possibility, an annihilating but just verdict is pronounced on the profane world [...] In allegorical perception, [...] the profane world is both elevated in rank and devalued. This religious dialectic of the content has its formal correlate in the dialectic of convention and expression. For allegory is both of these – convention and expression – and they are inherently in conflict with each other.[77]

This conflict is the one between convention – that is the totality of habit, the world of legally binding determination – and expression, that which in experience lets itself be known without being able to be presented through the means of determination. Allegory is the presentation of the conflict at work in presentation, it is going back to the experience of determinability to expose the antinomy at play in determination. As such, it inscribes "the activity and power of producing *into* the product that it brings

---

75 Menke (2020), 251.
76 Benjamin (2019), 197 f. (Bd. I, 360 f.)
77 *Ibid.*, 184. (Bd. I, 351)

about" –it "*co*-present[s] the act of presenting in the presentation."[78] But by doing so it creates both the fragmentation of meaning – opposed to the totality of symbolic presentation – and fundamental ambiguity – opposed to the principle of identity. Thus, the allegory is the conjuration of the myth of progression attached to the tragic cycle of symbolic unity, the cycle of lawmaking and law preserving determination, that always moves towards a new, better, more precise, determination. Benjamin describes this conjuration as the revelation of the transient character of history which obtains in allegory – as opposed to the eternal unity of the symbol:

> Whereas in the symbol, with the sublimation of downfall, the transfigured countenance of nature reveals itself fleetingly in the light of salvation, in allegory there lies before the eyes of the observer the *facies hippocratica* of history as petrified primal landscape. History, in everything untimely, sorrowful, and miscarried that belongs to it from the beginning, is inscribed in a face – no, in a death's head.[79]

The transient character of history, which obliges us to allegorical presentation, turns itself into a symbol: "a death's head." But the symbolical meaning of the death's head is the passing away. In the symbolic unity of meaning, historical becoming cannot be severed from death's head. The death's head symbolizes the need for allegorical presentation. But as much as one cannot expunge history from the death's head, one cannot abstract the individual existence that was attached to it. Not only are the mediations put back in the appearance of immediacy, but the particular is also re-established in its universal aspect:

> And though it is true that to such a thing all 'symbolic' freedom of expression, all classical harmony of form, and everything human is lacking, nevertheless in this figure, the most fallen in nature, is expressed meaningfully as enigma not only the nature of human existence in general but the biographical historicity of an individual.[80]

The restoration of meaning under the guise of transience in the death's head is what Benjamin calls the "core of the allegorical vision":

> This is the core of the allegorical vision, of the Baroque profane exposition of history as the Passion of the world – meaningful only in the stations of its decline. So much meaning, so much forfeiture to death, for at the deepest level death incises the jagged line of demarcation between physis and meaning. But if nature has at all times been subject to the power of death, it is also at all times allegorical. Meaning and death are brought to fruition in

---

78 Menke (2020), 251.
79 Benjamin (2019), 174. (Bd. I, 343)
80 *Ibid.* (Bd. I, 343)

> historical unfolding, just as they are closely intermeshed as seeds in the unredeemed state of sin of the creature.[81]

The allegorical portrayal attaches meaning not to the act of determination that for better or for worse, human beings are fatefully attached to as the act by which they free themselves from nature and by which they transform their relation to history as a determinate negotiation of their relationship with nature. Rather, allegory portrays that meaning appears in the decay of determination. Revolution as the alternative to the alternative – the alternative that is neither an alternative *to* right nor an alternative *in* right – is the presentation that presents why presentation needs to be repeated.

As Howard Caygill observed, "in the closing pages of *The Origin of German Trauerspiel* Benjamin imagines the allegorization of allegory, the revelation that the allegorical destruction of meaning is itself an allegory."[82] Allegory repeats itself as allegory because it replays its own ambiguity at every turn and portrays therefore its own limit. Contrary to the symbol for which its limit is an unpresented effect, allegorical portrayal acknowledges its limits, its failures.

> For it is precisely in visions of the intoxication of destruction, visions in which everything earthly turns to rubble, that there is revealed not so much the ideal of allegorical immersion as its limit. The bleak confusion of Golgotha, legible as schema of allegorical figures in a multitude of engravings and descriptions of the period, is not simply a symbol of the desert of human existence. In it, transience is not so much signified, allegorically presented (*allegorisch dargestellt*), as – itself signifying – performed as allegory (*dargeboten als Allegorie*). As the allegory of resurrection.[83]

The suspension of the cycle of lawmaking and law preserving determination is accomplished by allegory in its own allegorization. In it the transience of meaning is not merely signified, it becomes itself the ground of signification. Transience is significant because as much as it means that everything leads to the death of signification, this death is also the possibility of its own renewal, the resurrection of meaning in the everlasting transience, or the always available experience that could put an end to the tyranny of determination. The end of the *Trauerspiel* book then points back to the first sentence of the book, it points back to its origin – "The origin is the goal"[84] – the *Ursprung der Ursprung des deutschen Trauerspiel*: "It is proper to philosophical writing to stand, with every turn, before the question of presentation anew."[85]

---

81 *Ibid.* (Bd. I, 343)
82 Caygill, Howard (2010): "Walter Benjamin's concept of allegory". In: Rita Copeland and Peter T. Struck: The Cambridge Companion to Allegory. Cambridge: Cambridge University Press, 252.
83 Benjamin (2019), 254. (Trans. mod.) (Bd. I, 343)
84 Menke (2020), 251.
85 Benjamin (2019), 1. (Trans. mod.) (Bd. I, 207)

About the Author: William Ross is a postdoctoral fellow of the Social Science and Humanities Research Council of Canada, guest fellow in philosophy at the Goethe Universität Frankfurt am Main.

William Ross
william.d.ross85@gmail.com.

Kritik des Rechtssubjekts als absolutes Verhältnis des Tragischen zum Komischen

Zum Zusammenhang von Staat, Geschichte und Religion bei Rosenzweig und Hegel

KRISTIAN SCHÄFERLING

Critique of the Legal Subject as the Absolute Relation of the Tragic to the Comic

On State, History and Religion in Rosenzweig and Hegel

Abstract: The article attempts to critically reconstruct a systematic relation between objective and absolute spirit in Hegel. This involves retracing steps of the process of subjectivization of the political-theological nexus of the state, history and religion through the aesthetic mediation of the actuality of the internally divided absolute idea. In the *Phenomenology of Spirit* this question is put in terms of comedy and tragedy – the two privileged affect-forms underlying the individualization of the masses into subjects of the state. Setting out from a discussion of Rosenzweig's critique of Hegel, the article aims to point towards an opening in the legal subject from which a reconsideration of the subjectivization of a collective that has been excluded from history might resume.

Keywords: Actuality, State, History, Religion, Tragic, Comic

1 Einleitung

Rosenzweigs Verhältnis zum deutschen Idealismus ist verschieden facettiert. Dies zeigt sich auch in der Rosenzweig-Rezeption. Dort gibt es auf der einen Seite die starke Tendenz, das „neue Denken" dem Idealismus, insbesondere dem Hegelschen, diametral entgegenzusetzen; andere hingegen versuchen aufzuzeigen, dass eben eine solche Rosenzweig-Rezeption, beziehungsweise in vielen Formulierungen auch Rosenzweigs Hegel-Rezeption selbst, der Komplexität der idealistischen Systeme nicht gerecht werde und dass Rosenzweigs Denken vielmehr der idealistischen Konstruktion Wesentliches schulde. Die spannungsreichen Bezüge hierbei haben sicherlich auch mit der Frage danach zu tun, zu welchem Grad ein Austausch zweier Denkweisen, der deutschen Philosophie und dem jüdischen Denken, in der Arbeit deutsch-jüdischer Philosophen *in concreto* stattfand oder nicht.[1] Diese Debatten werden hier nicht weiter thematisiert, zumindest nicht explizit. Die folgenden Überlegungen wollen auch nicht etwa abwägen, wie weit Rosenzweigs Kritik des Idealismus nun entweder als gelungen verstanden werden kann oder aber warum es doch unmöglich sein soll, durch die religionsphilosophische Offenbarungstheologie in Rosenzweigs Schriften eine 'im eigentlichen Sinn' philosophische Stellungnahme zu begründen. Die Personalunion Rosenzweigs – im deutschen Universitätssystem sozialisierter Hegel-Gelehrter und dann auch gläubiger Jude – bringt die Nähe zweier gedanklicher Welten hervor. Es gibt ein tiefgreifendes Verhältnis zwischen dem jüdischen mythisch-religiösen Denken und Hegels Staatsdenken. Die hier vertretene These ist, dass es auf Grund dieses Verhältnisses möglich wird, im Hinblick auf die bei den beiden Philosophen jeweils unterschiedlich konzipierte Funktion der Religion zwischen objektivem und absolutem Geist weitere für das Verständnis der Hegelschen Rechtsphilosophie relevante kritische Fragen zu stellen. An diese These geknüpft wird auch zu diskutieren sein, wie das durchs Hegelsche Rechtssubjekt Hervorgebrachte ebenso wie das durch es Ausgeschlossene gleichermaßen an der Subjektivierung beteiligt sind, die insofern ebenso philosophisch-logisch wie auch staatsgeschichtlich und völkergeschichtlich zu interpretieren ist. Die folgende Untersuchung verfolgt so die Absicht, den ersten Entwurf eines Rahmens für eine Kritik des Rechtssubjekts aufzustellen. Dieser Entwurf kann insofern von Wert sein als er ein anderes Modell der Rechtskritik vorschlägt als dies im Zuge der sonst in der Rechtsphilosophie naheliegenden Formen der politisch-juridischen oder sozial-ökonomischen Kritik geschieht.

Der Artikel ist in drei Abschnitte gegliedert: Im ersten Abschnitt werden einige Eckpunkte von Rosenzweigs Kritik an Hegel in Form einer Skizze des Bezugs von Staat, Geschichte und Religion bei Rosenzweig dargestellt. Dadurch soll eine erste Vorstellung des internen Zusammenhangs zwischen den beiden Denkern aufgerissen werden. Der zweite Abschnitt wendet sich einer Betrachtung des Wirklichkeitsbegriffs bei Hegel im Kontext des Verhältnisses von Staat und Religion zu. Hier soll erörtert werden, inwiefern Wirklichkeit bei Hegel als eine gegen jegliche Transzendenz gerichtete Immanenz der Idee, des Begriffs und des Selbstbewusstseins vor dem Hintergrund von Hegels frühen Schriften zur jüdischen und christlichen Religion verständlich gemacht werden kann. Der dritte Abschnitt nimmt eine ästhetische Vermittlung des

---

1 Vgl. hierzu u. a.: Cohen, Hermann (1915): *Deutschtum und Judentum*. Gießen: Verlag von Alfred Töpelmann; Rosenzweig, Franz (1984): „Deutschtum und Judentum" (um 1915). In: Ders.: GS III, *Zweistromland. Kleinere Schriften zu Glauben und Denken*. Hg.: Mayer, Reinhold / Mayer Annemarie. Dordrecht: Martinus Nijhoff, 169–175; Scholem, Gershom (1970): „Wider den Mythos vom deutsch-jüdischen Gespräch". In: Ders.: *Judaica 2*. Frankfurt am Main: Suhrkamp, 7–11; Bienenstock, Myriam (2018): *Cohen und Rosenzweig. Ihre Auseinandersetzung mit dem deutschen Idealismus*. Freiburg/München: Karl Alber; Pollock, Benjamin (2009): *Franz Rosenzweig and the Systematic Task of Philosophy*. Cambridge, UK: Cambridge University Press.

Zusammenhangs von Staat, Geschichte und Religion in der Subjektivierung des Bewusstseins in den Blick. Spezifisch geht es um die Affekt-Formen des Tragischen und des Komischen, anhand derer sich die Konturen eines kritischen Modells des Rechtssubjekts abzeichnen lassen.

2 Rosenzweigs Kritik an Hegel

2.1 Individuum und Nation

Die kritische Perspektive auf den Hegelschen Idealismus, die Rosenzweig in *Hegel und der Staat* entwickelt, zielt auf das Problem der Ohnmächtigkeit nicht nur des Individuums sondern auch des kollektiven politischen Subjekts. So schreibt Rosenzweig: „[B]eide, Einzelmensch und Nation, sind so in gewissem Sinne dem Staat zu opfern, dem vergötterten Staat das Eigenrecht des Menschen wie die Ganzheit der Nation".[2] Anders als sein Lehrer Friedrich Meinecke, der Hegel als Theoretiker des preußischen Machtstaats las, welcher in seiner Lehre vom Staat nur leider die Individualität vernachlässigt habe,[3] vertritt Rosenzweig in *Hegel und der Staat* die These, dass Hegel in seiner politischen Philosophie die spätere geschichtliche Entwicklung zum preußischen Nationalstaat begrifflich eigentlich gar nicht vollzogen habe. Rosenzweig sieht die systematische Funktion des Staats bei Hegel vor allem darin, als Instanz zwischen objektivem und absolutem Geist zu vermitteln. Der Staat ist der Raum, worin sich die vollständige Durchbildung des Einzelnen zum Allgemeinen zu vollziehen hat – primär zum vernünftigen Allgemeinen und nicht so sehr zum Allgemeinen eines kollektiven Willens. Die dann nach Hegels Tod in der tatsächlichen historischen Herausbildung des preußischen Staats einflussreichere Idee der Nation als Staatskörper, als realem Träger des kollektiven Willens, verschwindet im Hegelschen Modell insofern der Struktur nach schon der Einzelmensch in die formale Konstruktion des Staats als Verwirklichung des vernünftigen Allgemeinen eingehe.[4] Demnach geht es Rosenzweig weniger darum nachzuweisen, dass ein unmittelbares Abhängigkeitsverhältnis zwischen Hegels Philosophie und der historischen Herausbildung des preußischen Staats bestünde. Die im Vergleich zu Meinecke umfassendere politische Kritik impliziert vielmehr einen besonderen philosophischen Anspruch. Rosenzweigs Kritik stützt sich so von Beginn an, wenn auch über Umwege, nicht primär auf die Analyse historischer und politischer Fakten, sondern zielt vielmehr auf den zu Grunde liegen-

---

2 Rosenzweig, Franz (2010): *Hegel und der Staat* (1920), Hg.: Lachmann, Frank. Mit einem Nachwort von Axel Honneth. Berlin: Suhrkamp, 530.

3 Meinecke, Friedrich (1924): „Hegel und die Anfänge des deutschen Machtstaatsgedankens im 19. Jahrhundert". In: *Zeitschrift für Politik*, Vol. 13, 197–213.

4 Rosenzweig (2010), 526–531.

den (politisch-)philosophischen Subjektbegriff.[5] Um Rosenzweigs Interpretation besser verständlich machen zu können, ist zu klären, inwiefern es sich hierbei trotz der klaren Stoßrichtung gegen die Hegelsche Philosophie letztlich nicht so sehr um deren Ablehnung rundum handelt, als eher um ein anderes Verständnis im Rahmen einer durchaus ähnlichen Fragestellung.[6]

2.2 Staat, Geschichte, Religion

Rosenzweig betont in *Hegel und der Staat* vor allem die systematische Rolle der Religion in der Herausbildung der Hegelschen philosophischen Form. Der Schritt weg vom Kantischen System der Transzendentalphilosophie, hin zum eigenen System ergab sich für Hegel in den Jahren vor 1800 aus der Reibung an Fragen der Theologie und Religionsphilosophie. In den Jugendschriften zur Religion lässt sich verfolgen, wie allmählich die Idee einer immanenten Wirksamkeit des Absoluten erschlossen wird, d. h. die Herausbildung des Bereichs, welcher im fertigen System der objektive Geist sein wird. Die historische Wirklichkeit der Freiheit lässt sich für Hegel niemals in einem Jenseits aufsuchen, sondern kann nur in den Formen des objektiven Geists als der Verwirklichung des freien Willens im Sozialen und Politischen im Verlauf der Geschichte existieren. In der Lehre vom objektiven Geist besteht Hegels wohl eigenste Erschließung an Neuland im Vergleich zu den anderen Zeitgenossen des deutschen Idealismus.[7] Die systematische Konstruktion erfordert eine Form der objektiven Wirklichkeit des absoluten Geistes. Diese Rolle hat die Religion inne. Sie ist die Ge-

---

5 Die problematische reale politische Bedeutung des Hegelschen Staatsbegriffs entfaltet sich demnach in einer indirekten Weise. Indem in der Wirklichkeit des preußischen Staats die scheinbar realere Idee der Nation als realer Körper des Allgemeinen an die Stelle der vernünftigen, allgemeinen Idee trat, ohne doch jemals über die unerbittliche (ethnische, kulturelle, politische etc.) Partikularität hinauswachsen zu können, lässt sich retrospektiv über das Hegelsche System sagen, dass die Idee eines wahrhaften Universalismus jener Leerstelle der Vernunft preisgegeben wurde, wo die unreinen Diskurse fortleben, welche der Materialismus des Hegelschen Idealismus zwar auf die Vergangenheit bezogen bisweilen so genau registriert, die aber auf die Zukunft hin nicht prophetisch ins System aufgehoben werden können.

6 Myriam Bienenstock hat diese Umwege der Annäherung Rosenzweigs an Hegels System im Sinne eines durch die Perspektive der Historiker Meinecke und Ranke beeinflussten Fehlverständnisses der Hegelschen Geistphilosophie rekonstruiert. Siehe: Bienenstock (2018), v. a. 123–145. Der Topos, wonach Rosenzweigs Auseinandersetzung mit Hegel zu einfach sei, ist wiederholt in der Rezeption anzutreffen. Vgl. hierzu z. B.: Fricke, Martin (2003): *Franz Rosenzweigs Philosophie der Offenbarung*. Würzburg: Königshausen & Neumann; oder auch Bienenstock, Myriam (1992): „Rosenzweig's Hegel". In: *The Owl of Minerva*, 23,1 (Spring 1992), 177–182. Unabhängig davon, zu welchem Grad diese Bewertungen gerechtfertigt sein mögen oder nicht, denke ich, dass die von vielen AutorInnen angemerkte Schwierigkeit, Rosenzweigs Hegel-Interpretation einzuordnen, wiederum in einer anderen Schwierigkeit begründet liegt, die mit einer Frage der Deutung des Hegelschen Werkzusammenhangs zu tun hat – insbesondere mit der Rolle der *Phänomenologie des Geistes* im Verhältnis zum fertigen System.

7 Hier zeigt sich auch das Problem der Verkehrung der reinen Vernunft in der Wirklichkeit. Hegel ist sich dessen voll im Klaren, spricht selber von dieser „verkehrten Welt". Vgl. Hegel, G. W. F. (1986g): *Phänomeno-*

stalt des absoluten Geistes, die im objektiven Geist auch institutionell erscheint, in ihm verkörpert ist. Systematisch gesehen ist die Legitimität des Staats – seines Zeichens wichtigstes Instrument einer immanenten Wirklichkeit des Vernünftigen in der Geschichte – für Hegel also durch die Religion begründet.

Aber paradoxerweise kann die immanente Ermächtigung der vernünftigen Konstruktion im Staat gerade auch die Ohnmacht des realen politischen Körpers implizieren. In diesem Zusammenhang steht bei Rosenzweig weniger das Verhältnis von Religion und Staat als vielmehr das von Religion und Geschichte im Fokus. Die offensichtlich eng an Hegel angelehnte, aber mit anderem Akzent gesetzte Fragestellung entspringt der Thematisierung eines Meta-Rahmens von Geschichtlichkeit, dessen Notwendigkeit sich Rosenzweig nach der Erfahrung einer Krise des Historismus im frühen 20. Jahrhundert aufdrängte. Vor diesem Hintergrund kann man auch Rosenzweigs wiedererwachtes Interesse am Judentum verstehen.[8] Was nun die Wirksamkeit einer solchen Konstruktion der Vernunft in der Geschichte angeht, votiert auch Rosenzweig, wie Hegel, für die Immanenz:

> Die Wirklichkeit des Ziels in der Welt der Wirklichkeiten, das ist was ich brauche. [...] Praktisch kommt es sogar nur darauf an, daß man mit dieser Wirklichkeit zusammenwächst. ‚Gott im Himmel' ist durchaus Nebensache. Es sind nicht die schlechten, sondern grade die guten Christen, die über dem ‚Herrn Jesus' den lieben Gott selbst ganz vergessen. Und nicht der ‚Monotheismus', sondern die Tora macht den Juden.[9]

Vernunft darf demnach nicht abstrakt bleiben. Gottes Willen und Geschichtlichkeit, Religion und Geschichte sind auch für Rosenzweig in einer immanenten Dialektik miteinander zu verbinden. Aber auch wenn Geschichte und Geschichtlichkeit in einem dialektischen Verhältnis zueinander stehen, kommt der Geschichte für Rosenzweig anders als für Hegel keine ontologische Dignität zu. In einem undatierten Brief an Rudolf Ehrenberg vom September 1910 stellt Rosenzweig eine ideengeschichtliche Abfolge des Verhältnisses von Gott zu der Welt, der Natur oder der Geschichte dar. Von dieser Abfolge, die ich im Einzelnen nicht wiedergeben möchte,[10] ist hier festzu-

---

logie des Geistes (1807), Werke 3. Frankfurt am Main: Suhrkamp, 127–136. Man kommt kaum umhin diese Verkehrung als diabolisch zu bezeichnen.

8 In der Desorientierung einer relativistischen kulturalistischen Geschichtsschreibung nach Rickert ist es für Rosenzweig der monotheistische Offenbarungsglaube, welcher Orientierung in Raum, Zeit und Geschichte, und damit Geschichtlichkeit, zu denken erlaubt. Vgl. den Brief an Gertrud Oppenheim vom 30 Mai 1917: Rosenzweig, Franz (1979): *GS I.1. Briefe und Tagebücher 1900–1918*. Hg.: Rosenzweig, R. / Rosenzweig-Scheinmann E., unter Mitwirkung von Casper, B. Haag: Nijhoff, 412 f. Siehe auch Mendes-Flohr, Paul (1988): „Franz Rosenzweig and the Crisis of Historicism". In: Ders. (Hg.): *The Philosophy of Franz Rosenzweig* [meeting held Apr. 20 – May 2, 1980 in Jerusalem]. Hanover/London: Brandeis University Press, 138–161.

9 Brief an Gertrud Oppenheim vom 31. Mai 1917. In: Rosenzweig, Franz (1979), 414.

10 Vgl. die Wiedergabe des unveröffentlichten Manuskripts aus dem Nachlass Rosenzweigs in Pollock, Benjamin (2012): „‚Within Earshot of the Young Hegel': Rosenzweig's Letter to Rudolf Ehrenberg of Sep-

halten, dass Rosenzweig Hegels Kritik an der Transzendenz Gottes zur Geschichte in Form einer Figur Gottes darstellt, der als Garant einer Geschichte aufrechterhalten wird, welche von der Schuld endlicher Kreaturen vorangetrieben wird. Gott versöhnt im sühnenden Schicksal, das durch diese Schuld hervorgerufen wird, deren Verfehlungen. Damit aber wird Gott selber radikal abhängig von den Opfern der endlichen geschichtlichen Akteure. Der Gott *der* Geschichte löst sich als Gott *in der* Geschichte auf. Hierdurch wird Geschichtlichkeit selber letztlich fraglich.

Anders als bei Hegel muss für Rosenzweig darum eine uneinholbare Transzendenz Gottes trotz seines immanenten Eingreifens in die Geschichte gewahrt bleiben. Hier nun wird die theoretische Bedeutung von Rosenzweigs Rückwendung zum Judentum verständlich: Das Judentum ist sowohl Religion wie Volkszugehörigkeit. Im Rahmen der Fragestellung nach einem Modell von Geschichtlichkeit explizit trotz des Christentums am Judentum festzuhalten,[11] obwohl das jüdische Volk in der Diaspora nach der Zerstörung des zweiten Tempels vor fast 2000 Jahren und vor der Gründung des modernen Staates Israel aus der Geschichte herausgetrieben worden war, lässt sich als ein Interesse verstehen, die in der Hegelschen Subjektivierungskonstruktion verschwundene Identität eines Volks (nicht nur des jüdischen) nachzukonstruieren. In diesem Sinne kann Rosenzweigs These, dass das Judentum eine der Geschichte enthobene Position in der Geschichte ausmacht, so gedeutet werden, dass es mittels ihrer möglich wird, einen anderen Bezug von Geschichte und Geschichtlichkeit zu denken. Wenn man die reine Immanenz des Absoluten im Sinne Hegels als Totalität der Geschichte begreift, kann ein Eingreifen Gottes in die Geschichte als ein Durchbrechen dieser Immanenz verstanden werden. Jenseits des Geschichtlichen gibt es einen Einflussbereich Gottes. Das Eingreifen Gottes in die Geschichte kommt dann einer geschichtlich nicht ableitbaren Geschichtlichkeit gleich. Das impliziert auch eine Umkehr der Richtung zwischen Staat und Geschichte. Es geht nicht länger die Geschichte aus dem Staat hervor, sondern der (ein) Staat aus der Geschichtlichkeit – ein unerhörter Vorgang, der das Schicksal der Juden begründet.

> Ohne Staat [...] keine Weltgeschichte. Der Staat allein läßt jene Spiegelbilder der wahren Ewigkeit in den Zeitstrom fallen, die als Epochen die Bausteine der Weltgeschichte bilden. Und darum muß die wahre Ewigkeit des ewigen Volks dem Staat und der Weltgeschichte allzeit fremd und ärgerlich bleiben.[12]

---

tember 1910". In: Wiese, Christian Wiese / Urban, Martina (Hg.): *German-Jewish Thought Between Religion and Politics, Festschrift in Honor of Paul Mendes-Flohr on the Occasion of His Seventieth Birthday*. Berlin/Boston: de Gruyter, 185–207.

11 So der englische Titel des gesammelten Briefwechsels zwischen Franz Rosenzweig und Eugen Rosenstock-Huessy. Vgl. Rosenstock-Huessy, Eugen (1969): *Judaism despite Christianity. The „Letters on Christianity and Judaism" between Eugen Rosenstock-Huessy and Franz Rosenzweig*. University of Alabama Press.

12 Rosenzweig, Franz (1976): *Der Stern der Erlösung* (1921). GS II., Einführung v. Reinhold Mayer. Haag: Nijhof, 371.

Das jüdische Volk figuriert hier als die konstitutive Ausnahme der Weltgeschichte. Als eine die zeitliche Ordnung übersteigende Existenz in der Zeit wurde Israel gleichwohl in die Geschichte gesetzt. Es ist Träger des ewigen und absoluten Gesetzes Gottes und damit der Zeitlichkeit des menschlichen Lebens entzogen, die Hegel als das absolute Movens der Geschichte selbst zur Geschichtlichkeit des Subjekts erhebt. Rosenzweig setzt gegen die Lebendigkeit der Zeit die Ewigkeit des Gesetzes:

> Solche Lebendigkeit wäre die, womit die Zeit ein Leben belohnt, das sich ihr untertan macht: eine rein zeitliche Lebendigkeit. Das ist die Lebendigkeit eines Lebens im Augenblick: daß es Leben in der Zeit ist, sich von der Vergangenheit davontragen läßt und die Zukunft heranruft. So leben Menschen und Völker. Diesem Leben entzog Gott den Juden, indem er die Brücke seines Gesetzes himmelhoch über den Strom der Zeit wölbte, unter deren Bogen sie nun in alle Ewigkeit machtlos dahinrauscht.[13]

Der oben bereits genannte undatierte Brief an Rudolf Ehrenberg verdeutlicht, dass es, Rosenzweigs persönlichem Glauben ungeachtet, nicht darum geht und letztlich nicht gehen kann, (eine) Religion als die dogmatische Antwort auf diese philosophischen Fragen zu präsentieren. Religion ist ein menschliches Verständnis des Verhältnisses Gottes zur Welt und dieses wird in unterschiedlichen Epochen anders dargestellt. Aber anders als für Hegel kann für Rosenzweig eine solche geschichtliche Abfolge philosophisch determinierbarer Gestalten dieses Verhältnisses keine philosophische Universalgeschichte geben. Während für Hegel die Geschichte durchs Christentum in den absoluten Geist aufgehoben wird, bleibt für Rosenzweig das Verhältnis von Geschichte und Religion offen, wobei der unterschiedliche Begriff der göttlichen Offenbarung in der Philosophie *auch ein Faktor* ist. Die Vermittlung von menschlicher Geschichte und Gottes Absicht ist demnach nicht nur historisch offen, sondern ontologisch nicht abgeschlossen. Wenn aber die Offenbarung noch nicht abgeschlossen ist, ist demnach auch die philosophische Vermittlung anders zu denken. Tatsächlich denkt Rosenzweig die göttliche Offenbarung in der interpersonalen Anrede Gottes hin an den Menschen, der mit seinem Namen angesprochen wird. Rosenzweig zieht die radikale Konsequenz, dass Gott selbst erst ein Ich wird, wo er ein Du mit Namen anspricht, das sich dann wiederum erstmals als Ich erfährt, welches Gottes Ich zu bezeugen in der Lage ist.[14] Dabei wird Identität nicht im Sinne einer Bestimmung einer schon vorab existierenden Entität spezifiziert, sondern konstituiert sich erstmals und nicht abschließend. Die individuell namentlich konstituierte Identität ist eine neue Allgemeinheit:

> Was einen eigenen Namen hat, kann nicht mehr Ding, nicht mehr jedermanns Sache sein; er ist unfähig, restlos in die Gattung einzugehen, denn es gibt keine Gattung, der es zu-

13 Ebd., 376.
14 Ebd., 207 f.

> gehörte, es ist seine eigene Gattung. Es hat auch nicht mehr seinen Ort in der Welt, seinen Augenblick im Geschehen, sondern es trägt sein Hier und Jetzt mit sich herum; wo es ist, ist ein Mittelpunkt, und wo es den Mund öffnet, ist ein Anfang.[15]

In der Offenbarung kommt die Identität erst hervor. Und das heißt, sie kann sich (jederzeit) radikal ändern. Identität in diesem Sinne ist keine Vermittlung des Selbstbewusstseins, sondern eine sich in der Offenbarung erst konstituierende Vermittlung. Im Gebot der Anrede Gottes an die Menschen offenbart sich die Ewigkeit des Gesetzes in der Zeit. Hier aber wird der Mensch zum Teilnehmer der göttlichen Ewigkeit. Erst dadurch wird der Augenblick göttlicher Wirklichkeit real präsente Ewigkeit. Geschichtlichkeit findet Eingang in die Geschichte wo das „Wachsen der Welt" und das „Wirken der menschlichen Seele" sich überkreuzen. Ohne den menschlichen Versuch, Gottes Reich herbeizuführen, das heißt: ohne die Zukunft vorwegzunehmen „ist die Zukunft keine Zukunft, sondern nur eine in unendliche Länge hingezogene, nach vorwärts projizierte Vergangenheit."[16]

3 Wirklichkeit bei Hegel

3.1 Wirklichkeit in der Religion, Logik und Phänomenologie

Der Grund für Rosenzweigs religionsphilosophische Erwiderung auf die Hegelsche Staatsphilosophie kann auf einem systematischen Zusammenhang bei Hegel beruhend weiter erläutert werden. Die Frage der Wirklichkeit des Geistes, die Hegel in der *Phänomenologie des Geistes,* der *Wissenschaft der Logik,* den *Grundlinien* und im fertigen System der *Enzyklopädie* begrifflich diskutiert, ist in seinen frühen Schriften zur Religion und den dortigen Überlegungen zum Verhältnis von Ideal und Wirklichkeit präfiguriert. Wirklichkeit wird hier vor allem als Anerkennung von Immanenz verstanden. Dabei wird die Gegenüberstellung von Transzendenz und Immanenz in Abgrenzung zum Judentum vorgenommen, dessen Wesen als die verpasste Chance zur Versöhnung mit der entzweiten Natur bestimmt wird – eine Versöhnung, die für Hegel erst durch die hellenisch-christliche Tradition vollzogen werden kann.

Die in den frühen Schriften anhand der Exegese des biblischen Texts vorgenommenen Überlegungen sollen hier zunächst nur insoweit referiert werden als sie Licht auf die Entstehung des Hegelschen Wirklichkeitsbegriffs zu werfen erlauben. Hegels Deutung nach wiederholt Moses, der den Israeliten das göttliche Gesetz übermittelt, eine Geste, die vor ihm Abraham und vor diesem bereits Noah ausgeführt hatten: das Ideal

---

15 Ebd., 208.
16 Ebd., 253 f.

von der Wirklichkeit abzutrennen. Das aber heißt nichts anderes als die Selbstgesetzgebung zu verunmöglichen. Abraham, der Stammvater der Israeliten, ist für Hegel keineswegs der Gläubige der singulären Verheißung, sondern der, dessen Vermögen zu lieben, d. h. sich mit dem Fremden zu verbinden, grundsätzlich gestört ist und der sich aller Festlegung in dieser Welt stets entzieht.[17] Wo hingegen Abrahams Nachkommen mächtiger wurden, seien sie tyrannisch geworden.[18] Der Stammvater ohne Verwurzelung in dieser Welt und das Volk der Nachkommen dann umso tyrannischer – Hegel suggeriert damit im Stamme Israels die wesenhafte Vermischung zweier noch weiter zurückliegender Charaktere, die bis an den Mythos heranreichen: Noah und sein verdecktes alter ego Nimrod. Durch „Aufnahme eines fremden Wesens [...] verunreinigte [sich der Geist dieses Volkes]".[19] Hegel ist nicht am Noah vor der Flut interessiert – dem als einzig Gerechten Auserwählten, dessen Geschlecht trotz der Sünde der mythischen Zeit noch tadellos war – sondern am Noah nach der Flut. Dieser nämlich setzte nach der mythischen Vernichtung – die zugleich eine Vernichtung des Mythos bedeutet – der Natur Schranken, indem er sich selbst der Beschränkung durchs Gesetz unterwarf. Noah folgt damit einer von zwei Möglichkeiten, die Hegel hier, anders als später, unterscheidet und einander entgegensetzt: nämlich der „Idee" und nicht der „Wirklichkeit". „Damit der Mensch gegen die Ausbrüche der nun feindlichen Natur bestehen könnte, so mußte sie beherrscht werden; und da das entzweite Ganze nur in Idee und Wirklichkeit entzweit sein kann, so ist die höchste Einheit der Beherrschung entweder in einem Gedachten oder in einem Wirklichen."[20] Weil die Idee als bloß gedachte zu schwach ist, um sich in einer Einheit mit der Wirklichkeit zu verbinden, liegt die Wahrheit der Idee jedoch nicht in ihr selbst, sondern in der Wirklichkeit. Dafür steht Nimrod, der kurzerhand in den „Menschen [die] Einheit [legte], [...] ihn zum Seienden ein[setzte], das die übrigen Wirklichen zu Gedachten mache, d. h. tötete, beherrschte".[21] Die Wirklichkeit präsentiert sich so als „das Gesetz des Stärkeren, aber eines Lebendigen".[22]

In seinen späteren Werken wird diese ‚Wirklichkeit' von Hegel dann begrifflich ausgearbeitet. Im Abschnitt über die Wirklichkeit in der *Wissenschaft der Logik* wird Wirklichkeit als Manifestation der absoluten Form oder als reflektierte Absolutheit bestimmt. Als Manifestation macht die absolute Form der Wirklichkeit eine gesetzte Einheit der logischen Modalität der Wirklichkeit (im Sinne einer real in sich reflektierten Existenz oder als Unmittelbarkeit) und Möglichkeit (im Sinne einer Reflexion in sich) aus, die als voneinander isolierte Momente noch nicht realisiert sind. Die Wirk-

---

17 Hegel, G. W. F. (1986b): „Der Geist des Judentums" / „Der Geist des Christentums und sein Schicksal" (1798–1800). In: Ders.: *Frühe Schriften*, Werke 1. Frankfurt a. M.: Suhrkamp, 274–418., hier 277 ff.
18 Ebd., 280.
19 Ebd., 274.
20 Ebd., 275.
21 Ebd., 276.
22 Ebd.

lichkeit kann so als eine Form der absoluten Gegenwart verstanden werden, wo das Absolute rein gegenwärtig und noch nicht entwickelt ist. Jedoch ist diese reine Wirklichkeit freilich in sich selbst nur logisches Moment des Wirklichen als Beziehung von Unmittelbarkeit und Reflexion, also Moment des Wirklichen im Sinne eines „in sich reflektiertes Sein[s], und dieses zugleich als unmittelbar existierendes."[23] Als solche, schreibt Hegel, ist Wirklichkeit Notwendigkeit. Die Wirklichkeit hebt so die Existenz auf und ist von da ab zuständig für die Realisierung der Existenz als unmittelbarer. Wenn diese rein logischen Bestimmungen wieder in den Bereich des ‚Wirklichen' zurückübersetzt werden, heißt das, dass Zukunft im Hegelschen System lediglich im Sinne der Erstreckung der absoluten Gegenwart aufscheinen darf. Zukunft ist relevant für Gegenwart nur im logischen Sinne der Wirklichkeit, d. h. im Sinne eines kontinuierlichen Werdegangs von einer Gegenwart in die nächste. Brüche können im Nachhinein festgestellt aber niemals als Verheißung antizipiert werden. Dass die Eule der Minerva erst zur Abenddämmerung mit ihrem Flug anhebt heißt, dass bei Hegel jede Naivität des Denkens ausgeschlossen ist in einem mit strenger Notwendigkeit am Tod orientierten Leben. Wirklichkeit und Ideal voneinander trennen zu wollen, wie dies Noah und Abraham getan hätten, ist hier schlicht widersinnig. Das Wahre, schreibt Hegel in der Vorrede zur *Phänomenologie des Geistes*, ist „nur als System wirklich" – und Substanz als Subjekt zu begreifen heißt das „Absolute als Geist" zu verstehen.[24] Das heißt, damit eine solche Identität des Wirklichen bestehen kann, muss es ein System der Bestimmungen geben, wo reale Bestimmungen als geistige in logische Bestimmungen aufgehoben werden können. Darin besteht die Übereinstimmung einer gesetzten Wirklichkeit mit sich selbst.

Die Funktion der Übersetzung vernünftiger Bestimmungen in reale und der Herausbildung vernünftiger Bestimmungen als realer hat im Hegelschen System des Geistes der Staat inne. In der *Enzyklopädie* spricht Hegel im letzten Paragraph über die Weltgeschichte (§ 552) das Verhältnis von Staat und Religion an. Auch in diesem Kontext spricht Hegel von Wirklichkeit und bestimmt diese hier als Vernunft, die im Staat verwirklicht wird, wobei das Staatsvolk durch die Sittlichkeit im Staat, deren Substantialität die Religion ist, geformt wird. Der Geist des sittlichen Selbstbewusstseins dieses Volks wird in einer „in der sittlichen Welt *wirklich* vollbrachte[n] Reinigung" zu seiner Wahrheit erhoben.[25] Nur in diesem Rahmen der substantiell religiösen Sittlichkeit des Staates ist es demnach möglich, eine „Negation"[26] zu denken, welche das Volk diszipliniert, sein Wissen reinigt und seinen Willen befreit. Der Staat ist dabei die „eigene, die

---

23 Hegel, G. W. F. (1986j): *Wissenschaft der Logik II* (1812/1816). Werke 6, Frankfurt am Main: Suhrkamp, 202.
24 Hegel (1986g), PdG, 28.
25 Hegel, (1986d): *Enzyklopädie der philosophischen Wissenschaften im Grundrisse* (1830). Dritter Teil. Die Philosophie des Geistes, mit den mündlichen Zusätzen, Werke 10, Frankfurt am Main: Suhrkamp, 354.
26 Ebd.

sich verwirklichende Vernunft [...]; die Sittlichkeit im Staate."[27] Religiöse Heiligkeit hingegen ist lediglich eine unfreie Vorstellung des sittlichen Inhalts, im Sinne einer jenseits des Selbstbewusstseins liegenden Ohnmächtigkeit des Guten. Es scheint hier als stünden Religion und Sittlichkeit einander entgegen. „[D]urch das Sicheinführen des göttlichen Geistes in die Wirklichkeit, die Befreiung der Wirklichkeit zu ihm wird das, was in der Welt Heiligkeit sein soll, durch die Sittlichkeit verdrängt."[28] Aber das heißt nicht, dass Sittlichkeit ohne seine religiöse Substantialität bestehen könnte. Hegel warnt geradezu vor der „Torheit neuerer Zeit" die Verschränkung von Sittlichkeit und Religion ineinander nicht länger wahrhaben und „Revolution ohne eine Reformation" machen zu wollen.[29] Sittlichkeit und religiöse Geistigkeit des Staates müssten sich vielmehr gegenseitig stützen. Hegel sucht also die Wirklichkeit des Geistes im Staat als seine Verwirklichung in der Sittlichkeit des Volkes auf. In der *Phänomenologie des Geistes* geht er in diesem Kontext davon aus, dass ein qualitativer Unterschied zweier Ebenen der Geschichte des Subjekts zu berücksichtigen ist. Der moderne Schritt zur absoluten Negativität des von der Substanz losgelösten Subjekts ist, einmal geschehen, unhintergehbar. Gleichwohl kann der politische Bruch in den Gesellschaften der Moderne zu den traditionellen Formen der Sittlichkeit scheitern, wenn die Freiheit des modernen Individuums bloß liberal in der Form des Rechtssubjekts gedacht wird. Eine Emanzipation von kollektiver Unfreiheit kann ihrerseits regressiv sein.

3.2 Selbst und Schicksal

Die lebendige Wirklichkeit des Gesetzes kann für Hegel nur bei dessen Immanenz garantiert werden. Diese Immanenz sieht Hegel seit seinen frühen Schriften im Christentum erreicht. Aber das Problem, das in den Figuren Noahs und Nimrods als ein externer Gegensatz von Idee und Wirklichkeit dargestellt wurde, wiederholt sich im Christentum nun als interner Gegensatz. In der dialektischen Immanenz wird der Gegensatz von Idee und Wirklichkeit nicht in dem Sinne aufgehoben, dass er verschwände und ein von irgendwoher kommendes Drittes, etwa die Gnade des Christentums, an seine Stelle träte, um den Widerspruch zu schlichten; vielmehr wird der Gegensatz *im* Christentum selbst aufgehoben, d.h. bewahrt, oder vielmehr bewährt.[30] Die Wirklichkeit selbst ist geistig und die Idee wirklich, weil sie in der Wirklichkeit etwas bewirkt. Die dialektische Synthesis ist der Blick auf den Gegensatz selbst von der Per-

---

27 Ebd., 359.
28 Ebd., 358.
29 Ebd., 360.
30 Hier zeigt sich, dass sich die Hegelsche Dialektik von einem generellen Klischee von Dialektik unterscheidet, wonach die Synthese als versöhnendes Drittes zu These und Antithese hinzutritt. Solch eine Auflösung wäre für Hegel überhaupt keine Dialektik, sondern schlechter Dualismus; nicht immanent begründet, sondern unbegründete Transzendenz.

spektive einer der Positionen des Gegensatzes aus gesehen. Entsprechend findet die Wirklichkeit einen Weg, in ihrer Aufhebung in die Idee zu überleben, ganz so wie das Böse einen Weg fand zu überleben, obwohl die mythische Flut alle Unreinheit hätte vertilgen sollen. Durch die Dialektik Hegels überlebt das Böse, indem es als Schlechtes präsentiert wird: anstelle des (nicht einlösbaren) Anspruchs, *das Gute zu tun*, tritt der Anspruch, *etwas gut zu tun*. Das Objekt wird fallengelassen, bzw. als Modus des Subjekts in dieses aufgenommen.

Man muss die These aufwerfen, dass an dieser Stelle die den objektiven Geist begründende, im eigentlichen Sinne moralische *Verkehrung* stattfindet. In „Der Geist des Christentums“ interpretiert Hegel nun nach den jüdischen Schriften auch das Neue Testament:

> Richtet nicht, so werdet ihr nicht gerichtet, denn mit welchem Maß ihr messet, wird euch wieder gemessen. Das Maß sind Gesetze und Rechte. Jenes Gebot kann doch nicht heißen: Was ihr anderen wider die Gesetze nachseht und erlaubt, das wird euch auch nachgesehen werden – ein Bund schlechter Menschen erteilt jedem Einzelnen die Erlaubnis, schlecht zu sein –, sondern: Hütet euch, das Rechttun und die Liebe als eine Abhängigkeit von Gesetzen und Gehorsam gegen Gebote zu nehmen und sie nicht als aus dem Lebendigen kommend zu betrachten. Ihr erkennt [sonst] eine Herrschaft über euch [an], über die ihr nichts vermögt, die stärker ist als ihr; eine Macht, die nicht ihr selbst seid.[31]

Es wird gesagt, dass das Gebot keine Erlaubnis zur *Schlechtigkeit* gebe. Aber Hegel redet wohlweislich von schlecht, nicht von *böse*. Auf diese Weise kann das *Gute* als Gegensatz des *Schlechten* präsentiert werden und ist damit gerade kein absolutes moralisch Gutes mehr, das dem Bösen entgegengesetzt wäre. Als Gegenteil des Schlechten betrifft das Gute eher eine praktische Klugheitsregel, eine Regel, wie man in besserer Weise *tun* könne – *was* tun bleibt dabei sekundär. Es geht also um ein Gerichtetsein aufs Gesetz als Objekt, das eine Praxis des Umgangs mit dem Gesetz beinhaltet. Aber die angeratene Weise des Umgangs mit dem Gesetz macht eben gerade nicht den Umgang mit dem Gesetz, sondern das Gesetz selbst zum Problem. Das Gesetz ist für Hegel deshalb ein Problem, weil es eine Macht ist, die nicht vom Selbst kommt, insofern sie als ein jenseitiges Absolutes behauptet wird.

Das Zitat geht bei Hegel folgendermaßen weiter:

> Ihr setzt für euch wie für andere vor der Tat ein Fremdes, ihr erhebt zu einem Absoluten ein Fragment des Ganzen des menschlichen Gemütes; stellt darin eine Herrschaft der Gesetze und Knechtschaft der Sinnlichkeit oder des Individuums auf und setzt auf diese Art Möglichkeit von Strafen, nicht eines Schicksals, jene von außen her, von einem Unabhän-

31 Hegel (1986b), 352.

gigen kommend, dieses [d. h. das Schicksal !, K. S.] durch eure Natur, obzwar als ein jetzt Feindseliges bestimmt, aber noch nicht über euch, sondern nur gegen euch.[32]

Das Verhältnis des Subjekts zum Gesetz, das Hegel hier der Predigt Jesu entnehmen will, ist der eines Selbstbezugs. Das absolute Gesetz ist demnach eigentlich als solches ein von den Menschen gesetztes. Unmenschliche Übermacht gegen das Individuum, die Knechtschaft der Sinnlichkeit und die Möglichkeit der Strafe von einem unabhängigen Außen sollen als menschlich produziert erkannt werden. *Gegen* eine falsche Abtrennung vom Selbst steht hier das Schicksal. Wie Hegel an der Stelle sagt, ist das Schicksal zwar noch als ein „Feindseliges bestimmt". Aber es ist auf der gleichen Ebene wie das Selbst: „noch nicht über euch, sondern nur gegen euch". Das Modell dieses Verhältnisses ist nicht Noah, sondern Nimrod. Das Schicksal ist vom Selbst handhabbar.

Dieser sich um das Jahr 1800 herum in der Deutung von Judentum und Christentum herausbildende Schicksalsglauben tritt an die Stelle des für den Hegel vor der Frankfurter Zeit bestimmenden kantianischen Freiheitswillens. Strukturell gesehen verdrängt der Schicksalsbegriff das kategorische Sittengesetz ebenso wie den absolut transzendenten Gott des jüdischen Volks. Funktional gesehen kommt das einer Ersetzung der Kategorie der Sünde durch die dialektische Einheit von Schuld und Schicksal im Ganzen des Lebens gleich. Während Sünde (trans-)objektive Bedingung ist, ist Schuld hingegen subjektiv gewirkt und bringt als solche ein objektives Schicksal hervor. Der Schritt ist erstaunlich: Er lässt die absolute Indifferenz der dualistischen Nicht-Beziehung von Subjekt und Objekt bestehen, bringt sie aber zugleich in die immanente Einheit der Lebens-Form. Zwar ist die Trennung vom Leben Schuld und zieht so auch mit schicksalhafter Notwendigkeit Strafe, d. h. Konsequenzen nach sich; zwar kann das Schicksal nicht hintergangen werden, zwar ist es absolut notwendig – doch die Schuld trifft nur das Selbst, kein Fremdes. Abtrennung und Entzug von der historischen Entfaltung des Lebens bewirkt Schuld, jedoch Schuld an sich selbst, nicht gegen Gott. Ebendieser geschlossene Kreislauf der Schuld ist Schicksal. Als Leben begreift das Schicksal seine eigene Kontingenz in sich. Es ist nicht ewig unversöhnlich wie das verletzte äußere Gesetz der Juden oder das verletzte innere Gesetz Kants. Der Hegelsche Geist des Christentums *ist* das, was hier Schicksal heißt, also vereinende Versöhnung des Jenseits mit dem Diesseits, von Subjekt und Objekt, Objekt und Subjekt. Das Schicksal ist lebendiges Selbstbewusstsein. Schuld und Strafe stehen zwar in notwendigem Verhältnis zueinander, aber Schuld, selbstgemachte Trennung, kann eben auch wieder vernichtet werden.

[D]a sie nicht von einem fremden Gesetze über den Menschen kommt, sondern aus dem Menschen erst das Gesetz und Recht des Schicksals entsteht, so ist die Rückkehr zu dem ursprünglichen Zustand, zur Ganzheit möglich, denn der Sünder ist mehr als eine exis-

32 Ebd., 352 f.

> tierende Sünde, ein Persönlichkeit habendes Verbrechen; er ist Mensch, Verbrechen und Schicksal ist in ihm, er kann wieder zu sich selbst zurückkehren, und wenn er zurückkehrt [sind sie] unter ihm.[33]

Das Schicksal versöhnt sich selbst – mit gesetzhafter Notwendigkeit, sei es auch im Durchlauf seiner eigenen kontingenten Bewegung. So bleibt es sich selbst gleich und wird zugleich anders. Denn auch wenn das Ich Prinzip dieses Selbstbewusstseins ist, überschreitet sich das Prinzip selbst. Ontologisch geht das Schicksal des Selbstbewusstseins über das Selbstbewusstsein des Ich hinaus, wird objektive Geschichte oder Unbewusstes des Ich, welches im absoluten Subjekt doch erfassbar sein soll. Es *hat* eine Geschichte, weil es Geschichte, objektiver Geist *ist*.

4 Vom tragischen zum komischen Subjekt

Vor diesem Hintergrund wird nun die Relevanz der eingangs aufgeführten von Rosenzweig vorgenommenen ontologischen Verschiebung im Zusammenhang von Religion, (Staats-)Volk und Geschichte besser verständlich. Wie gesehen umfasst dieser Bereich bei Rosenzweig einen noch nicht geschichtlich vermittelten Bereich, der weder einfach dem Individuum noch dem Kollektiv zugeordnet werden kann, wo die Geschichtlichkeit Gottes in die Geschichte eingeführt wird. Wie ebenfalls gesehen spricht Hegel keineswegs nur von Geschichte – der ontologische Rahmen der Geschichtlichkeit wird auch hier über die Religion eingeführt; dann ans Selbst gebunden. Es soll nun hier vertreten werden, dass Hegels Deutung der Vollendung des Prozesses vom Tod Gottes am Kreuz und seiner Wiederauferstehung als das Sich-Finden des absoluten Selbstbewusstseins des Geistes es erforderlich macht, die Betrachtung des Zusammenhangs von Geschichte und Religion in eine (meta-)affekttheoretische Betrachtung des Subjektivierungsprozesses zu überführen, bzw. diese Betrachtung an jene anzuschließen. So operiert auch die Hegelsche Frage der Subjektivierung im Zusammenhang von Religion und Geschichte. Damit ist eben gesagt, dass es hier nicht nur um das Individuum geht sondern auch um eine kollektive Einheit des Nationalvolks. Darüber hinaus geht es eigentlich aber auch um die Allgemeinheit der Menschen schlechthin, also um die *Unmenge aller Menschen* oder um die Massen. Wie diese beiden Ebenen eines bestimmten, also partikularen staatlichen Kollektivs und die wahre Allgemeinheit aller letztlich zueinander stehen ist nicht abschließend geklärt. Hegel führt hier jedenfalls die ästhetischen Formen der Komödie und der Tragödie – bzw. die Affekte oder Affektparadigmen des Komischen und des Tragischen – ein, um eine Sphäre des Geistes zu markieren, die sich nicht einfach geschichtlich deuten lässt, die aber angenommen

---

33 Ebd., 353 f.

werden muss, um die Subjektvierung des Verhältnisses von Religion und Geschichte setzen zu können. Weil die Subjektivierung sich hier im Rahmen des objektiven Geistes zwischen Individuum und partikularem (Staats-)Kollektiv abspielt, betrifft sie, obwohl sie doch allgemein sein sollte, nicht alle Menschheit. Somit ist sie jedenfalls nicht *nur* logisch.

In der *Phänomenologie des Geistes* werden das Tragische und das Komische – diese beiden affektiven Grundregister der Subjektivierung – im Schritt vom traditional-sittlichen Subjekt zum modern-sittlichen Subjekt von Hegel nun zweimal aufgerufen: zuerst im Kontext des Rechts und später noch einmal im Kontext der Religion. Im Abschnitt über die sittliche Handlung lässt Hegel zunächst anhand der Antigone-Tragödie die Form der modernen Rechtsperson aus dem Zusammenbruch der organischen antik-sittlichen Gemeinschaft hervorgehen. Dieser Rückzug der alten Ordnung folgt der strengen „Notwendigkeit des leeren Schicksals, [...] das *Ich* des Selbstbewußtseins."[34] Im Stufengang der Selbstentfaltung des Geistes ist der Rechtszustand aber selbst nur eine der Durchgangsstationen in der Vermittlung des absoluten Selbstbewusstseins. Und so spricht Hegel an späterer Stelle in der *Phänomenologie* nochmals von Tragödie und Komödie, und zwar im Kapitel über die Kunstreligion. Hier geht es dann darum, das ungebändigte Ich wieder zu bändigen und der Vernünftigkeit zuzuführen. Vor dem Hintergrund des bisher Gesagten werden die beiden Kontexte verständlich: Weil Individuen und eine unbestimmte Menge des Volks nicht dasselbe sind, ist die Wiederholung oder Zweistufigkeit der Subjektivierung nötig. Hier bringt die Subjektivierung, zuerst im Modus eines Bruchs, die Rechtsperson hervor: aus der Zerstörung der antiken Sittlichkeit entspringt erstmals die Form des modernen Individuums. Es geschieht die *Einschreibung des Subjekts in die Substanz*. Die zweite Stufe oder Wiederholung der Subjektivierung steht dann im Zusammenhang der Religion und bedeutet *die Einschreibung des absoluten Geistes in die Universalgeschichte*. Einmal der Aufstieg des natürlichen Bewusstseins und einmal das Herabsteigen des wahren Wissens. Es gilt ein Individuum herauszubilden, das als solches doch auch die kollektive Einheit repräsentiert, ein Individuum also, das denken kann, welches Leichtsinn und unglückliches Bewusstsein gleichermaßen überwunden hat und weiß: mein Schicksal geht mit dem des Staatskollektivs einher.

Wenden wir ins nun genauer zunächst dem ersten Kontext zu. Die moderne sittliche Substanz wird in der *Phänomenologie* als eine durch die individuelle Tat entzweite vormoderne Substanz dargestellt, deren Unversöhntheit mit sich selbst sich in der schicksalhaften Bewegung ihrer selbst aufhebt. Diese immanente Entzweiung und Rückkehr in die Einheit der Substanz-als-Subjekt wird in der Form der griechischen Tragödie dargestellt. Die Welt der traditionellen Sittlichkeit steht mit dem Bewusstsein der einzelnen in Übereinstimmung. Das Verhältnis des sittlichen Bewusstseins

34 Hegel (1986g), PdG, 355.

auf das sittliche Wesen ist noch durch „einfache reine Richtung" bestimmt.[35] Es gibt also ein unmittelbares Umsetzen der Substanz in sittlichen Agenten, die ihrer Pflicht folgen. Im sittlichen Bewusstsein gibt es kein wirkliches Individuum, individuelle Tätigkeit gibt es erst im Selbstbewusstsein. „Die Tat" schreibt Hegel, „ist das wirkliche Selbst."[36] In der Tat entleeren sich sowohl Substanz und Individuum gegenseitig. Denn was als einseitig ausgerichtete, ruhige Übereinstimmung erschien ist eigentlich ein unruhiges Ineinander-Übergehen von Gegensätzen und wird zu der

> negativen Bewegung oder der ewigen Notwendigkeit des furchtbaren *Schicksals,* welche das göttliche wie das menschliche Gesetz sowie die beiden Selbstbewußtsein[e], in denen diese Mächte ihr Dasein haben, in den Abgrund seiner *Einfachheit* verschlingt – und für uns in das *absolute Fürsichsein* des rein einzelnen Selbstbewußtseins übergeht.[37]

Dieses Auseinandertreten von Substanz und Individuum wird der Tragödie zugeordnet. So wird als der nicht-wissentliche Verbrecher gegen das Gesetz Ödipus genannt, als die wissentliche (und darum reinere) Verbrecherin Antigone.[38] Und an späterer Stelle werden mehrere Bestimmungen gegeben, welche die Entzweiung der sittlichen Substanz in den Kontext der Tragödie stellen. Um nur einige zu nennen: so liegt in der Tragödie eine Zusammenfassung der „Zerstreuung der Momente der wesentlichen und handelnden Welt" vor.[39] Oder: „die *Substanz* des Göttlichen tritt *nach der Natur des Begriffs* in ihre Gestalten auseinander".[40] In den absoluten Charakteren der Tragödie wird die Individualität wesentlich, verliert ihren Charakter der Zufälligkeit und Inkonsequenz.[41] Gleichzeitig wird der Gedanke des Tragischen aber relativiert. Im Abschnitt über die sittliche Handlung tauchen die Bezeichnungen ‚Tragödie' oder ‚tragisch' nicht auf – wohl aber fällt das Wort ‚komisch'. Das Tragische wird ins Komische transformiert. Ja, die tragische Kollision wird tatsächlich als komisch bezeichnet. So heißt es: „Komisch aber ist die Kollision der Pflichten, weil sie den Widerspruch, nämlich eines *entgegengesetzten Absoluten,* also Absolutes und unmittelbar die Nichtigkeit dieses sogenannten Absoluten oder Pflicht, ausdrückt."[42]

Vom Standpunkt des Absoluten aus gesehen gibt es einen immanenten Widerspruch. Das Absolute setzt sich selbst einander entgegen, weil es sich gleichermaßen als göttliches wie als menschliches Gesetz darstellt. In diesem Sinne sind Tragödie und Komödie hier aufeinander bezogen. Die Antigone-Tragödie zeigt das: Das Gesetz der *polis,* das durch Kreon behauptet wird, steht dem Gesetz der Familie oder der Götter,

---

35 Ebd., 342.
36 Ebd.
37 Ebd.
38 Ebd., 347 f.
39 Ebd., 534.
40 Ebd.
41 Ebd., 540.
42 Ebd., 343.

auf das Antigone sich beruft, um den Staatsfeind, ihren Bruder Polyneikes, würdig zu bestatten, entgegen. Weil der Widerspruch der absoluten Substanz selbst immanent ist, ist er unvermeidlich. Nur deshalb bleibt er nicht in der Ohnmacht, sondern entwickelt überhaupt eine praktische Wirkmacht. Damit aber wird er auch unausweichlich zur Schuld: Indem das Selbstbewusstsein zur Tat schreitet, erhebt es sich aus der und gegen die einfache Gerichtetheit auf die ihm substantiell vorgegebene sittliche Pflicht, die ihm als unmittelbare Wahrheit noch unfraglich ist. Stattdessen setzt es die Entzweiung, die „Trennung seiner selbst in sich als das Tätige und in die gegenüberstehende, für es negative Wirklichkeit."[43] Darum wird das Selbstbewusstsein zur Schuld. Es wählt eine Seite, wendet sich einem Gesetz zu – dem göttlichen oder dem menschlichen Gesetz – und verletzt damit notwendig das andere Gesetz. Die Schuld zeigt sich in seiner Tat. Und das Tun ist das Wesen dieses Selbstbewusstseins, das sonst nicht wirkliches wäre. Die Schuld zieht unweigerlich Strafe nach sich, aber weil beide Seiten innerlich ineinander verschlungen sind und aneinander schuldig werden, zieht die Tat auch den Zusammenbruch beider Seiten nach sich. Damit aber glätten sich gewissermaßen wieder die Wellen. Die Schuld hebt sich selbst im Schicksal auf.[44]

Hier liegt bei Hegel der entscheidende Übergang zwischen Tragödie und Komödie. Die Tragödie kippt unmittelbar in die Komödie. Denn nichts anderes *ist* bei Hegel die Komödie: der Zusammenbruch dessen was ohnehin nicht haltbar war, ohne dass dabei das Wesentliche zerstört worden wäre – war doch alle Schuld nur Schuld des Selbst an sich. Es muss daher bis zum Verschwinden anders werden ohne doch jemals sich selbst zu verlassen. Der formale Aspekt allein macht das Selbst zum Komischen. Das komische Subjekt, sagt Hegel in seinen Vorlesungen zur Ästhetik, „[kann] sich in freier Heiterkeit aus diesem Untergange erheben."[45]

Vom Standpunkt des einzelnen Bewusstseins aus gesehen ist die moderne Subjektivität tragisch, weil sie in einem notwendigen Auseinandertreten von Substanz und Individualität beruht. Aber vom Standpunkt des Absoluten aus gesehen ist die moderne entzweite Subjektivität komisch, weil sie sich, sich selbst bewahrend, in sich selbst aufhebt. In der Tragödie wird das Selbst zwar als den einander gegenüberstehenden Charakteren zugeteilt dargestellt. Eigentlich aber, schreibt Hegel, ist das Selbst „in der Tat die negative Macht, die Einheit des Zeus, des *substantiellen* Wesens und der *abstrakten* Notwendigkeit; es ist die geistige Einheit, worein alles zurückgeht."[46]

Trotz dessen, dass damit also die negative Macht einer geistigen Einheit erreicht ist, in der was erscheinend entspringt doch auch verbleibt, scheint damit das Ziel noch nicht erreicht: Warum spricht Hegel hier von einer Einheit des substantiellen Wesens

---

43 Ebd., 345 f.
44 Ebd., 349 ff.
45 Hegel (1986i): *Vorlesungen über die Ästhetik III* (1820–1829). Werke 15, Frankfurt am Main: Suhrkamp, 529.
46 Hegel (1986g), PdG, 541.

und der *abstrakten* Notwendigkeit? Der Grund hierfür liegt darin, dass die nun aus dem Zusammenbruch der sittlichen Einheit hervorgehende komische Einheit nichts anderes ist als die Basiseinheit der Gestalt des Geistes, die in den *Grundlinien der Philosophie des Rechts* als abstraktes Recht bezeichnet wird: So *komisch* das vielleicht klingen mag – aus den Trümmern der vormodernen, substantiellen sittlichen Allgemeinheit erhebt sich in freier Heiterkeit die von Hegel sogenannte „formelle Allgemeinheit" der Rechtsperson.[47] Am Beginn des Abschnitts zum Rechtszustand in der *Phänomenologie* heißt es: „Die allgemeine Einheit, in welche die lebendige unmittelbare Einheit der Individualität und der Substanz zurückgeht, ist das geistlose Gemeinwesen [...] eine *Gleichheit*, worin *Alle* als *Jede*, als *Personen* gelten."[48] Die Person des Rechts ist abstrakt, weil sie nicht wirklich allgemein ist, sondern nur formell allgemein, Einheitsmodul eines Durcheinanders. Deswegen beschreibt Hegel hier dann auch, wie die leere, inhaltslose Selbstständigkeit des Rechts nur „allgemeine Verwirrung und gegenseitige Auflösung" hervorbringt und damit nur „unwirklicher Gedanke" bleibt.[49] Denn die formelle Gleichheit geht sehr wohl mit realer Ungleichheit einher. Der hier gewährte komische, abstrakte, formelle Selbstgenuss des, wie Hegel schreibt, „ungeheuren Selbstbewusstseins" ist der einer „ebenso ungeheureren Ausschweifung".[50] Eben den formellen Charakter der Person zeigt uns die Komödie – den Schauspieler scheinbar direkt vereint mit der dramatischen *Person*, anders als in der Tragödie ohne Maske, aber nicht als Individuum, sondern als abstrakter Typus:

---

47 Ebd., 354.
48 Ebd., 355.
49 Ebd., 355 f.
50 Ebd., 358. In einem frühen Fragment unterscheidet Hegel noch zwischen einem Staat, dessen Prinzip „das Eigentum" ist und einem Staat, dessen Prinzip „das Ganze" ist. Vgl. Hegel, G. W. F. (1986e) „Fragmente historischer und politischer Studien aus der Berner und Frankfurter Zeit" (ca. 1795–1798). In: Ders.: *Frühe Schriften*, Werke 1, Frankfurt am Main: Suhrkamp, 428–448, hier 444. Partikulares Eigentum und Staatsganzes sind hier also noch im Sinne eines äußerlichen Gegensatzes begriffen. Wenige Jahre später, kurz nach 1800, wird das Eigentum hingegen selbst, nur konsequent, zum Teil des immanent entzweiten, und deshalb auszurichtenden Ganzen des Staats: „Eine Menschenmenge kann sich nur einen Staat nennen, wenn sie zur gemeinschaftlichen Verteidigung der Gesamtheit ihres Eigentums verbunden ist." Hegel, G. W. F. (1986c): „Die Verfassung Deutschlands" (1800–1802). In: Ders.: *Frühe Schriften*, Werke 1, Frankfurt am Main: Suhrkamp, 461–581, hier 472. Abermals einige Jahre später führt Hegel im Naturrechtsaufsatz aus, wie dieser immanente Widerspruch letztlich zu schlichten wäre: „[W]as wäre mit solchem Pöbel anzufangen, der auch in allem beaufsichtigt, was Privatsache ist, noch weniger ein öffentliches Leben führt und der hiermit zum Bewußtsein des gemeinsamen Willens und zum Handeln im Geist eines Ganzen schlechthin nicht, sondern allein zum Gegenteil gebildet ist [?]" Die Antwort liegt in der Totalisierung von Zwang. „[D]as Sittliche, welches nach dem Verhältnis allein gesetzt wird, oder die Äußerlichkeit und der Zwang, als Totalität gedacht, [hebt] sich selbst auf. [...] Indem –A ein Äußeres gegen die Bestimmtheit +A des Subjekts, so ist es durch dies Verhältnis in fremder Gewalt; aber dadurch, daß es sein +A als eine Bestimmtheit ebenso negativ setzen, aufheben und entäußern kann, bleibt es bei der Möglichkeit und bei der Wirklichkeit fremder Gewalt schlechthin frei. Indem es +A sowohl als –A negiert, ist es *bezwungen*, aber nicht *gezwungen*". Hegel, G. W. F. (1986h): „Über die wissenschaftlichen Behandlungsarten des Naturrechts, seine Stelle in der praktischen Philosophie und sein Verhältnis zu den positiven Rechtswissenschaften" (1802/03). In: Ders.: *Jenaer Schriften*, Werke 2, Frankfurt am Main: Suhrkamp, 434–530, hier 475–479.

> Das Selbst, hier in seiner Bedeutung als Wirkliches auftretend, spielt es mit der Maske, die es einmal anlegt, um seine Person zu sein; aber aus diesem Scheine tut es sich ebenso bald wieder in seiner eigenen Nacktheit und Gewöhnlichkeit hervor, die es von dem eigentlichen Selbst, dem Schauspieler, sowie von dem Zuschauer nicht unterschieden zu sein zeigt.[51]

Der komische Genuss, der darin liegt, das Selbst unmittelbar und abstrakt, als formelle Rechtsperson, zum absoluten Wesen zu erklären ist aber laut Hegel schlicht Leichtsinn: „Die *einfache Einzelheit* [man beachte die Kursivsetzung von ‚Einzelheit' *und* ‚einfach'!, K. S.] […] erhebt sich aus [dem] Inhalte [der erfüllten Allgemeinheit des sittlichen Lebens], und ihr Leichtsinn reinigt sie zur Person, zur abstrakten Allgemeinheit des Rechts."[52] Diese Komödie des Rechts ist leichtsinnig, weil von der abstrakten Allgemeinheit des Rechts her noch weiter gedacht werden muss. Der konkrete, vernünftige Inhalt des Rechts muss hergeleitet werden und eben das geschieht bei Hegel in der Religion, dem zweiten Kontext der Subjektivierung durchs Komische und Tragische. Nach dem Aufstieg des Bewusstseins aus der substantiellen Unmittelbarkeit der sinnlichen Gewissheit hinauf bis zur Vernunft, muss der absolute Geist doch auch wieder den Abstieg ins Materielle hinein unternehmen. Es gibt also zunächst einen Übergang des Tragischen ins Komische. Aber weil man hier nicht stehenbleiben kann, wird das Komische wieder aufgegeben. Ohne Zweifel sieht Hegel in der Einheit der Form des absoluten Selbst, die als solche Tragödie und Komödie gleichermaßen umfasst, das Tragische als die wirklichere, das heißt: als die Gegenwart erzwingende Position. Die Hegelsche Komödie erfordert so notwendig eine Wiederkehr der Tragödie – ja sie *ist* selbst deren Wiederholung. Die Komödie bei Hegel wiederholt die Tragödie. Damit drückt die Komödie die tragische Ironie des sich selbst reflektierenden Schicksals aus. So bleibt das politische Subjekt bei Hegel real ohnmächtig, gerade weil es in der Theorie als Versöhnung seines selbst gestifteten Schicksals gesehen wird. Wo es wirkt, ist es tragisch, aber es ist tragisch weil es seiner Form nach komisch, d. h. in sich selbst (befangen) ist. Es ist aber nur komisch, insofern es die Tragödie seiner Subjektvierung wiederholt. Und deren wirkendes Movens bleibt tragisch, wie somit letztlich auch das Subjekt selbst.[53] Die Möglichkeit eines komischen Subjekts, welches nicht vom Tragi-

---

51 Hegel (1986g), PdG, 542.

52 Ebd., 546.

53 Diese letztlich tragische Komödie im Sittlichen charakterisiert Hegel im Naturrechtsaufsatz so: „[D]ie Komödie überhaupt [fällt] auf die Seite der Schicksallosigkeit […]; entweder daß sie innerhalb der absoluten Lebendigkeit [fällt] und also nur Schattenbilder von Gegensätzen oder Scherze von Kämpfen mit einem gemachten Schicksal und erdichteten Feinde [darstellt] – oder innerhalb der Nichtlebendigkeit fällt und also nur Schattenbilder von Selbständigkeit und von Absolutheit darstellt." Hegel, G. W. F. (1986h), 496. Das Schicksal fängt diese Schicksallosigkeit wieder ein: „Die Komödie trennt die zwei Zonen des Sittlichen so voneinander ab, daß sie jede rein für sich gewähren läßt, daß in der einen die Gegensätze und das Endliche ein wesenloser Schatten, in der anderen aber das Absolute eine Täuschung ist. Das wahrhafte und

schen bestimmt wäre, fehlt hingegen. Die Wahrheit der unerfüllten Abstraktion, die Hegel auch als stoische Selbstständigkeit des Denkens bezeichnet, ist darum das unglückliche Bewusstsein. Die Tragik kehrt wieder: „Wir sehen", schreibt Hegel,

> daß dies unglückliche Bewußtsein die Gegenseite und Vervollständigung des in sich vollkommen glücklichen, des komischen Bewußtseins ausmacht. In das letztere geht alles göttliche Wesen zurück, oder es ist die vollkommene *Entäußerung* der *Substanz*. Jenes hingegen ist umgekehrt das tragische Schicksal der an und für sich sein sollenden *Gewißheit seiner selbst*. Es ist das Bewußtsein des Verlustes aller *Wesenheit* in *dieser Gewißheit* seiner und des Verlustes eben dieses Wissens von sich – der Substanz wie des Selbsts; es ist der Schmerz, der sich als das harte Wort ausspricht, daß *Gott gestorben ist.*[54]

An die Stelle Gottes tritt das Ich, welches sich seiner selbst auch als das Ansich gewiss sein soll. Als Subjekt dann geht es in die gesellschaftlich wirksame rechtlich-formale Konstruktion des Staats ein, der für die bestimmte Vernünftigkeit der materiellen Wirklichkeit Sorge trägt. Die politische Einheit der Moderne muss zwar einmal durch die Wirklichkeit der abstrakten Negativität des reinen – oder bloßen – Ichs hindurch. Es aber dabei zu belassen ist ausgeschlossen. Schon in der frühen Schrift von 1798 zur Wahl der Magistrate in Württemberg hat Hegel dem durch jahrhundertelange Erbmonarchie herabgekommenen Volke nicht die Fähigkeit zur freien politischen Entscheidung zugetraut.[55] Ausschweifend, pöbelhaft und orientierungslos wie diese Volksmassen sind können sie politisch unmöglich sich selbst überlassen werden. Sie wüssten gar nicht, was mit einer solchen Freiheit anzufangen wäre. Das Verhältnis von Allgemeinheit und Einzelheit ist darum auf substantieller Ebene des Bewusstseins durchzubilden. Die *einfache Einzelheit* muss zur *allgemeinen Einzelheit* geformt werden. Der Prozess der Subjektivierung des Selbstbewusstseins umfasst seine eigene Wiederholung oder die Dopplung seiner Hälften. Im Staat soll die affirmative Unendlichkeit des Absoluten, die Negation der Negation als Korrektur einer internen Abweichung in der rekursiven Logik dieser Subjektivierung denkbar werden. Der Staat erst ist absoluter und objektiver Geist zugleich, „Bild und Wirklichkeit" der Vernunft.[56] Er ist seine eigene Manifestation, d. h. immanente Wirklichkeit, oder die wirkliche Form der absoluten Wirklichkeit. Er bringt hervor, was in ihm möglich ist.

---

absolute Verhältnis aber ist, daß die eine im Ernste in die andere scheint, jede mit der anderen in leibhafter Beziehung [ist] und daß sie füreinander gegenseitig das ernste Schicksal sind; das absolute Verhältnis ist also im Trauerspiel aufgestellt." Ebd., 499.

54 Hegel (1986g), PdG, 547.

55 Hegel, G. W. F. (1986a): „Daß die Magistrate von den Bürgern gewählt werden müssen [Über die neuesten inneren Verhältnisse Württembergs ...]" (1798). In: Ders.: *Frühe Schriften*, Werke 1. Frankfurt am Main: Suhrkamp, 268–273.

56 Siehe hierzu § 360 der *Grundlinien*: Hegel, G. W. F. (1986f): *Grundlinien der Philosophie des Rechts oder Naturrecht und Staatswissenschaft im Grundrisse* (1820), Werke 7. Frankfurt am Main: Suhrkamp, 512.

5 Schluss

Es wurde der Versuch unternommen, einen erweiterten Rahmen eines kritischen Modells des Rechtssubjekts zu skizzieren. Dabei wurden philosophische, theologische und staats- bzw. völkergeschichtliche Elemente zum Material der Überlegungen gemacht. Die Gegenüberstellung von Rosenzweig und Hegel im Bezug auf den jeweils unterschiedlich konzipierten Zusammenhang von Staat, Geschichte und Religion mag so dazu beitragen, das politisch-philosophische Subjekt anders zu konzipieren. Während Rosenzweigs Kritik des Hegelschen Idealismus durch ein verändertes Verständnis der göttlichen Offenbarung einen Fokus auf die Verbindung von Geschichte und Religion legt, um einen Raum zu markieren, wo in nicht vorhersehbarer Weise der Geschichtlichkeit Gottes ein aus der Geschichte ausgeschlossenes Subjekt zu entspringen vermöchte, legt Hegel vielmehr den Fokus auf die Verbindung von Geschichte und dem Staat als dem Subjekt der Geschichte. Religion dichtet hier im Sinne der Sittlichkeit die immanente Wirklichkeit des Staats als eines solchen Subjekts ab.

Bei Hegel wird der Raum der Subjektivierung, der – zwischen Individuum und Kollektiv – letztlich niemals ganz vorhersehbar ist, durch die subjektivierenden Affekte des Tragischen und des Komischen an den Staat gebunden. Es hat sich herausstellt, dass das Komische hierbei letztlich im Tragischen verschwindet. An dieser Stelle müssten nun vertiefte Überlegungen dazu anschließen, welche Implikationen aus diesem Verschwinden des Komischen folgen; aber auch weitere dazu, ob und in welcher Weise das Komische anders wieder eingeholt werden könnte. Im Zuge dessen wäre es erforderlich danach zu fragen, in welcher Form ein Komisches, das nicht Wiederholung des Tragischen ist, existieren könnte. Die reale Existenz einer solchen Affekt-Form hinge daran, wie eine Offenbarung denkbar würde, die nicht Manifestation von Wirklichkeit wäre.

Zur Person: Kristian Schäferling promoviert in der Politischen Philosophie in Dundee und Frankfurt am Main.

Kristian Schäferling
kristian.schaeferling@yahoo.de.